Baden-Powell:
The Early Campaigns

Baden-Powell:
The Early Campaigns

The Matabele Campaign 1896

and

The Downfall of Prempeh, a Diary of Life
With the Native Levy in Ashanti, 1895-6

R. S. S. Baden-Powell

Baden-Powell: The Early Campaigns
The Matabele Campaign 1896
and
The Downfall of Prempeh, a Diary of Life With the Native Levy in Ashanti, 1895-6
by R. S. S. Baden-Powell

FIRST EDITION

First published under the titles
The Matabele Campaign 1896
and
The Downfall of Prempeh

Leonaur is an imprint
of Oakpast Ltd

Copyright in this form © 2013 Oakpast Ltd

ISBN: 978-1-78282-219-6 (hardcover)
ISBN: 978-1-78282-220-2 (softcover)

http://www.leonaur.com

Publisher's Notes
The views expressed in this book are not necessarily those of the publisher.

Contents

The Matabele Campaign 1896   7

The Downfall of Prempeh, a Diary of Life With
the Native Levy in Ashanti, 1895-6   275

A Matabele warrior making disparaging remarks

# The Matabele Campaign 1896

Contents

Preface	11
Outward Bound	13
State of Affairs in Matabeleland	25
Our Work at Buluwayo	35
Scouting	59
The Rebels Decline to Surrender	77
Campaign in the Matopos	89
Our Work in the Matopos	102
Fighting in the Matopos	114
The Final Operations in the Matopos	129
The Situation in Matabeleland and Mashonaland	141
The Downfall of Uwini	153
Shanghani Column—Through the Forest	168
Shangani Patrol—Return March	180
In the Belingwe District	189
The Downfall of Wedza	203
Clearing the Mashona Frontier	219
Through Mashonaland	235

The Situation in Rhodesia	249
After War—Peace	259
L'envoi	271

Preface

Umtali, Mashonaland,
12th December, 1896.

My dear Mother,—It has always been an understood thing between us that when I went on any trip abroad, I kept an illustrated diary for your particular diversion. So I have kept one again this time, though I can't say that I'm very proud of the result. It is a bit sketchy and incomplete, when you come to look at it. But the keeping of it has had its good uses for me.

Firstly, because the pleasures of new impressions are doubled if they are shared with some appreciative friend (and you are always more than appreciative).

Secondly, because it has served as a kind of short talk with you every day.

Thirdly, because it has filled up idle moments in which goodness knows what amount of mischief Satan might not have been finding for mine idle hands to do!

R. S. S. B.-P.

To the Reader

The following pages contain sketches of two kinds, namely, sketches written and sketches drawn. They were taken on the spot during the recent campaign in Matabeleland and Mashonaland, and give a representation of such part of the operations as I myself saw.

They were jotted down but roughly, at odd hours, often when one was more fit for sleeping than for writing, or in places where proper drawing materials were not available—I would ask you, therefore, to look leniently upon their many faults.

The notes, being chiefly extracts from my diary and from letters written home, naturally teem with the pronoun, "I," which I trust you will pardon, but it is a fault difficult to avoid under the circumstances. They deal with a campaign remarkable for the enormous extent of country over which it was spread, for the varied components and inadequate numbers of its white forces, and especially for the difficulties of supply and transport under which it was carried out—points which, I think, were scarcely fully realised at home. The operations were full of incidental interest, and of lessons to those who care to learn.

Personally, I was particularly lucky in seeing a good deal of Matabeleland, and something of Mashonaland, as well as in having a share in the work of organisation in the office, and in afterwards testing its results in the field. Incidentally I came in for a good taste of the best of all arts, sciences, or sports—"scouting." For these reasons I have been led to offer these notes to the public, in case there might be aught of interest in them.

The "thumbnail" sketches claim the one merit of having been done on the spot, some of them under fire.

Several of the illustrations have also appeared in the *Graphic* and *Daily Graphic*, and are here reproduced through the courtesy of the proprietors of those journals.

R. S. S, B.-P.

Marlborough Barracks, Dublin,
19th March, 1897.

CHAPTER 1

Outward Bound
2nd May to 2nd June.

War Office, S.W., 28th April, 1896.
Sir,—Passage to Cape Town having been provided for you in the s.s. *Tantallon Castle*, I am directed to request that you will proceed to Southampton and embark in the above vessel on the 2nd May by 12.30 p.m., reporting yourself before embarking to the military staff officer superintending the embarkation.
You must not ship more than 55 cubic feet.
I am further to request you will acknowledge the receipt of this letter by first post, and inform me of any change in your address up to the date of embarkation.
You will be in command of the troops on board.
I have the honour, &c., Evelyn Wood, Q.M.G.

What better invitation could one want than that? I accepted it with greatest pleasure.

I had had warning that it might come, by telegraph from Sir Frederick Carrington, who had that day arrived in England from Gibraltar *en route* to South Africa. He was about to have command of troops in Matabeleland operating against the rebels there. His telegram had reached me at Belfast on Friday afternoon, when we were burying a poor chap in my squadron who had been killed by a fall from his horse. I had a car in waiting, changed my kit, packed up some odds and ends, arranged about disposal of my horses, dogs, and furniture, and just caught the five something train, which got me up to town by next day morning. At midday the general sailed for South Africa, but his orders were that I should follow by next ship; so, after seeing him off, I had several days in which to kick my heels and live in constant

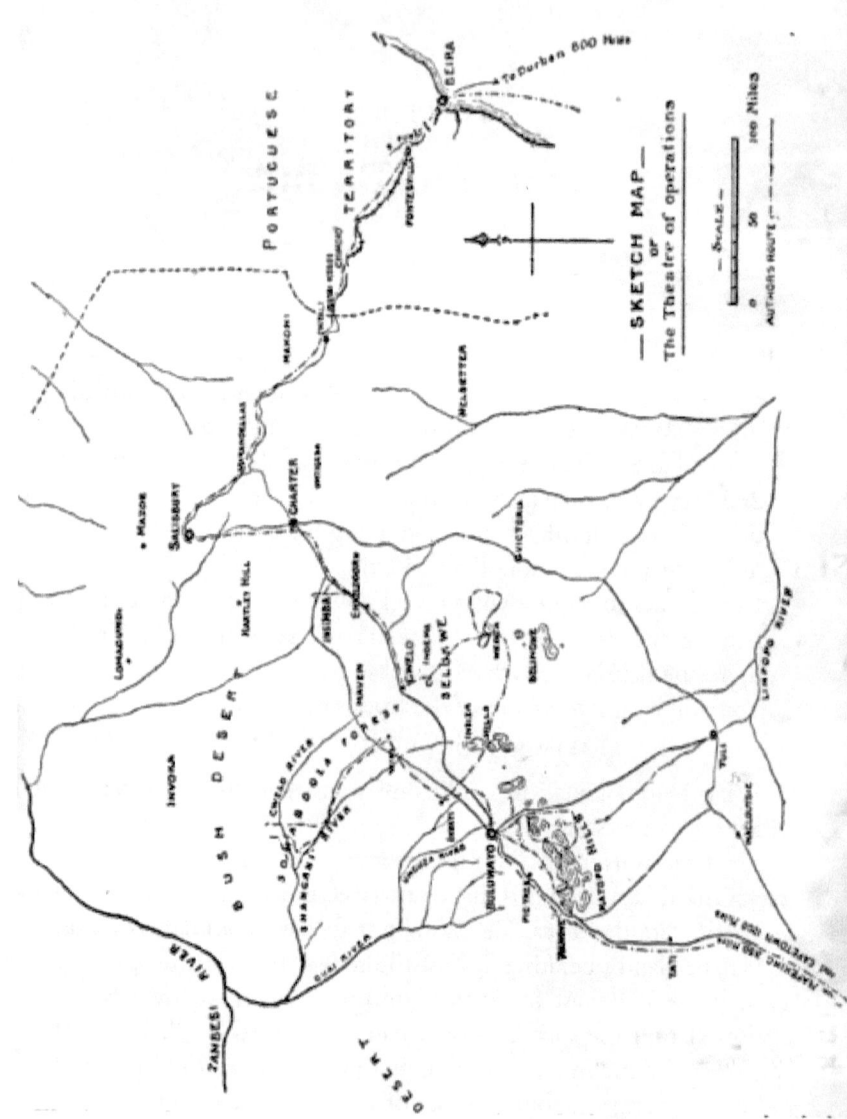

dread of being run over, or otherwise prevented from going after all. But fortune favoured me.

2nd May,—Embarked at Southampton in the *Tantallon Castle* (Captain Duncan) for Cape Town. On board were 480 of the finest mounted infantry that man could wish to see, under Colonel Alderson; also several other "details." Then, besides the troops, the usual crowd of passengers, 200 of them—German Jews, Cape Dutch, young clerks, &c., going out to seek their fortunes in El Dorado. (You don't want details, do you, of this, my fourth voyage to the Cape?)

4th May.—Perfect weather, palatial ship, and fast. Delightful cabin all to myself. Best of company. Poorish food, and a very good time all round.

6th May.—Madeira. You know. Breakfast *with fruit* at Reid's Hotel. The flowers and gardens. Scramble up on horses to the convent, up the long, steep, cobbled roads, and the grand toboggan down again in sliding cars. How I would like to live there for—a day! Then back on board, and off to sea by eleven. Deck loaded up with Madeira chain and fruit skins.

8th May.—Daily parades, inspection of troop decks, tugs of war, concerts on deck, and gradual increase in personal girth from sheer over-eating and dozing. Our only exercise is parade for officers at seven every morning in pyjamas, under a sergeant-instructor, who puts us through most fiendish exercises for an hour, and leaves us there for dead.

We just revive in time to put the men through the same course in their turn, stripped to the waist, so that they have dry shirts to put on afterwards. "Knees up!" I'd like to kill him who invented it—but it does us all a power of good.

10th to 13th May.—Hot and muggy off the coast of Africa from Cape de Verd to Sierra Leone, though out of sight of land. Not many weeks since I was here, homeward bound from Ashanti—same old oily sea, with rolling swell, and steamy, hot horizon.

14th May.—A passenger, who so far had spoken little except to ask for "another whisky," found dead in bed this morning, and buried overboard. Poor chap! He had opened a conversation with me the night before, and seemed a well-intentioned, gentle soul, although a drunken bore.

15th to 18th May.—Athletic sports, tableaux, concerts, and the fancy dress ball, and our dinner party to the captain.

The ball was interesting in showing the diverse taste of diverse nationalities. Four Frenchmen and one lady so prettily and well got up. The British officer, save in one or two instances (of which, alas! I wasn't one), could not rise to anything more original than uniform. An ingenious young lady put us all to shame, appearing as Britannia, "helmet, shield, and pitchfork too," all complete. (Nose and helmet didn't hit it off—at least—yes—the nose did hit it (the helmet) off, and the hat had to be worn the wrong way round to allow more room.)

BRITANNIA

Now was the best part of the voyage as far as climate went—bright, breezy days and deep blue sea, and the ship just ripping along—perfection.

19th May.—At 4 a.m. I awake with an uncanny feeling. All is silence and darkness.; The screw has stopped, the ship lies like a log, the only sound is the plashing of the water pouring from the engine, and occasionally sharp footsteps overhead.

And looking from my port, I see, looming dark against the stars, the long, flat top of grand old Table Mountain—its base a haze from which electric lights gleam out and shine along the water.

A busy day. No news except that Sir Frederick had gone on up to Mafeking, and I was now to follow.

General Goodenough inspected our troops upon the wharf among the Cape carts, niggers, cargo, trollies (drawn by the little Arab-looking horses), and the Cape Town dust. The troops go off by train to Wynberg camp to await Sir Frederick's orders.

Old Cape Town just the same as ever. Same lounging warders and convicts digging docks, Malays and snook fish everywhere. Adderley Street improved with extra turreted, verandahed buildings. The castle, venerable, low, and poky as of yore, and—of course—under repair. Short visits there, to Government House, and to that beautiful old Dutch house in Strand Street where one learns the Dutch side of the questions of the day.

By nine o'clock at night we're all aboard the train for Mafeking—a thousand well-remembered faces seem to be there on the platform cheering us away as we steam out into the night.

Hard beds, cold night, bumpity flap we go.

20th May.—Battling along over the Karoo. Stony plains with frequent stony hills and mountains. The clearest atmosphere, and air like draughts of fresh spring water. Up hill, down dale—the train crawling up at foot's pace with heart-breaking, laboured panting of the engine, then down the other side rattling and swaying about like a runaway coster's barrow.

Three times in the day we stop at wayside stations where there's a kind of *table d'hôte* prepared—much as it is in India, only less so.

Very little life along the line, beyond an occasional waggon with its lengthy team of oxen or of donkeys, creeping at its very slowest pace along the plain.

Our own pace, however, is not much to boast about; we don't go fast, and often stop to execute repairs.

The scenery remains much the same, except that the stony plain gives place to white grass *veldt* sparsely dotted with little thorn-bushes—its only beauty (and that is matchless of its kind) the wonderful colours of the distant hills, especially at dawn or sunset.

We pass by little groups of iron-roofed houses—sanatoria where people come to live—or die—whose lungs are gone.

Kimberley. Miles of mine-heads, mounds of refuse, town of tin houses and dust, a filthy refreshment-room,—and on we go.

22nd May.—At last, after three nights and two days jogging along in the train, we rattle into Mafeking at 6 a.m.

"Into Mafeking?" Well, there's a little tin (corrugated iron) house and a goods shed to form the station: hundreds of waggons and mounds of stores covered with tarpaulins, and on beyond a street and market square of low-roofed tin houses. Mafeking is at present the railway terminus. The waggons and the goods are waiting to go north to Matabeleland, but here they're stranded for want of transport, since all the oxen on the road are dying fast from rinderpest. However, every train is bringing up more mules and donkeys to use in their stead.

Near to the station is the camp of the 7th Hussars and mounted infantry of the West Riding and the York and Lancaster Regiments. These troops are waiting here in case they may be wanted in Matabeleland.

Thus Mafeking is crowded.

Sir Frederick is here, and we, the staff, take up our quarters for a few days in a railway carriage on a siding. The staff consists of Lieutenant-Colonel Bridge, A.S.C., as Deputy Assistant Adjutant-General (for Transport and Supply), Captain Vyvyan, Brigade Major; Lieutenant V. Ferguson, A.D.C.; my billet is Chief Staff Officer.

While here at Mafeking we are the guests of Mr. Julius Weil, the genius—in both senses—of this part of South Africa. He works the machinery of transport and supply of the Chartered Company; his "stores" have in them everything that man could want to buy. "Weil's Rations" are known half the world over as the best tinned foods for travellers; he owns the best of dogs and horses; he is Member of the Legislative Assembly of the Cape: and withal he is young and lively!

23rd May.—Our only news from Matabeleland is that Cecil Rhodes has safely got across from the East Coast, through Mashonaland, to Buluwayo, with a column under Beal. And that Plumer's force, specially raised here in the south, had got within touch of Buluwayo without fighting. Rhodes had said the neck of the rebellion now was broken—and with it go the necks of all our hopes. But still we shove along.

Packed up our kits, and in the afternoon embarked, the four of us (the General, Vyvyan, Ferguson, and self), in the coach for Buluwayo. The coach a regular Buffalo-Bill-Wild-West-Deadwood affair; hung by huge leather springs on a heavy, strong-built under-carriage; drawn by ten mules. Our baggage and three soldier-servants on the roof; two coloured drivers (one to the reins, the other to the whip). Inside are four transverse seats, each to hold three, thus making twelve "insides." Luckily we were only four, and so we had some room to stretch our legs. We each settled into a corner, and off we went, amid the cheers of the inhabitants of Mafeking. One, more eager than the rest,— a former officer of Sir Frederick's in the Bechuanaland Police,— jumped on, and came with us for thirty miles, trusting to chance to take him back again.

MAFEKING TO BULUWAYO
Ten days and nights by coach.

That night we reached Pitsani, a single roadside inn,—the starting-place of Jameson's raid into the Transvaal. We stopped, and supped, and slept, and started on at daybreak. This stopping to sleep was but a luxury which we did not come in for afterwards along the road.

24th May.—Does it bore you, a daily record of this uneventful journey? Well, if it does, you easily can skip it, which is more than we could do, alas!

All day over a sandy track, on open, white grass *veldt*, which generally changed into hilly country, dotted with thorn-bushes. All waterless. The mules, of which we get a change every ten or twelve miles, in very poor condition—so our pace is very slow. Reached Ramoutsa after dark, after 65-mile drive. Tin hotel, and large native *kraal* town (said to have 10,000 inhabitants in its mass of beehive huts). Boyne living here; a well known hunter on the Kalehari, and had shot with "Ginger" Gordon (15th Hussars). A native "reed dance" was going on in the *"stadt"* (as they call the native town),—every man blowing a reed whistle which gives two notes, and, played in numbers, gives a quaint, harmonious sound. The men dance in a circle, stamping the time; the women waggle round and round the circle, outside it. Altogether a very "or'nery" performance, especially as all were dressed in European store-clothes.

25th May.—Struggling on with weak mules to Gaberones (18 miles in 5½ hours). And on again. Every mile now began to show the grisly, stinking signs of rinderpest. Dead oxen varied occasionally with dead mules—the variety did not affect the smell—*that* remained the same. Occasionally we passed a waggon abandoned owing to the loss of animals.

The road at times was hard, but generally soft red sand. The scenery had a sameness of level, white grass land and thorn-bush.

Reached a big *kraal* (Matchudi's) of 700 inhabitants, at midnight. Deep sandy road. It took our fresh (!) team over half an hour to get us outside the village. Our pace was now so slow, and the whacking of the whip so painful merely to listen to (happily, the mules don't seem to feel it half so much as we), that we did much of the journey walking on ahead. Sun baking hot, and flies as thick as dust, and that was bad.

27th May.—By walking with a gun we managed to get a good supply of partridges and guinea-fowl as we went along. Today we passed the downward coach, in which was Scott-Montague, M.P. He gave us lots of information; and we felt we were not having the worst of the journey, when we saw him packed in with twelve other "insides," one of whom a woman, and another her baby, *which wasn't very well!*

Reached Pala—a group of stores—at midnight. Here were collected some two hundred waggons, stopped by loss of all their oxen from rinderpest. Three thousand two hundred beasts dead at this one place!

28th May.—We trekked along all day. Bush country; lots of partridges. One of our mules died on the road. Passed through Captain Lugard's camp about 11 p.m. Only Hicks, his manager, awake. He had thirteen waggons, and nearly two hundred mules and donkeys. He is taking an exploring expedition of eleven white men to the Lake N'Gami district, prepared to remain away two years if necessary.

29th May.—Outspanned, 4.30 a.m., and had our first wash since starting, in liquid mud from water-holes. The road was now through heavy sand. We walked over 20 miles of our journey on foot.

Reached Palapchwe (Khama's capital) at midnight.

Found a dozen telegrams awaiting us, describing fights round Buluwayo, such as put some hopes into us again. Here we slept in beds!

30th May.—Before breakfast, who should stroll in, all by himself, but Khama! Thin, alert, and looking quite young, in European clothes.

He had not much to say. He knew me as George's brother, and asked about the baby niece.

His town is certainly well-ordered, and he manages everything himself.

There are three or four European stores; otherwise the town is an agglomeration of *kraals*, and thus stands in several sections, each under its own headman. It is situated on an under-cliff of a bush-grown ridge; is fairly well supplied with water; and commands a splendid view over 100 miles of country. Khama had moved his people here only a few years ago, from Shoshong, which used to be his capital farther west. He rules his country effectively. No liquor may be sold, even among white men; and all along the road while in his country we found the rinderpest carcasses had been burned.

But he might with advantage do something for the road. Leaving Palapchwe at 10 a.m., we bumped and jolted down the stony hill in a manner calculated to mash up not only the coach and its insides, but *their* insides as well. Any person or persons afflicted with liver should go and live a week at Palapchwe, and drive down this hill daily—once a day would be enough!

And then beyond—across the plains, grown with *mopani* bush—the road was all deep sand. We merely crept along. But still we had broken the back of our journey—

Mafeking to Palla	220 miles
Palla to Palapchwe	110 ,,
Palapchwe to Tati	107 ,,
Tati to Buluwayo	115 ,,
Total	557 ,,

A certain sameness of scenery and want of water all the time, but compensated for by the splendid climate, the starry nights, and the "flannel-shirt" life generally.

Every one of the few wayfarers, in waggons or otherwise, along the road is interesting, either as a hunter, gentleman-labourer, or enterprising trader. They all look much the same: Boer hat, flannel shirt, and breeches—so sunburnt that it is hard at first to tell whether the man is English, half-caste, or light *kaffir*.

One we met today, creeping along with a crazy, two-wheeled cart drawn by four donkeys. He himself had only been two months in South Africa: came from Brighton. Heard that food and drink were at a premium in Buluwayo; so had loaded up this drop-in-the-ocean of a cargo of meal and champagne, and was steadily plodding along with it to make his fortune. We lightened his load by two pints, and weightened his pocket with two pounds. And we afterwards heard he sold his whole consignment at a very good profit long before he got to Matabeleland.

31st May.—All day and all night we go rocking and pitching, rolling and "scending" along in the creaking, groaning old coach: just *exactly* like being in the cabin of a small yacht in bad weather—and the occasional sharp swish of the thorn-bushes along the sides and leathern curtains sounds just like angry seas. Then frequently she heels over to a very jumpy angle, as if a squall had struck her. One of these days the old thing will go over.

Strange that in all this endless, uninhabited, and bushy wilderness there is scarcely any game.

We carry our own food, chiefly tinned things, with us, and at convenient outspans (when we are changing mules) we boil our kettle and have a meal of sorts and thoroughly enjoy it—especially the evening meal, under the stars.

1st June.—Reached Tati Gold Fields, 1 a.m. A collection of three or four tin stores, one of them an hotel, where we rolled into bed for a short rest.

We breakfasted with Mr. Vigers, the resident commissioner. Tati is a British Protectorate of older standing than the Chartered Company, and independent of it. It has its own administrative machinery,—a mining population of whites and blacks and "wasters," and yet not a single policeman! "Wasters?"—oh, it's a South African word, and most expressive; applies to the specious loafer who is so common in this country,—the country teems with him in high grades as well as low, *hinc multæ lacrimæ* in the history of South African enterprises.

Twenty miles beyond Tati we crossed the dry bed of the Ramakan River, the border of Matabeleland. Close by the river stands the ruin of a "prehistoric" fort, built of trimmed stones. There are several similar forts about the country, offshoots of the famed Zimbabye ruins near Victoria.

We nearly killed our general today in crossing a dry river bed. The descent into the drift was so steep that the wheelers could not hold back the coach, so our drivers sent them down it at a gallop. Half-way down there was a sill of rock off which the coach took a flying leap into the sand below. We inside were chucked about like peanuts in a pot, and Sir Frederick was thrown against the roof and his head and neck were stiff for some time afterward.

Had dinner (!) at a roadside shanty "hotel," where the waiter smoked while he served us.

2nd June.—Signs of war and of colonization at last. We reached Mangwe, 6.30 a.m. An earthwork fort with a waggon encampment outside it. In this *laager* were all the women and children, chiefly Dutch, from farms around; the men acting as garrison under command of Van Rooyen and Lee,—two well-known hunters, who were here in Lobengula's time.

In the fort they showed with pride some half a dozen Matabele prisoners they had captured in a fight. I looked well at them, fearing that they might be the only enemy that I should see. Happily I might have spared my eyes.

We now went through the Mangwe Pass. The road here winds its way through a tract of rocky hills and *koppies*, which are practically the tail of the Matopo range, running eastward hence for sixty miles.

It would have been a nasty place to tackle had the Matabele held it. They might easily here have cut off Buluwayo from the outer world, but their *M'limo*, or oracle, had told them to leave this one road open as a bolt-hole for the whites in Matabeleland. They had expected that when the rebellion broke out, the whites would avail themselves en masse of this line of escape; they never reckoned that instead they would sit tight and strike out hard until more came crowding up the road to their assistance.

The scenery is striking among these fantastic mounts of piled-up granite boulders, with long grass and bushy blades between. For ten miles the road runs between these *koppies*, then emerges on the open downs that constitute the Matabele plateau,—the watershed, 4.000 feet in altitude, between the Zambesi and Limpopo.

Now we come to the forts every six or eight miles along the road for protection of the traffic. They are each manned by about thirty men of the local defence force,—men in the usual shirt-sleeve costume, but fine, serviceable-looking troops. Some forts are the usual earthwork kind; others are such as would make a sapper snort, but are none the less effective for all that. They are just the natural *koppie*, or pile of rocks, aided by art in the way of sandbag parapets and thornbush abattis fences,—easily prepared and easily held. One we came to had been threatened by Matabele the previous night, and some rebels had been reported near the road this same morning,—so things were getting a little more exciting for us.

By-and-by we met a troop of mounted men twenty-five miles from Buluwayo. These had come out to act as escort. At first glance, to one fresh from Aldershot or the Curragh, they looked a pretty ragged lot on thin and unkempt ponies; but their arms and *bandoliers* were all in first-rate order, and one could see they were the men to go anywhere and do anything that might be wanted in the fighting and campaigning line. However, we did not take them with us, Sir Frederick telling them to follow on at leisure, a couple of scouts from a fort being sent ahead of us at the worst part to see that the road was clear.

The coach in which Lord Grey, the Administrator, had come a short time before us had been seen and pursued by Matabele, but we had no excitement, and soon after midnight we rolled into Buluwayo.

CHAPTER 2

State of Affairs in Matabeleland

3rd June.—Unpacked ourselves at 1 a.m. from our lairs in the corners of the coach, with something akin to regret at leaving the old thing after ten days and nights in her. But it *was* a blessing to bed down in a house, and the bath on waking was worth gold. (Bathroom was the verandah in the main street.)

Our lodging was next door to the club buildings, now used as a barrack for Grey's Scouts, and defended with a small bastion of tin biscuit-cases and sacks filled with earth. By breakfast-time I had investigated Buluwayo.

A red earth flat laid out by ditches, in blocks and streets, over two miles long and half a mile wide. The centre portion of the town well filled with buildings, all single-storied, some brick, some tin, some "paper" (*i.e.* wire-wove, ready-made in England, sent out in pieces), all with verandahs. The more outlying blocks only boasting a house or shanty here and there. Most of the houses built with a view to ultimate extension; *e.g.* one consisted of evidently, the scullery, back kitchen, and "offices," the front to be added later, when better times came round. The gardens, streets, and vacant lots richly sown with broken bottles, meat tins, rags, and paper; scarcely a garden, shrub, or tree in the place. The houses generally, if they are not "Bottle stores" (*i.e.* public houses), are either dry-goods stores or mining syndicate offices. Everywhere enterprise and rough elements of civilization— not forgetting the liquor branch.

Half a mile southward of the town lies a bush-covered rising ground, on which are a good number of "villas," with their two or three acres of bush fenced in to form their gardens in the future. At present they are deserted, the owners living in town while the Matabele are about.

In the centre of the town is the market square with its market house—a big brick building which is now used as the main refuge and defence of the town. Round the market house is drawn up a rectangular laager of waggons, built up with sacks full of earth to form a bullet-proof wall. Outside the *laager* the ground for twenty or thirty yards is rendered impassable by means of "entanglements" of barbed wire and a fence of the same, as well as by a thick sprinkling of broken bottles all over the ground itself.

Up on the roof of the hall is a look-out turret, from which, by touching a button, an observer can at will fire any of the electric mines which have been laid in the various approaches to the market square.

Although most of the people who have houses in Buluwayo are now living in their homes again, there are numbers of families from suburban or outlying farms who are still living in the *laager*. And at the western end of the town is another smaller *laager* of waggons round a house, in which a number of Boer farmers, with their families, are living.

We had a very nice house "commandeered" (*i.e.* taken over by government at a fair rental), and handed over to us for our use as a dwelling-house, ready supplied with furniture, &c.; and then the offices of one of the gold-mining companies were similarly commandeered and assigned to us for offices. In a very short time we had settled down and were hard at work—and there was lots to do.

Of course our first business was to interview all the heads of affairs, and so to form an idea of the situation.

Sir Richard Martin (with whom I had served previously, when on the mission to Swaziland, under Sir F. de Winton) is deputy commissioner, appointed since Jameson's raid to regulate the use and moves of the armed forces in the Chartered Company's territories, so as to prevent any further adventurous departures on their part. Lord Grey is Administrator of the Government of the whole country of Rhodesia, which includes Matabeleland and Mashonaland, &c.—a tract of country 750,000 square miles in extent, or equal to Spain, France, and Italy together. Mr. Cecil Rhodes, while bearing no official position, practically represents the management of the country as well as of the company, and his advice and experience are of the greatest value, since all the other "heads" are new arrivals in the country.

And it is in this number of heads that our danger would apparently, and our difficulty will most certainly be. Virtually, of course, the general is *the* head while active operations are in progress, but he has to cut his cloth according to the style approved by the deputy commissioner, according to the expense sanctioned by the administrator, and according to the general design required by the high commissioner, while not totally disregarding the local experience of Mr. Rhodes and others. Altogether the principle of strategy, which directs that "the general in command should merely have his objective pointed out to him, and a free hand given him," seems to be pretty well trenched upon by the present arrangement, though, under the circumstances, it could not well be helped. This, however, has always been the case in the history of South African warfare—frequently with fatal results—so it is nothing new; the only thing is to make the best of it, and pull together as much as possible.

And this is what we find is the situation of affairs.

Matabeleland had been captured by the Chartered Company's troops, acting from Mashonaland, in 1893, and Lobengula driven to his death as a fugitive. Since then the country had been go-warned by the Administrator and his magistrates and Native commissioners in the various districts into which the country was divided.

By 1896 the white population had increased to nearly four thousand, guarded by an armed police force distributed about the country. At the end of 1895 the greater part of this police was taken from Rhodesia, in order to take part in Jameson's raid into the Transvaal.

Just about the same time the terrible scourge of rinderpest came down upon the land. Three years before it had made a start in Somaliland, and had steadily and persistently worked its way down the continent of Africa—and it now crossed the mighty barrier of the Zambesi, and was sweeping over the great cattle-country, Matabeleland. With a view to checking its ravages, the government took all possible steps for preventing the transmission of infection, and, amongst others, that of slaughtering sound cattle was adopted. This procedure was perfectly incomprehensible to the native mind, and before long it was mooted among them that the white man's idea in slaughtering the cattle was to reduce the native to the lowest straits, and to starve him to death.

The natives had only been very partially beaten in the war in 1893, and the memory of it rankled strongly in their mind. They had thought the war was merely a passing raid, and it was only now they were realising that the whites had come to stay, and to oust them from their land. They were only waiting for their opportunity to rise and drive out their invaders.

Then, ever since the war, there had been a partial drought over the land, and what little crops there were had been devoured by unprecedented flights of locusts. All these misfortunes tended to spread among the people a general feeling of sullen discontent.

And this was increased to a feeling of bitter resentment against the whites, because they, the Matabele, found that the one remedy for want which in the old days they had been wont to ply so readily—namely, the wholesale raiding of their weaker neighbours—was under the new *régime* denied them. Nowadays, not only was every such raid prevented or punished as unlawful, but even in their home life their liberties were interfered with, and trifling thefts of cattle from a neighbour's herd, or the quiet putting away of a lazy slave, or of a quarrelsome stepmother, were now treated as crimes by policemen of their own blood and colour, but creatures of the white man, strutting among them with as much consequence and power as any of the royal *indunas*.

These things developed their hatred against the whites, and served as plausible reasons for their conduct when the chiefs came to be questioned later on in giving in their surrender.

Meanwhile, the chiefs and headmen, hoping to get back their ancient powers, fomented this feeling for all that they were worth. And they had a ductile mass to handle, for to the vast majority of their people the question of rights and wrongs was an unknown quantity, but the lust of blood—especially blood of white men, when, as they anticipated, it could be got with little danger to themselves—was an irresistible incentive.

The withdrawal of the armed forces from the country for the Transvaal raid gave them their opportunity.

The Matabele have no regular religion beyond a reverence for the souls of ancestors, and for an oracle-deity adopted from the Mashonas, whom they call the *M'limo*. The *M'limo* is an invisible god, who has three priests about the country, one in the north-east beyond Inyati, one in the south in the Matopo hills, and one south-west near Mangwe. The pure-bred Matabele, as well as the aboriginal natives, the Makalakas and the Maholis, all go to consult these priests of the *M'limo* as oracles, and place a blind belief in all they say. In addition to the three high priests, there are four warrior-chiefs of the *M'limo*. These men working in with the priests brought about the outbreak of rebellion. Three of these warrior-*indunas* are Matabele, the fourth—Uwini—heads the Makalakas.

Choosing well their opportunity, when, as they thought, all the white fighting men had left the country, and none but women, children, and dotards were left behind, they spread the message through the land—with that speed which only native messages can take. They called on all the tribes to arm themselves, and to assemble on a certain moon round three sides of Buluwayo. The town was to be rushed in the night, and the whites to be slaughtered without quarter to any. The road to Mangwe was to be left conspicuously open, so that any whites who might escape their notice would take the hint and fly from the country.

Buluwayo was not to be destroyed, as it would serve again as the royal *kraal* for Lobengula, who had returned to life again. After the slaughter at Buluwayo the army would break up into smaller *impis*, and go about the land to kill all outlying farmers and to loot their farms. The *M'limo* further promised that the white men's bullets would, in their flight, be changed to water, and their cannon-shells would similarly turn into eggs. The plan was not a bad one, but in one important particular it miscarried, and so lost to the *kaffirs* the very good chance they had of wiping out the white men.

About 24th March the outbreak began—but prematurely. In their eagerness for blood some bands of rebels, acting contrary to their instructions, worked their wicked will on outlying settlers and prospectors before attempting the night surprise on Buluwayo. *That* was their mistake—it gave the alarm to the whites in town, and enabled them to prepare their defence in good time.

Among the Insiza Hills, some thirty-five miles east of Buluwayo, on that fateful day, seven white men with their coloured servants were butchered at Edkins Store, and at the Nellie Reef Maddocks a miner was murdered, while a few miles farther on a peaceable farming family were brutally done to death. The white-haired old grandfather, the mother, two grown-up girls, a boy, and three little yellow-haired children—all bashed and mangled. At another place a bride, just out from the peace and civilization of home, had her happy dream suddenly wrecked by a rush of savages into the farmstead. Her husband was struck down, but she managed to escape to the next farm, some four miles distant—only to find its occupants already fled. Ignorant of the country and of the people, the poor girl gathered together what tinned food she could carry, and, making her way to the river, she made herself a grassy nest among the rocks, where she hoped to escape detection. For a few terrible days and nights she existed there,

GOING OUT FOR A FIGHT
Grey's Scouts riding out to Buluwayo to "have a "shy" at the enemy.

till the Matabele came upon her tracks, and shortly stoned her to death—another added to their tale of over a hundred and fifty victims within a week.

The only comfort is that their gruesome fate saved many other lives, for the news spread fast, and as more reports from every side came in of murdered whites, those in Buluwayo realised that the rising was a general one, and merciless. They promptly took their measures for defence.

The *laagers* were formed, as I have described, to accommodate the seven hundred women and children in the place; while the eight hundred men were organised in troops, and armed and horsed in an incredibly short space of time.

Patrols were promptly sent out to bring in outlying farmers, and to gather information as to the rebels' moves and numbers.

Ere long the rebel forces were closing round Buluwayo. North, east, and south they lay, to the number of seven thousand at the least. Throughout the country their numbers must have been but little under ten to thirteen thousand.

Nearly two thousand of them were armed with Martini-Henry rifles. A hundred of the Native Police deserted, and joined them with their Winchester repeaters. Many of them owned Lee-Metfords, illicitly bought, stolen, or received in return for showing gold-reefs to unscrupulous prospectors. And numbers of them owned old obsolete elephant guns, Tower muskets, and blunderbusses. So that in addition to their national armament of *assegais, knobkerries*, and battle-axes, the rebels were well supplied with firearms and also with ammunition.

In saying that the Native Police deserted and joined the rebels, I must in justice add that it was chiefly the younger members of the force who did so: the old hands remained loyal, and though at first they were disarmed as a precautionary measure, they proved most useful to our side later on, though very few in numbers. Much has been said against them as having been the cause of the revolt, through their overbearing conduct. I am perfectly convinced that the rebellion would have occurred just the same had there been no such body as the Native Police in existence.

At the same time, I don't mean to say that they did not abuse their powers. I should think that they most probably did, but that is no reason why they should incontinently be done away with. I don't see, for one thing, how proper government of the natives is going to be carried out without a native police: the only thing is that the force must be very closely and effectively commanded. The same difficulty has been encountered, and has thus been dealt with, by us in Natal, in India, in West Africa, everywhere, in fact, where natives form a large proportion of the population.

But I am wandering from my point into discussion and argument, which are not in my line. I am supposed to be giving you a *résumé* of what had been happening up to the time of Sir Frederick's taking over command in Matabeleland.

Directly after the outbreak, Colonel Napier, with his usual energy, lost no time in getting together a few men, and, with a party of sixty, he went off to the Shangani, thirty miles north-east of Buluwayo, and brought into safety over forty white settlers.

At the same time, Captain the Hon. Maurice Gifford, with forty-four men, made a dash to Cumming's Store, through difficult country in the Insiza Hills, fifty miles east of Buluwayo, and rescued over thirty people, losing one man killed and six wounded.

Captain F. C. Selous raised a troop of forty mounted men the same day, and made a bold reconnaissance southward of Buluwayo for thirty miles, to the Matopos.

Three days later (29th March), Captain. MacFarlane, with thirty men, went out to Jenkins' Store, and relieved Pittendrigh's party, who were hard pressed there. One man was killed and two wounded in this affair.

On 4th April, Maurice Gifford again went out, with 140 men, to Fonsecas, just north of Buluwayo, where he was hotly attacked by the enemy, losing four men killed and seven wounded. He himself lost his arm on this occasion, and Captain Lumsden, who took his place, was mortally wounded. MacFarlane, with sixty men, relieved him.

Brand and Niekerk took a strong patrol down to the mining camp in the Gwanda district, to find the miners had already safely got away south. On their return journey this patrol was attacked and very nearly cut off in passing through the eastern end of the Matopos. Out of their total of a hundred they lost five killed and fifteen wounded, besides thirty horses killed; but with sheer hard fighting they got through in the end.

Then, when the enemy closed on Buluwayo, as if to swamp it, Bisset led the garrison out in a sortie on 22nd April. There was a stubborn fight, in which neither side gained any ultimate decisive advantage, but it was remarkable for the fact that perhaps in no fight in history have there been so many deeds of gallantry performed among so small a body of men. No less than three men have since been recommended for the Victoria Cross for separate acts of heroism in this fight.

Three days later. Captain "Mickey" MacFarlane—an old friend of ours in the 9th Lancers—again led out the Buluwayo Field Force, and this time dealt the enemy a very heavy blow, such as changed the aspect of affairs, and relieved Buluwayo from any immediate danger of being rushed.

In these early fights and patrols the Buluwayo Force had lost twenty men killed and fifty wounded, while over two hundred settlers in surrounding districts had been murdered. Meanwhile, a relief force was being organised at Salisbury in Mashonaland, three hundred miles to the north, under Colonel Beal, and another at Kimberley and Mafeking, nearly six hundred miles to the south, under Colonel Plumer of the York and Lancaster Regiment. In the last week in May these two forces appeared in the neighbourhood of Buluwayo from their opposite directions, Cecil Rhodes arriving with that from the north; Lord Grey arriving about the same time as Colonel Plumer's from the south.

Meanwhile, Colonel Napier, with the bulk of the Buluwayo Force, had gone out to meet the Salisbury Force, and in combination with it did much to clear the country east of Buluwayo.

(P.S.—A most interesting detailed account of the outbreak, and of these early operations—including the acts of individual gallantry on the part of Baxter, Crewe, Henderson, Grey, and others—will be found in Captain F. C. Selous' book. *Sunshine and Storm in Rhodesia*.)

Colonel Plumer had raised, organised, and equipped his force of eight hundred Cape Colony men and horses in an incredibly short space of time; but that is one beauty of South Africa—that it teems with good material for forming a fighting force at a moment's notice. Nor did the "M.R.F." (Matabele Belief Force), as Plumer's corps was styled, lose any time in getting to work after its arrival at Buluwayo. For three days (23rd—26th May) it was hammering at the various *impis* threatening Buluwayo on the north and east with complete success.

Thus, when we arrived a week later, we found that the immediate neighbourhood of Buluwayo had been cleared of the enemy, but the *impis* were still hanging about in the offing, and required to be further broken up.

The general's plan, accordingly, was to send out three strong columns simultaneously to the north-east, north, and north-west, for a distance of some sixty to eighty miles, to clear that country of rebels, and to plant forts which should prevent their reassembly at their centres there, and would afford protection to those natives who were disposed to be friendly. The southern part of the country, namely, the Matopo Hills, was afterwards to be tackled by the combined forces on their return from the north. Such was the situation in the beginning of June. And now I'll continue the diary.

CHAPTER 3

Our Work at Buluwayo

4th June.—Office work from early morning till late at night. To say there is plenty of work to be done does not describe the mountain looming before us. The more we investigate into such questions as the force and strong points of the enemy, and the resources at our command wherewith to tackle him, the more huge and hopeless seems the problem.

Our force is far too small adequately to cope with so numerous and fairly well-armed an enemy, with well-nigh impregnable strongholds to fall back on, and with his supply and transport train ample and effective—as furnished by his wives and children.

Our force, bold as it is, is far too small, and yet we cannot increase it by a man, for the simple reason that if we did, we could not find the wherewithal to feed it. There is practically no reserve of food in the country, rinderpest has suddenly destroyed the means of bringing it, and here we lie, separated from the railway by a sandy road 587 miles in length!

Nor on the spot has any adequate provision been made to meet the future wants of the small force we have. All the food-stuffs in the place have been brought together, and the commissariat organisation and system has so far amounted to showing to an officer requiring rations for his troop a pile of stores, with "There you are! Take what you want."

One of the first steps has been to telegraph for Colonel Bridge, who had been left at Mafeking, to come and organise a system of transport and supply. Then we have to make a medical staff and an ordnance department.

In the meantime three columns are organised, and such provision as is possible is being made for their supply for patrols of about three weeks' duration, to the northward of Buluwayo. And we hope to start them off tomorrow.

During the brief intervals from office work for breakfast, lunch, and dinner, one has most interesting glimpses of the sunny street, crowded with throngs of "swashbucklers," each man more picturesque than his neighbour. Cowboy hat, with *puggree* of the colour of his corps, short-sleeved canvas shirt, cord breeches, and puttees, with bandolier across his chest, and pistol on his hip, is approximately the kit of every man you meet. The strong brown arms and sunburnt faces, the bold and springy gait, all show them soldiers, ready-made and ripe for any kind of work. Good shots and riders, and very much at home upon the veldt, no wonder that they form a "useful" crew—especially when led, as they are, by men of their own kidney.

Among the leaders are Mickey MacFarlane, erstwhile the dandy lancer, now a bearded buccaneer and good soldier all the time; Selous, the hunter-pioneer of Matabeleland; Napier and Spreckly, the light-hearted blade, who is nevertheless possessed of profound and business-like capacity; Beal, Laing, and Robertson, cool, level-headed Scotsmen with a military training; George Grey, "Charlie" White, and Maurice Gifford, for whom rough miners and impetuous cowboys work like well-broken hounds.

Indeed, the Volunteer troops seem to have thoroughly adapted themselves to the routine of soldiering, as well as to the more exciting demands of the field of action.

Night guards, daily standing to arms before sunrise, patrols, and other uncongenial duties are all carried out with greatest regularity; but the following amusing account of a morning patrol—which appeared in the *Matabele Times* this week—shows some of the drawbacks under which they carry on their work:—

> Standing to arms at 4 a.m. is not in itself a joy, but its cruelty is accentuated when the troop orderly takes that opportunity of informing you that you are to leave the *laager* at 5.30 and go on patrol to Matabele Wilson's, in company of three other unfortunates, for the purpose of ascertaining whether the road be clear travelling.
>
> On the occasion of which I write this was my fate, and our little party, with noses that needed constant attention with a handkerchief, and numbed fingers clasping cold rifles, stood shivering outside the stable gates, viewing life despondently and

swearing at the remount staff. All things, pleasant and otherwise, have an end, and at last, in response to frequent knocks, the gate opened, and we followed a depressed-looking official to where four alleged horses, with drooping heads and downcast mien, disconsolately champed the half-ton of rusty iron which South Africans call a bit, and dreamed of oats. Each man chose a horse, and with the assistance of sundry stable-boys induced him to leave his empty manger and move wearily out into the street. Here great care was necessary in mounting, as it was yet to be ascertained whether the crocks could stand up straight under the weight of a rider, but at last we fell in, and by dint of spur and rein reached the *laager*.

The corporal in charge of the patrol then went to wake up the orderly officer and get his orders, and my horse edged sideways towards the windmill; he wanted something to lean against. By-and-by out comes the corporal, we awakened our mounts, and started. 'Our orders are to go out to Wilson's and meet a patrol from the Khami River, then return to town,' and 'You're not to gallop all the way,' added the corporal. We at once said we wouldn't, and just then one of the horses fell down in endeavouring to step over a gutter. We dismounted and put the turn-out on its feet again, and proceeded.

Just past the Dutch *laager* someone said, 'By Jove, the *laager* smells peculiar.' Another man said, 'Yes, the big *laager* is just the same.' We passed a bush and struck the source of the odour, a dead ox; and promptly apologized to the *laagers*.

"All went well for a mile or so, and the corporal says, 'Let's have a trot.' We rammed in the spurs and shook the reins; one horse started a feeble lolloping trot which he maintained for at least twenty yards before he fell down; two horses shook their heads and whisked their tails, but took no further notice of the appeal for more speed; and the fourth, a grey, with fine prominent points, stopped dead short. We all passed a few remarks about the gentlemen who had selected the horses for duty, and resumed our wonted 'crawl march.'

More rinderpest, and my horse made a movement as if to lean against the smell, but it was too strong for him, and he moved on, to prevent being knocked over. On passing dead horses and cattle we used to draw in a long breath and endeavour to spur up a trot that would carry us out of range, before we were again compelled to breathe or 'bust,' but our horses used generally to land us in the middle of the stink and then pull up. You would see a man get black in the face trying to hold his breath, and at last have to burst out and refill his lungs with the very richest of the odour.

Passing the remains of the *kraal* where the transport riders, Potgieter and his mate, were murdered, we saw the heaps of earth piled over the victims' bodies. Here one of our number dismounted to light his pipe. This was the last we saw of him; he never caught up, though we only walked our horses; and he finally rolled up at the fort, half an hour after we had arrived, on foot, having tied his horse on to a tree. He said he found it considerably; easier walking. Dawson's Fort is splendidly placed, and commands a fine view of the surrounding country; the walls are built up with stone topped with two courses of sandbags, shelter for the garrison being afforded by sails; permanent running water passes the foot of the hill.

A number of donkey waggons were outspanned on the road beneath the fort, and out by Wilson's house, where now a hotel flourishes with the success usual in Matabeleland, we could see the coolies working in the gardens, planting to renew the crops of vegetables reaped with zeal and thoroughness by troops and travellers evidently determined that the enemy shouldn't have them any way. Rinderpest is very much in evidence round the fort, and oxen lie dead literally in troops, long regular lines of carcasses lying together.

At the foot of the hill leading to the fort one of the horses gave out altogether, having clean knocked up in five miles of travelling, the whole of which was done at a walking pace.

"If the loudly expressed wishes of the unfortunate wight who had to walk and carry a heavy rifle from Wilson's to Buluwayo under a hot sun, have any effect on the official who was responsible for sending horses barely strong enough to move their own shadows on a duty in the course of which speed might have been necessary to save their riders' lives, he will some day find himself on a weak horse as per sample supplied to us, and a score of Matabeles with sharp *assegais* and a taste for fancy experiments in the torture line after him, with the certainty that he will have to get off and try his individual sprinting powers before reaching a place of safety.

Not that there could be the least spice of danger between here and Wilson's, but that the official who would allow horses which to the most unversed eye are only fit for the sick lines to leave the stable at all, would just as readily send the same variety of mounts on hazardous service.

5th June.—Colonel Plumer's column, 460 strong, moved off to the country of the Guai River, north-west of Buluwayo.

And Macfarlane's column of 400 went away to the north. Spreckley's column was to make its start next day, but the unexpected happened to prevent it.

At ten o'clock at night, just as Sir Frederick was thinking we had done enough office work for the day, Sir Charles Metcalfe and the American scout Burnham rode up and came into the office, looking a bit dishevelled and torn. They had been riding out in the evening to visit Colonel Beal's column from Salisbury, which was camped about three miles out of the town. Seeing fires close to the road, and near to where they thought the camp must be, they had ridden up to them, and found themselves in the camp of a large *impi* of the enemy! They only escaped by making their way home by a detour through the bush. The news seemed almost too improbable to be true, and yet the bearers of it were not men to get excited and bring in a false report.

So I telephoned to a piquet we had at Government House (about two miles out of town) to send a patrol to investigate. But the subsequent reports were not wholly satisfactory, and I roused up Spreckley in the middle of the night to show me the way, and we rather upset the sleep of the inhabitants of Government House by appearing there to make further inquiries at about three in the morning. Nothing satisfactory to be learned there; so back to Buluwayo, and, getting a fresh horse and a police-trooper as guide, I went out again towards Beal's camp.

There, in the early dawn, I was at last able to see the enemy clear enough. On the opposite bank of the Umgusa River they were camped in long lines, fires burning merrily, and parties of them going to and from the stream for water. I took my information on to Beal's camp. I was much taken with the coolness with which the news was received there. It was not above two miles and a half from that of the enemy. The men were ordered to get their breakfasts without delay, and a patrol of a sergeant and two men was sent out to the stream to see if there were good water there, and also (apparently as an after-

The Umgusa Fight: 6th June

thought) whether they, too, could see any enemy there. Before we had finished breakfast they returned.

"Well, is it all right? Is there water there?"

"Yes."

"Is it good water?"

"I couldn't tell."

"Why not?"

"Because the Matabele were there, and wouldn't let us come near."

So we saddled up and moved off towards the spot to await the arrival of more troops from Buluwayo,. for I had sent my police-trooper back with a note to tell them there that "it was good enough," and asking that Spreckley's mounted column should be sent out to join us. Presently they came up, followed by a few volunteers in carts who wanted to join in the fun.

Our strength was 250 mounted men, with two guns and an ambulance.

The country was undulating *veldt* covered with brush, through which a line of mounted men could move at open files.

As we advanced, we formed into line, with both flanks thrown well forward—especially the right flank under Beal, which was to work round in rear of the enemy on to their line of retreat—a duty which was most successfully carried out. The central part of the line then advanced at a trot straight for the enemy's position.

The enemy were about 1200 strong, we afterwards found out. They did not seem very excited at our advance, but all stood looking as we crossed the Umgusa stream, but as we began to breast the slope on their side of it, and on which their camp lay, they became exceedingly lively, and were soon running like ants to take post in good positions at the edge of a long belt of thicker bush. We afterwards found that their apathy at first was due to a message from the *M'limo*, who had instructed them to approach and to draw out the garrison, and to get us to cross the Umgusa, because he (the *M'limo*) would then cause the stream to open and swallow up every man of us. After which the *impi* would have nothing to do but walk into Buluwayo and cut up the women and children at their leisure.

But something had gone wrong with the *M'limo's* machinery, and we crossed the stream without any *contretemps*. So, as we got nearer to the swarm of black heads among the grass and bushes, their rifles began to pop and their bullets to flit past with a weird little *"phit," "phit,"* or a jet of dust and a shrill "*wh-e-e-e-w*" where they ricocheted off the ground. Some of our men, accustomed to mounted infantry work, were now for jumping off to return the fire, but the order was given: "No; make a cavalry fight of it. Forward! Gallop!"

Then, as we came up close, the niggers let us have an irregular, rackety volley, and in another moment we were among them. They did not wait, but one and all they turned to fly, dodging in among the bushes, loading as they ran. And we were close upon their heels, zigzagging through the thorns, jumping off now and then, or pulling up, to fire a shot (we had not a sword among us, worse luck!), and on again.

The men that I was with—Grey's Scouts—never seemed to miss a shot.

The Matabele as they ran kept stopping behind bushes to fire. Now and again they tried to rally, but whenever a clump of them began to form or tried to stand, we went at them with a whoop and a yell, and both spurs in, and sent them flying. Of course, besides their guns they had their *assegais*. Several of our horses got some wounds, and one man got a horrid stab straight into his stomach. I saw another of our men fling himself on to a *kafir* who was stabbing at him; together they rolled on the ground, and in a twinkling the white man had twisted the spear from its owner's hand, and after a short, sharp tussle, he drove it through the other's heart.

In one place one of the men got somewhat detached from the rest, and came on a bunch of eight of the enemy. These fired on him and killed his horse, but he himself was up in trice, and, using magazine fire, he let them have it with such effect that before they could close on him with their clubs and *assegais*, he had floored half their number, and the rest just turned and fled. And farther on a horse was shot, and, in the fall, his rider stunned. The niggers came looping up, griming at the anticipated bloodshed, but Sergeant Farley, of Grey's Scouts, was there before them, and hoisting up his comrade on to his horse, got him safe away.

Everywhere one found the *kafirs* creeping into bushes, where they lay low till some of us came by, and then they loosed off their guns at us after we had passed.

I had my Colt's repeater with me—with only six cartridges in the magazine, and soon I found I had finished these—so, throwing it under a peculiar tree, where I might find it again, I went on with my revolver. Presently I came on an open stretch of ground, and about eighty yards before me was a *kaffir* with a Martini-Henry.

EIGHT TO ONE

He saw me and dropped on one knee and drew a steady bead on me. I felt so indignant at this that I rode at him as hard as I could go, calling him every name under the sun; he aimed,—for an hour, it seemed to me,—and it was quite a relief when at last he fired, at about ten yards distance, and still more of a relief when I realised he had clean missed me. Then he jumped up and turned to run, but he had not gone two paces when he cringed as if some one had slapped him hard on the back, then his head dropped and his heels flew up, and he fell smack on his face, shot by one of our men behind me.

At last I called a halt. Our horses were done, the niggers were all scattered, and there were almost as many left behind us hiding in bushes as there were running on in front.

A few minutes spent in breathing the horses, and a vast amount of jabber and chaff, and then we reformed the line and returned at a walk, clearing the bush as we went.

I had one shave. I went to help two men who were fighting a *kaffir* at the foot of a tree, but they killed him just as I got there. I was under the tree when something moving over my head caught my attention. It was a gun-barrel taking aim down at me, the firer jammed so close to the tree-stem as to look like part of it. Before I could move he fired, and just ploughed into the ground at my feet. He did not remain much longer in the tree. I have his *knobkerrie* and his photo now as mementoes.

At length we mustered again at our starting-point, where the guns and ambulance had been left. We found that, apart from small scratches and contusions, we had only four men badly wounded. One poor fellow had his thigh smashed by a ball from an elephant gun, from which he afterwards died. Another had two bullets in his back. Four horses had been killed.

And the blow dealt to the enemy was a most important one. A prisoner told us that the *impi* was composed of picked men from all the chief regiments of the rebel forces, and that a great number of the chiefs were present at the fight.

(P.S.—We learned some months afterwards from refugees and surrendered rebels that this was true, and that no less than fifteen headmen had been killed, as well as more than two hundred of their men.)

Of course this was a very one-sided fight, and it sounds rather brutal to anyone reading in cold blood how we hunted them without giving them a chance—but it must be remembered we were but 250 against at least 1200. Lord Wolseley says "when you get niggers on the run, keep them on the run" (this we did, for half a mile beyond the spot where we pulled up, Beal with his column cut in from the flank and bashed them from a new direction), and our only chance of bringing the war to a speedy end is to go for them whenever we get the chance, and hit as hard as ever we can; any hesitation or softness is construed by them as a sign of weakness, and at once restores their confidence and courage. They expect no quarter, because, as they admit themselves, they have gone beyond their own etiquette of war, and have killed our women and children. We found one wounded man who had hanged himself after the fight. This is not an uncommon occurrence in these fights.

(P.S.—I did not at the time fully realise the extraordinary bloodthirsty rage of some of our men when they got hand to hand with the *kaffirs*, but I not only understood it, but felt it to the full myself later on, when I too had seen those English girls lying horribly mutilated, and the little white children with the life smashed and beaten out of them by laughing black fiends, who knew no mercy.)

Don't think from these remarks that I am a regular nigger-hater, for I am not. I have met lots of good friends among them—especially among the Zulus. But, however good they may be, they must, as a people, be ruled with a hand of iron in a velvet glove; and if they writhe under it, and don't understand the force of it, it is of no use to add more padding—you must take off the glove for a moment

THE BITER BIT

I had stopped for a moment under a tree to look at a man who had just been shot, when there was a slight movement among the branches above me, and a Matabele who was hiding there fired down, but missed me. He was immediately afterwards shot—and I photographed him later.

and show them the hand. They will then understand and obey. In the present instance they had been rash enough to pull off the glove for themselves, and were now beginning to find out what the hand was made of.

After the fight I made tracks for Buluwayo, got in in time for late lunch, made up for lost time in the office, and was quite ready to go to bed soon after dinner. But I called in at the club on my way, to have a peep at the wonderfully picturesque collection of warriors, who were, many of them,—most of them in fact,—still in their fighting-kit (for many had no other), talking over the day's doings.

7th June.—Rode out early, with a police-orderly to guide me, to inspect the fort at Hope Fountain, ten miles south of Buluwayo, from which one could just see the tops of Matopo Mountains, in which so many of the rebel chiefs are said to be taking up their position. This fort had been attacked about ten days ago, but the enemy never came on with any boldness, and drew off after losing eleven killed. The mission station close by, a very pretty little homestead with nice gardens and trees, had been looted and burnt by the rebels.

I got back to Buluwayo just in time to see Spreckley's column march off to patrol the country north-east of Buluwayo. A fine body of 400 of the roughest, most workman-like fighters one could wish to see. It comprised both infantry and mounted infantry, artillery, and a levy of wild-looking friendly Matabele. In the afternoon I rode over yesterday's battlefield with Vyvyan, recovered my gun,—which, by the way, Sir Frederick has christened "Rodney,"—and photographed the chap who potted me out of the tree.

8th and 9th June.—Office work from early morning up to late at night.

10th June.—Lunched with Maurice Gifford, who had lost his arm in one of the first fights of the war. He is not really in a fit state to be about,—it still hurts him badly, poor chap, and he is a bit feverish,—but quite anxious to have another go at the enemy. He says he feels the pain as if it were in his hand, whereas the arm was taken off at the shoulder.

News came in from MacFarlane of a skirmish he had had near Redbank.

In the afternoon I rode out with Vyvyan to Taba-s'-Induna, a flat-topped hill that stands up bold and abruptly out of the sea-like *veldt* ten miles from Buluwayo. It was the place of execution for many of

Lobengula's Indunas. Beautiful view from the top over a widespread yellow prairie, with sharp blue mountains on the horizon.

11th June.—The hospital, which has a number of wounded men among its sick, stands away at one corner of the town, and is fortified and garrisoned in case of attack. Eight nuns work their lives out nursing there, and the men, if not demonstrative, are to the full appreciative and grateful, and would do anything for them.

Close to the hospital, on a rise, stands the "Eiffel Tower": a skeleton look-out tower about eighty feet high, from which the country round for many miles can be watched. The look-out man today says he can see a fight going on in the far distance to the north, apparently somewhere in MacFarlane's direction.

De Moleyns, adjutant of the 4th Hussars, arrived from England, anxious for a job, and we took him on as head of the Remount Department.

12th June.—Office as per usual. But vague rumours of what the enemy are doing in the Matopos made me impatient, especially owing to their vagueness. So in the evening I started off with Burnham, the American scout, to go and investigate. Delightful night ride to Kami Fort, sixteen miles south-west of Buluwayo. Jam, cookies, and tea with the two officers there, and a few hours' sleep on that best of beds—the *veldt* tempered with a blanket and a saddle.

13th June.—At 4 a.m. we were off again, Burnham and I and Trooper Bradley of the Mounted Police, who knew this part of the country well.

We got to Mabukutwane Fort—one of the natural *koppies* strengthened with sandbags, &c.—in time for breakfast. Here we found some excitement, as a transport rider in charge of waggons had just come in from the road, reporting that he had been fired on by Matabele about two miles out. A patrol was sent out, and we sent warnings to waggons and to the coach, which was due to pass today, telling them to wait at the fort till the road had been reconnoitred. It ended in nothing—the patrol returned, having found no Matabele nor any spoor of them.

So, having been joined by Taylor, the Native commissioner, we rode off across the *veldt* towards the Matopos, some six miles distant from the fort. On arriving at Mapisa's *kraal*, a friendly chief, we off-saddled our horses (but never let our guns out of our hands, for even friendlies are not to be too blindly trusted), and, taking two or three of his scouts with us, we climbed up into some *koppies* which commanded a view of the enemy's position, and of the Matopos generally. Awful country, a weird, jumbled mass of grey granite boulders thickly interspersed with bush, and great jagged mountains.

The Matabele had never before been reduced to the necessity of taking to these mountain fastnesses, but they were the regular refuge of the Makalakas, the original inhabitants of the country, when raided by their Matabele conquerors. This particular stronghold before us, the Inugu Mountain, with its neighbouring gorges and its labyrinths of caves, had been chosen by Lobengula as the safest refuge in the country, and consequently he had made it the home of his favourite queen, Famona.

It is now held by an *impi* of about a thousand Matabele. Their outposts, in talking with some of Mapisa's spies (they shout to each other at a safe distance across a valley), have said that they mean to draw the white troops on when they come to attack them, till they have got them well inside the gorge under the mountain, and then to "give them snuff."

(P.S.—A month later, as will presently be seen, they tried this on with Laing's and Nicholson's columns.)

While we were staring our eyes out at the position, taking bearings, and making sketches, &c., I suddenly saw a distant cow, and, by getting on to a better rock, I soon discovered a herd of cattle feeding in the valley below the enemy's position. Here was a chance for a lark—to mount, swoop down, and round up the cattle under their very noses, before they had time to interfere! But to my surprise, on mooting the idea, the niggers with us let out that these cattle did not belong to the

INUGO MOUNTAIN STRONGHOLD

enemy, but to another friendly chief, Farko, who lived near by.

That the enemy should leave these cattle untouched was a revelation to me, and I then saw that the so-called friendlies were on pretty good terms with the rebels. But for this chance eye-opener—of having, in the first instance, seen a solitary cow in the distance—I might have been led to trust to friendlies and their reports. It was well I didn't.

Having seen all we could, and made a map, Burnham and I started out for home; reached Kami in the middle of the night, and early next day were back in Buluwayo.

Burnham a most delightful companion on such a trip; amusing, interesting, and most instructive. Having seen service against the Red Indians, ho brings quite a new experience to bear on the scouting work here. And, while he talks away, there's not a thing escapes his quick-roving eye, whether it is on the horizon or at his feet. We got on well together, and he much approved of the results of your early development in me of the art of "inductive reasoning"—in fact, before we had examined and worried out many little indications in the course of our ride, he had nicknamed me "Sherlock Holmes."

(P.S.—We planned to do much scouting together in the future, but, unfortunately, it never came off, as he was soon afterwards compelled, for domestic reasons, to go down country.)

SCOUT BURNHAM

The following is an extract from a business-like offer I received today one of the developments of war in modern times :—

We, A—— and B——, certified engineers, wish to place our services at the disposal of the Chartered Company in any offensive or defensive operations against the rebels. Speciality—Construction of forts, bridges, and dynamite operations. References, &c., &c.

It is another step towards carrying on war by contract.

14th and 15th June.—Office again, up till late into the night. Colonel Bridge arrived with his staff-clerks, and much relieved our pressure of work by taking over the commissariat and transport arrangements, which are our main anxiety. Indeed, we are on half-rations of tinned meat now; fresh meat unprocurable, and prospects of immediate further supply rather vague.

16th June.—Yesterday, with the arrival of Colonel Bridge, our clouds seemed to be lightening up a bit. Today a thunderclap has come. Telegrams from Salisbury (sent round by Victoria and Macloutsie, owing to the direct wire being cut) tell us of murders of whites in three widely separate parts of Mashonaland. It almost looks as though the Matabele rebellion were repeating itself there. If so, the outlook is very bad indeed. Salisbury is 270 miles from here by road. We have here a number of troops who were sent from Salisbury to help us, and now their want will be acutely felt over there. In Mashonaland they have only one line of road to the coast for their supplies, and if that gets cut, we cannot help them; we have not sufficient for ourselves.

Indeed, if we cannot manage to get up immense supplies within the next two or three months (it takes over a month for a mule-waggon to get here from Mafeking), I don't see how we are going to hold on to the country. The rains may set in in October, and, once they have begun, the transport of supplies and troops becomes impossible; the *veldt* becomes a bog, and the rivers rise into turgid torrents.

Our only chance of maintaining our hold on the country is to plant outlying posts, and to fill them up with a sufficient stock of food to keep them throughout the four months of the rainy season. And, in the meantime, we must also thoroughly smash up the enemy.

Owing to rinderpest, it seems almost impossible to get sufficient waggons in Cape Colony to bring up the required supplies. So that we're in a quandary. Either we smash up the enemy, and get up sup-

A Cape Boy Sentry

plies for outlying posts before the rains come on, or else we draw in our horns, concentrate nearer to our base, organising our measures for a real effective campaign directly the rains are over. But the loss of prestige, of time, and of property involved in this second course would be deplorable, so we mean to have a good try to gain the first, and win the race against weather, rinderpest, and other bad luck.

11th June.—Having heard of some Matabele firing on a party of our men, about three miles out on the Salisbury Road, yesterday, De Moleyns and I took an early morning ride with one of the morning patrols. Started in the dark at 4 a.m., and moved out along that road. Presently we came upon an armed nigger squatting at the roadside, so muffled up in a blanket and a sack that he did not hear us coming. We captured him, and then found that he was a sentry of one of our own outlying "Cape Boys'" piquets.

I said to him, "Where is your piquet?"

He replied, with much haughtiness, "I not carry a ticket; I am soldier!"

(*Explanation.*—All ordinary natives have to carry a "ticket" or pass, so that they may not be taken up and shot as spies.)

We went on, but saw no signs of Matabele. At daybreak we got to Beal's camp, had a cup of coffee there with Daly (formerly in the 13th), and got home in time for breakfast, much refreshed by our morning's ride, and especially as we saw, on our way home, *paauw*, guinea-fowl, hares, and pheasants. Office all day.

More outbreaks telegraphed from Mashonaland. No doubt now that it is rebellion there too.

It is a curious experience sitting with Sir Richard Martin, Lord Grey, and the general, in the telegraph office, and listening to a conversation being ticked to us from Salisbury, some 800 miles away, just as if the sender (Judge Vintcent) were in the next room—the message being a string of startling details of more murders, *impis* gathering, heroic patrols making dashing rescues, preparations for defence, and state of food supplies and ammunition.

18th to 21st June.—Days of office-work, literally from daylight till—well, long, long after dark. Not a scrap of exercise, nor time to write a letter home.

Office work, however interesting it may be, would incline sometimes to become tedious, were it not for rays of humour that dart in from time to time through the overcharged cloud of routine. Here are some items that have come to us in the past few days, and which have tended to relieve the monotony of the work.

A letter from a lady, who writes direct to the general, runs as follows (she desires information as to the whereabouts of her brother):—

> I apply to you direct, in preference to my brother's commanding officer, because it is said, '*Vaut mieux s'adresser au bon Dieu qu' à tous ses saints.*'
> If anything has happened to my brother, I hold Mr. Ch—— accountable for it, as, but for his playing lickspittle to Oom Kruger—but for his base betrayal of the Johannesburgers, which has made England the laughingstock of all her enemies, there need have been no kissing at all. Probably the poor natives hoped to be magnanimous, à la Kruger, by screwing £25,000 out of each of their prisoners, and that England would follow suit by trying our chief defenders at bar as convicts, in spite of a protesting jury.

Then, from the officer commanding one of the outlying forts, comes a letter to say:

> This being only a small fort, and no fighting to be done, I

consider it only a waste of time to remain here. If you cannot place me in a position where active service can be done, I beg respectfully to submit my resignation.

I have had many letters of that kind from various volunteer officers.

Then, from England:

Dear Sir,—Could you kindly give me any details as to the death of my brother Charles? He is supposed to have been eaten by lions about four years ago in Mashonaland.

My orderly (a volunteer) was not to be found today when I wanted him, but a loafer, hanging about the office door, said that the orderly had left word with him that "he was going out to lunch, but would be back soon, in case he were wanted."

One volunteer trooper, apparently anxious that the routine of soldiering should, in his corps at any rate, be carried out in its entirety, takes it upon himself to write to me as follows :—

I beg to request that the following charges may be made the subject of inquiry by court martial:—
(1) I charge the orderly officer, whoever he may be, with neglect of duty, in that he did not visit the guard-room last night when I was there.
'(2) I charge the corporal of the guard with neglect of duty, in that he was absent from the guard-room at 9.32 p.m., at the Spoofery.
(3) I charge the same corporal of the guard with not officially informing the guard that there was a prisoner in the guard-room.
(4) I charge the corporal of the guard with using unbecoming language, in that he used the phrase, 'Why the h—l don't you know?' to me.
&c. &c. &c.

Another trooper, not quite so enthusiastic, writes to tell me that at his fort the drill and discipline are *"heartrending."*

An Italian surgeon writes that he is "anxious to be engaged in the British Army in Matabeleland." He hopes that the general will "approve his generous intention," and will "grant him the admission in the army which many persons, not more worthy than him, so easily obtain."

Among the many interesting experiences of a campaign, carried on, as this one is, under a varied assortment of troops, is that entailed in receiving reports from officers of very diverse training. Some are verbose in the extreme, others are terse to barrenness. But the latter is a most rare fault, and may well be called a fault on the right side. As a rule, reports appear to be proportioned on an inverse ratio to work performed.

The man who has done little, tries to make it appear much, by means of voluminous description. I often feel inclined to issue printed copies, as examples to officers commanding columns, of Captain Walton's celebrated despatch, when, under Admiral Byng, he destroyed the whole of the Spanish fleet off Passaro—

> Sir,—We have taken or destroyed all the Spanish ships on this coast; number as per margin.—
>
> Respectfully yours, G. Walton, Capt.

There is no superfluous verbosity there.

Vyvyan ill with a very bad throat, and Ferguson away with one of the columns, so I have plenty to keep me occupied.

The outbreak in Mashonaland ever spreading like wildfire, till it covers an area of 500 miles by 200—some 2000 whites against 18,000 to 20,000 blacks.

We have asked for imperial troops to be sent up without delay, both to Matabeleland and Mashonaland, only to the extent of about 500 in each country, for every nerve will have to be strained to feed even these—but we haven't a chance of winning our race without them. It is a great relief to realise that they are on their way, bringing with them their own transport and supplies.

22nd June.—Spreckley's column returned from its three weeks' patrol without having found the enemy in force, but it broke up his "bits" into smaller pieces, destroyed many *kraals*, took prisoners, and, best of all, captured much cattle and corn.

23rd June.—Dined at Spreckley's house in the "suburban stands," as the wooded slope outside the town is termed. A very pretty "paper" house. These "paper" houses are common in Buluwayo—they are really wire-wove, with wooden frames, iron roofs, cardboard walls, with proper fireplaces, windows and doors, verandahs, &c. Just like a stone-built house in appearance, but portable; sent out from Queen Victoria Street in pieces.

Spreckley himself is an ass[1] in one respect, namely, because he did not take up soldiering as his profession instead of gold and pioneering—successful though he has been in this other line. He has all the qualifications that go to make an officer above the ruck of them. Endowed with all the dash, pluck, and attractive force that make a man a born leader of men, he is also steeped in common sense, is careful in arrangement of details, and possesses a temperament that can sing "Wait till the clouds roll by" in crises where other men are tearing their hair.

Owing to all the extra work in the office due to the Mashonaland outbreak, I had been unable to go on a little expedition with Burnham. A rumour had reached us that the natives in the south-west of the country intended rising. Hitherto they had remained quiet, and the road towards Mafeking had not been stopped; but now there appeared the danger of this road being blocked, and of our supplies, &c., being cut off from us. At the western end of the Matopos lived a priest of the *M'limo*, and the people took their orders from him. If he now were to direct them to rise, our line of communications would be in great danger. So we wanted him captured. The difficulty was that if a large party went there, he would have early intimation of its coming, and would decamp in good time. So a young fellow named Armstrong, the Native commissioner of that district, and Burnham volunteered to go alone and capture, or, if necessary, shoot him.

Today we had a telegram from Burnham giving the result of it. He had gone to Mangwe, and, accompanied only by Armstrong, he had ridden over to the cave of the local priest of the *M'limo*—pretended that if the *M'limo* would render him invulnerable to Matabele bullets he would give him a handsome reward—saw the priest begin to go through the ceremony (so there was no mistake as to his identity), and then shot him. It was a risky game, as in the next valley were camped a large number of natives who had come for a big ceremony with the *M'limo* the next day. But the two men got away all right, having to gallop for it. The natives never rose to stop the road.

26th June.—I had not been outside the office for four days, and was feeling over-boiled with the sedentary work, so after dinner I saddled up and rode off ten miles in the moonlight to Hope Fountain.

---

1. This was not intended for publication, and if it should happen to meet the eye of the gentleman alluded to, I trust he will be magnanimous enough not to sue me for libel—especially as I make the statement believing it to be true.

SILENCING THE ORACLE

The *M'limo* is an invisible deity believed in by the Makalakas and Matabelo alike. In different districts of the country are priests of the *M'limo* living in caves, who are consulted by the people as mouthpieces of the god. These priests gave out the order for the rebellion.

Here I roused out Pyke, the officer in command. (Had lost an arm in the previous Matabele war when with Forbes' Patrol down the Shangani after Lobengula.) He roused out Corporal Herbert, and we rode down in the dark to the Matopos, and had a very interesting look round there in the early morning. I much enjoyed it. Was back in the office by 10.30, all the better for a night out.

Pyke is one of three fine, athletic brothers who are all serving here in different corps.

This evening we had a cheery little dinner at the hotel, to which came Sir Richard Martin, Colonel and Mrs. Spreckley, Captain and Mrs. Selous, Captain and Mrs. Colenbrander—all heroes and heroines of the rebellion.

How Spreckley made us laugh, fooling around the piano as if he were just going to sing!

It is daily a source of wonder to me how the general manages to handle some of the local officers and men. Of course, with the better class it is impossible not to get on well, but there are certain individuals who to any ordinary Imperial officer would be perfectly "impossible." Sir Frederick, however, is round them in a moment, and either coaxes or frightens them into acquiescence as the case demands; but were any general, without his personal knowledge of South Africa and its men, to attempt to take this motley force in hand, I cannot think there would be anything but ructions in a very short space of time. A little tact and give-and-take properly applied reaps a good return from Colonial troops, but the slightest show of domineering or letter-of-the-regulations discipline is apt to turn them crusty and "impossible." A very good instance of the general feeling that seems to influence the local troops is shown in the following letter which the general has received. (The writer of it leaves it to the discretion of the general where to insert commas and stops.)

> To Mr. Frederick Carrington—General.
> Sir Seeing in the papers and news from the North the serious phase that affairs are taking I am willing to raise by your permission a set of Good hard practical colonials here that have seen service Farmers Sons and Chuck my situation and head them off as a Yeomanry Corps I have been under you Sir in the B.B.P. (Bechuanaland Border Police) and am well acquainted with the Big gun Drill and a Good Shot with the maxim. We will consider it an honour to stand under you sir but object to

eye glasses and kid gloves otherwise
                    Yrs to command
                                H——

"Eyeglass and kid gloves" standing in the estimation of this and other honest yeomen of the colony for "Imperial officer."

Unfortunately the colonials have had experience of one class or another of regular officers, which has not suited their taste, and his defects get on their nerves and impress themselves on their minds, and they are very apt to look on such individual as the type of his kind, and if they afterwards meet with others having different attributes, they merely consider them as exceptions which prove the rule. No doubt there are certain types among us, and our training and upbringing in the service are apt to gradually run us in the groove of one type or another.

The type which perhaps is most of a red rag to the colonial is the highly-trained officer, bound hand and foot by the rules of modern war, who moves his force on a matured, deliberate plan, with all minutiae correctly prepared beforehand, incapable of change to meet any altered or unforeseen circumstances, and who has a proper contempt for nigger foes and for colonial allies alike. And there is, on the other hand, the old-woman type, fussy, undecided, running ignorantly into dangers he wots not of; even in a subordinate position his fussiness will not allow him to be still, and so he fiddles about like a clown in the circus, running about to help everybody at everybody's job, yet helping none.

Happily—and the colonials here are beginning to realise it—these types are not the rule in the service, but the exception. What is now more often met with is the man who calmly smokes, yet works as hard and as keenly as the best of them.

Quick to adapt his measures to the country he is in, and ready to adopt some other than the drill-book teachings where they don't apply with his particular foe. Understanding the principle of give-and-take without letting all run slack. The three C's which go to make a commander—coolness, common sense, and courage—are the attributes *par excellence* of the proper and more usual type of the British officer. For be it understood that "coolness" stands for absence of flurry, pettiness, and indecision; "common sense" for tactics, strategy, and all supply arrangements; while "courage" means the necessary dash and leadership of men.

CHAPTER 4

Scouting

26th June to 14th July.

14th July.—A bit of a break in the diary, not because there was nothing doing, but just the opposite.

For one thing, we have been pretty busy in sending off three small columns to the assistance of Mashonaland. And also, personally, I have been fully occupied in another way: that is, in repeating my experiences of the 26th June, and frequently by day, and very often by night, I have been back in the Matopos, locating the enemy's positions. I go sometimes with one or two whites, sometimes with two or three black companions; but what I prefer is to go with my one nigger-boy, who can ride and spoor and can take charge of the horses while I am climbing about the rocks to get a view.

It may seem anomalous, but it is in the very smallness of the party that the elements of success and safety lie. A small party is less likely to attract attention; there are fewer to extricate or to afford a target, if we happen to get into a tight place; and I think that one is more on the alert when one is not trusting to others to keep the look-out.

Then we have a nice kind of enemy to deal with. Except on special occasions, they don't like going about in the dark, and cannot understand anybody else doing it; and they sleep like logs, and keep little or no look-out at night. Thus one is able to pass close through their outposts in the dark, to reconnoitre their main positions in the early dawn (when they light up fires to thaw away their night's stiffness), and then to come away by some other route than that by which you entered.

So long as you are clothed, as we are in non-conspicuous colours, you can escape detection even from their sharp eyes; but you must not move about—directly you move, they see you, and take steps to catch you. Half the battle in keeping yourself hidden, while yet seeing everything yourself, is to study the colour of your background; thus, if clothed in things that match the rocks in colour, you can boldly sit out in front of a rock, with little risk of detection, so long as you remain motionless; if you are hiding in the shadow alongside of a rock or bush, take care that your form thus darkened is not silhouetted against a light background behind you. To show even your hand on a skyline would, of course, be fatal to your concealment.

(P.S.—Do not wear any bright colours about you. I noticed that after I had been on the sick list and resumed my scouting expeditions, the enemy caught sight of me much more quickly than they used to, though I took just as much care, and remained just as motionless; and I then came to the conclusion that this was due to the fact that I had, in accordance with the doctor's advice, taken to wearing a flannel cummerbund wound round my waist—and the only flannel at that time procurable was of a brilliant red; and this was what caught their eye.)

Of course, anything liable to glitter or shine is fatal to concealment; rifle, pistol, field-glasses, wrist-watch, buckles, and buttons should be dulled, abolished, or held in such a way as not to catch the rays of the sun by day or of the moon by night.

For efficient scouting in rocky ground, in the dry season, india-rubber-soled shoes are essential; with these you can move in absolute silence, and over rocks which, from their smoothness or inclination, would be impassable with boots. It is almost impossible to obliterate your spoor, as, even if you brush over your footprints, the practised eye of the native tracker will read your doings by other signs; still, it is a point not to be lost sight of for a minute when getting into position for scouting, and a little walking backwards, doubling on one's tracks over rocky ground, lighting a fire where you are not going to cook your food, or one of a hundred similar subterfuges may often relieve you from the attentions of a too-inquisitive enemy.

When they have found you watching them, they will not, as a rule, come boldly at you, fearing that you are merely a lure to draw them on into some ambuscade or trap,—for that is one of their own pet games to play,—but they will work round to get on to the track you have made in getting to your positions. Having found this, and satisfied themselves that you are practically alone, their general rule is to lie in ambush near the track, ready to catch you on your return. Naturally one never returns by the same path. (P.S.—Once I had to do it, later on, at Wedzas, when there was no other way, and nearly paid the penalty.)

SOLITARY SCOUTING

Scouting alone gave better results than reconnaissance in parties. Accompanied by a reliable "boy," who could keep a good look-out and take care of the horses, one was able to do a lot of effective scouting. We generally moved by night, and worked in the early dawn.

Sometimes they try to shoot or to catch one; but so long as one keeps moving about, they do not seem to trust much to their marksmanship; and I have heard them shouting to each other, "Don't shoot at the beast, catch him by the hands, catch him by the hands!" Then they would come clambering over the rocks, but clambering awkwardly—for, lithe and active though they be, the Matabele are not good mountaineers, especially in that part of it which Montenegrins say is the most difficult (possibly because they themselves shine pre-eminently at it), namely, in getting rapidly downhill. Consequently, if one is wearing india-rubber-soled shoes (not hobnailed boots, for with them you merely skate about the slippery boulders), it is not a difficult matter to outpace them, provided you have the natural gift or requisite training for "placing" your feet. I am a fair blunderer in most things, but I was taken in hand in the days of my youth by a devotee of the art of skirt-dancing, and never, till I was forced by dark-brown two-legged circumstances to skip from rock to rock in the Matopos, did I fully realise the value of what I then learned, namely, the command of the feet.

The enemy are also full of tricks and ruses for catching us by luring us into ambuscades. Thus they will show scouts, cattle, women, and, at night, fires, in the hope of our coming close to capture or investigate, and so putting ourselves in their hands. But even if we were so simple as to be tempted, we should probably see something of their spoor which would put us on our guard. And in this respect the stupidity of the native is almost incredible; be gathers his information almost entirely by spooring, and yet it is only occasionally that he seems to remember that his own feet are all the time writing their message to his enemies. Now and again he thinks of it, and leaps across a path or sandy patch; but I suppose that, knowing the hopelessness of trying effectually to conceal his trail, he has acquired the habit of disregarding its importance.

There is naturally a strong attraction in reconnoitring, for, apart from the fun of besting the enemy, the art of scouting is in itself as interesting as any detective work.

It is almost impossible to describe all the little signs that go to make up information for one when scouting. It is like reading the page of a book. You can tell your companion—say a man who cannot read—that such and such a thing is the case.

"How do you know?" he asks.

"Because it is written here on this page."

THE VALUE OF SKIRT-DANCING

"Oh! How do you make that out?"

Then you proceed to spell it out to him; letters that make words, words that make sentences, sentences that make sense. In the same way, in scouting, the tiniest indications, such as a few grains of displaced sand here, some bent blades of grass there, a leaf foreign to this bit of country, a buck startled from a distant thicket, the impress of a raindrop on a spoor, a single flash on the mountain-side, a far-off yelp of a dog,—all are letters in the page of information you are reading, and whose sequence and aggregate meaning, if you are a practised reader, you grasp at once without considering them as separate letters and spelling them out—except where the print happens to be particularly faint. And that is what goes to make scouting the interesting, the absorbing game that it is.

A small instance will show my meaning as to what information can be read from trifling signs.

The other day, when out with my native scout, we came on a few downtrodden blades of common grass; this led us on to footprints in a sandy patch of ground. They were those of women or boys (judging from the size) on a long journey (they wore sandals), going towards the Matopos. Suddenly my boy gave a "How!" of surprise, and ten yards off the track he picked up a leaf. It was the leaf of a tree that did not grow about here, but some ten or fifteen miles away; it was damp, and smelt of *kaffir* beer. From these signs it was evident that women had been carrying beer from the place where the trees grew towards the Matopos (they stop up the mouth of the beer-pots with leaves), and they had passed this way at four in the morning (a strong breeze had been blowing about that hour, and the leaf had evidently been blown ten yards away). This would bring them to the Matopos about five o'clock. The men would not delay to drink up the fresh beer, and would by this time be very comfortable, not to say half-stupid, and the reverse of on the *qui vive*; so that we were able to go and reconnoitre more nearly with impunity—all on the strength of information given by bruised grass and a leaf.

There should have been no reason for my going out to get information in this way had we had reliable native spies or fully trained white scouts. But we find that these friendly natives are especially useless, as they have neither the pluck nor the energy for the work, and at best are given to exaggerating and lying; and our white scouts, though keen and plucky as lions, have never been trained in the necessary intricacies of mapping and reporting. Thus, it has now fallen to my lot to be employed on these most interesting little expeditions.

Under present conditions we, staff and special service officers, have to turn our hand to every kind of job as occasion demands, and one man has to do the ordinary work of half a dozen different offices. It is as though, the personnel of a railway having been suddenly reduced by influenza or other plague just when the bank holiday traffic was on, a few trained staff were got from another company temporarily to work it. We find a number of porters, stationmasters, cleaners, firemen, &c., available, but we have to put in a lot of odd work ourselves to make the thing run; at one minute doing the traffic management, at the next driving an engine, here superintending clearing-house business, then acting as points-men, and so on. It makes it all the more interesting, and in this way I have dropped in for the scouting work.

The net result of our scouting to date is that we have got to know the nature of the country and the exact positions of the six different rebel *impis* in it, and of their three refuges of women and cattle. Maps have been lithographed accordingly, and issued to all officers for their guidance. These maps have sketches of the principal mountains to guide the officers in finding the positions of the enemy.

The Matopo district is a tract of intricate, broken country, containing a jumble of granite-boulder mountains and bush-grown gorges, extending for some sixty miles by twenty. It lies to the south of Buluwayo, its nearest point being about twenty miles from that town. Along its northern edge, in a distance of about twenty-five miles, the six separate *impis* of the enemy have taken up their positions, with their women and cattle bestowed in neighbouring gorges.

On the principle, "*Gutta cavat lapidem non vi sed saepe cadendo*," we have taken innumerable little peeps at them, and have now "marked down" these *impis* and their belongings in their separate strongholds, a result that we could never have gained had we gone in strong parties.

Commencing at the western end, near the Mangwe road is the stronghold of the Inugu Mountain (see A in map), a very difficult place to tackle, with its cliffs, caves, and narrow gorges. The *impi* occupies the mountain, while the women and cattle are in the neighbouring Famona valley.

Five miles N.E. of this is the Chilili valley, (B), which are women and cattle of Babyan's *impi*. This *impi* is located deep in the hills near Isibula's *kraal* on the Kantol Mountain (D); while Babyan himself, and probably the priest of the *M'limo*, are in a neighbouring valley at (C).

Eighteen miles to the eastward, eight miles south of Dawson's

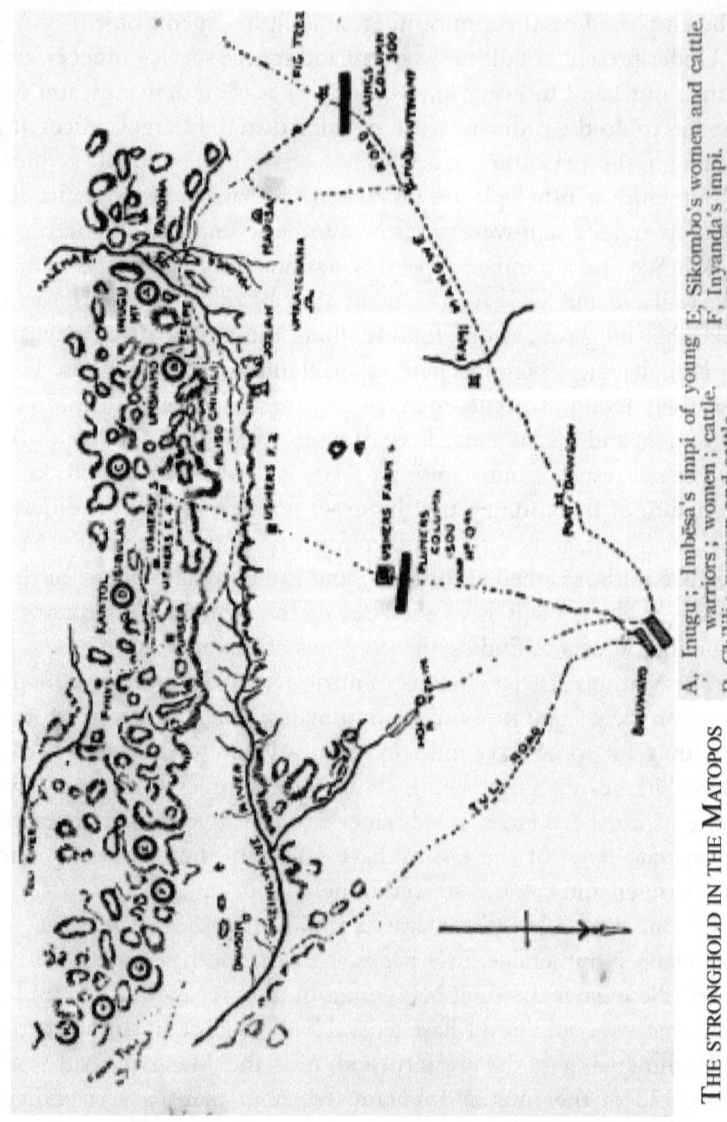

THE STRONGHOLD IN THE MATOPOS

A, Inugu; Imbēsa's impi of young warriors; women; cattle.
B, Chilili; women and cattle.
C, Babyan and Priest of M'limo.
D, Babyan's impi.
E, Sikombo's women and cattle.
F, Inyanda's impi.
G, Sikombo's impi.
H, Mnyakavula's impi.
K, Umlugulu's impi.

Our outposts were at Hope Fountain, Kami, Mabukutwane, and Fig Tree. From these we reconnoitred, passing, through the enemy's scouts on the north bank of the Umzingwane, and marking the positions of the impis in the hills by their fires, tracks, etc.

Store on the Umzingwane River, we come to a bold peak (F), that is occupied by Inyanda's people, with a valley behind it (E), in which are Sikombo's women and cattle.

A couple of miles farther west, Sikombo's *impi* is camped behind a dome-shaped mountain (G) close to the Tuli road.

On the west side of this road Umlugulu's *impi* was stationed when we first began our reconnaissance, but he moved nearer to Sikombo at (H), with Mnyakavula close by on (K). Each *impi* numbered roughly between one and two thousand men. Their outposts were among the hills along the northern bank of the Umzingwana River. We used to pass between these by night, arriving near the strongholds at daybreak.

INUGU MOUNTAIN, A

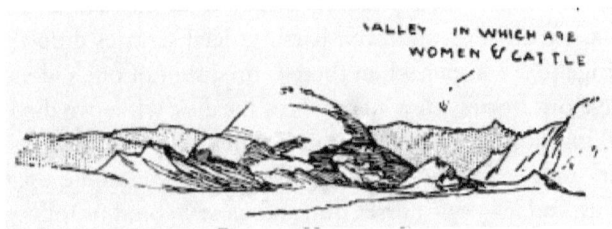

CHILILI VALLEY, B

INYANDA'S, SIROMRO'S, AND UMLUGY'S POSITIONS
Looking South

The following account, taken from the *Daily Chronicle*, gives an idea of what one meets with when out on reconnaissance with a patrol:—

Is it the cooing of doves that wakes me from dreamland to the stern reality of a scrubby blanket and the cold night air of the upland *veldt*? A plaintive, continuous moan, moan, reminds me that I am at one of our outpost forts beyond Buluwayo, where my bedroom is under the lee of the sail (waggon tilt) which forms the wall of the hospital. And through the flimsy screen there wells the moan of a man who is dying. At last the weary wailing slowly sobs itself away, and the suffering of another mortal is ended. He is at peace. It is only another poor trooper gone. Three years ago he was costing his father so much a year at Eton; he was in the eleven, too—and all for this.

I roll myself tighter in my dew-chilled rug, and turn to dream afresh of what a curious world I'm in. My rest is short, and time arrives for turning out, as now the moon is rising. A curious scene it is, as here in shadow, there in light, close-packed within the narrow circuit of the fort, the men are lying, muffled, deeply sleeping at their posts. It's etiquette to move and talk as softly as we are able, and even harsh-voiced sentries drop their challenge to a whisper when there is no doubt of one's identity. We give our horses a few handfuls of mealies, while we dip our pannikins into the great black 'billy,' where there's always cocoa on the simmer for the guard. And presently we saddle up, the six of us, and lead our horses out; and close behind us follow, in a huddled, shivering file, the four native scouts, guarding among them two Matabele prisoners, handcuffed wrist to wrist, who are to be our guides.

Down into the deep, dark *kloof* below the fort, where the air strikes with an icy chill, we cross the shallow *spruit*, then rise and turn along its farther bank, following a twisting, stony track that leads down the valley. Our horses, though they purposely are left unshod, make a prodigious clatter as they stumble adown the rough, uneven way. From force of habit rather than from fear of listening enemies, we drop our voices to a whisper, and this gives a feeling of alertness and expectancy such as would find us well prepared on an emergency. But we are many miles as yet from their extremest outposts, and, luckily for us, these natives are the soundest of sleepers, so that one might almost in safety pass with clattering horses within a quarter of a mile of them.

There must be some merit in wrapping up your head when cold,—even at the expense of your nether limbs,—for here in Southern Africa the natives have identically the same way as the men of Northern India have of keeping up their warmth, and as they feel the cold increase, so do they 'peel' their legs to find the wherewithal to further muffle up their heads. The keen crispness of the air is in keeping with our spirits, as, all awake, we trek along the hazy veldt. And what a lot of foes one sees when one is looking out for them! Surely that's a man—yes—no—an upright bush! Ah, there! I saw one move. It is but the sprig of a nearer tree deluding a too-watchful eye; the *kaffirs* do not move about as a rule alone at night, while if one is seen, you may be sure there is a party close at hand, and so one needs to keep a very sharp look-out. By going thus at night, we are hoping that we may slip past the Matabele outposts stationed on the hills, and so gain the country that we want to see beyond. Were we to attempt this feat by day, or with a larger party, we should undoubtedly attract attention and have to take a longish circuit. As it is, we make our way for some ten miles along this valley, keeping off the stony path and in the grass, so as to deaden sound as far as possible. High above on either hand the hills loom dark against the stars, and on their summits our enemy's outposts, we know, are quietly sleeping.

Now and again we cross a transverse *donga* or tributary watercourse that runs into our stream, the *donga* sometimes rising to the dignity of a ravine with steep and broken sides. And when we have found a place, and safely crossed it, we turn and approach it from the other side, so that should we happen later on to be pursued and want to get across it in a hurry, we shall know the landmarks that should guide us to the 'drift.' The stars are palpitating now and striving hard to increase their gleam, which means that dawn is at hand. The hills along our left (we are travelling south) loom darker now against the paling sky. Before us, too, we see the hazy blank of the greater valley into which our present valley runs.

Suddenly there's a pause, and all our party halts. Look back! there, high up on a hill, beneath whose shadow we have passed, there sparkles what looks like a ruddy star, which glimmers, bobs, goes out, and then flares anew. It is a watch-fire, and our foes are waking up to warm themselves and to keep their watch. Yonder on another hill sparks up a second fire, and on beyond, another. They are waking up, but all too late; we've passed them by, and now are in their ground. Forward! We press on, and ere the day has dawned we have emerged from out the defile into the open land beyond. This is a wide and undulating plain, some five miles across to where it runs up into mountain peaks, the true Matopos. We turn aside and clamber up among some hills just as the sun is rising, until we reach the ashes of a *kraal* that has been lately burned.

The *kraal* is situated in a cup among the hills, and from the *koppies* round our native scouts can keep a good look-out in all directions. Here we call a halt for breakfast, and after slackening girths, we go into the cattle *kraal* to look for corn to give our horses. (The *kaffirs* always hide their grain in pits beneath the ground of the 'cattle *kraal*' or yard in which the oxen are herded at night.) Many of the grain-pits have already been opened, but still are left half-filled, and some have not been touched—and then in one—well, we cover up the mouth with a flat stone and logs of wood. The body of a girl lies doubled up within. A few days back a party of some friendlies, men and women, had revisited this *kraal*, their home, to get some food to take back to their temporary refuge near our fort. The Matabele saw them, and just when they were busy drawing grain, pounced in upon them, *assegaing* three—all women— and driving off the rest as fast as they could go. This was but an everyday incident of outpost life.

And having fed our horses, each of us now got his 'billy' out,—a 'billy' (cooking-tin) is carried here by every officer and trooper in a case upon his saddle,—and, having lit a fire, we got our coffee boiled, and breakfast under way. Then two of us, taking with us our two prisoners, clamber up a *koppie*, from whose top we hope to get a view of the enemy's country. There is something ludicrous in, and yet one cannot laugh at, this miserable pair. Linked wrist to wrist, they move as would a pair of sullen Siamese twins. The grass is prickly hereabouts, and both want to keep to the tiny goat-track that we are following, and so they have to sidle up like crabs, going hand in hand along it.

At length we gain the top; there is a splendid panorama, and now that the sun is well up, the mountains out across the plain look but a few hundred yards away, so clear is every rock, so deep the shadows. The prisoners have no hesitation in telling us exactly where their friends are camped upon the mountains, and where they keep their women and their cattle. We sit and stare for half an hour, and then agree that, having come so far without accident, we may as well go farther, and get a nearer view of these redoubtable strongholds. We return down to our party, and as we descend, we remember that our native scouts and the prisoners have had a pretty long walk as it is. They had shown us what we had come out to see, and we now proposed to send them back.

So, having seen them shuffling homeward, we turned our horses' heads towards the mountains, and continued our way across the open valley. On and on, keeping everywhere a bright look-out against surprise. The *veldt* was rolling grassy downs, all covered, sometimes sparsely, sometimes densely, with bushes,—mostly thorns. Every open speck of sand, every track, was keenly scrutinized for 'spoor' (or tracks of men), and though there was not a soul to be seen about the *veldt*, the signs of their propinquity were here too glaring to be missed.

Leaving our horses, with the remainder of the men, well hidden behind a rise, we two walked on on foot, each carrying a rifle with him. It was an anxious time, as very soon the bush had shut us out of sight of our support, but still we kept along, anxious to gain the summit of a rounded, rocky hill, whence we could see all round, and so foresee all danger.

Now, on the paths before us were fresh tracks of an ox, behind whom had walked a man with naked feet, and going a little lame on one—the left toes dragged, he used a stick. They had passed along before sunrise, because across the tracks there ran the spoor of guinea-fowl heading towards their feeding-ground in yonder patch of maize. A single ox thus driven in the night assuredly meant a pack-ox smuggling in supplies to one of the rebel strongholds. More paths converged into the one we followed, bringing more and more people, women's feet and children's, oxen and donkeys, all fresh, and heading in the same direction.

Then, mounting on the rocks, we followed with our eyes the

direction of the path through thicker bush until it reached a solitary mountain. There we could see a thin wreath of smoke curling up from the bush, and, looking through our powerful telescope, we soon could see some other fires high up the hillside close to some mighty caves. Dogs were barking, cattle lowing, at the back of one particular shoulder of the hill; and while we stared to try and distinguish figures in the rocks, a sudden flash up near the mountain-top just caught our eye. Then, focussing the glass upon it, soon we saw the dark brown figures of some twenty natives squatting up about the sky-line, and the frequent glint and sparkle showed they carried guns and *assegais*.

Nearer and nearer we crept, gaining another *koppie*, whence we had a better view, and from here we marked the line that our attacking parties ought to take, and where to post our guns with best advantage. We might have stayed there longer, for it was a tempting spectacle to sit and watch. But the niggers in the hills are calling to each other, evidently suspicious, if not actually aware of our presence—and they have eyes as strong as telescopes. Now some crows fly startled from the bush a few hundred yards to our right. Someone is moving there! Up springs a plover screaming farther on—they're on the move. We have seen all that we want to see. To stay in one place for long when scouting is risky at any time; today it looks even dangerous. So we quietly slip away—not by the path we came—for that is the way you run into your enemy's ambuscades.

Then, as we went along, a novel footprint caught our eye, and struck us much as Friday's must have struck old Crusoe. A deep indented hollow of the fore part of a foot showed plainly in the grass to one side of the path, heading as to cross it, and in the grass beyond the other side the deep indent was seen of a heel in the earth. This was the spoor of a man, running much in the same direction as ourselves, yet wishing to avoid notice, because he jumped the path. Evidently a messenger going out the way we had come, and knowing of our presence there, and on his way to warn the outposts, through whom we had passed in the dark, to catch us on our homeward road.

Our horses now had had their second feed, the men had had a kind of meal, and so we started on again. We had to visit two more hills, but found them both unoccupied. And then we turned our heads for home. Caution became more than ever necessary now. There was only left the short afternoon of daylight, our horses were no longer over fresh, and we had five-and-twenty miles to go, ten of them along a defile valley. So with an advanced file sent well ahead, and one dropped well in rear, we journeyed on, each man keeping an ever-restless, bright look-out.

And though we talked and chatted from time to time for many a weary mile, you never saw your neighbour's eyes look at you for a moment. While talking, one had still to keep one's eyes afield. And what a mixture in our little band of eight!—Under the similar equipment of cocked-up Boer or cowboy hat, with ragged shirt and strong cord pants, with cartridge-*bandolier*, and belt from which hung knife and pipe, tobacco-bag and purse, all grimy and unkempt, and sunburnt to a rich, dark brick colour, each individual was an interesting study in himself. Here is one with *pince-nez*—(*pince-nez* on a trooper!)—a Cambridge man of highest education, who thought he would take to farming in Rhodesia; but his plans are interrupted by the war, and while that lasts he takes his place, like others, in the ranks.

Beside him rides a late A.B. seaman in the Royal Navy, a fine young fellow, full of pluck, who will press on where devils fear to tread, but he is disappointing as a scout, for, after having been close up to the enemy, he cannot tell how they are posted, what their strength, or any other points that the leader wants to know. This other man an architect, and yon a gold-prospector—in fact, there's a variety enough among them to suit almost any taste.

The sun has set and darkness has drawn on before we are well out of the defile; but we are now beyond the rebel outposts, and getting nearer home, so there's nothing much to—*bang! phit!*—and a bullet flits just over our heads! It came from behind; we halt and hear the clatter of hoofs as the man who was left as rearguard comes galloping up the road. A moment later he appears in the dusk rounding the next turn. He no sooner sees us than he halts, dismounts, drops on one knee, takes aim, and fires straight at us.

We shout and yell, but as he loads to fire again, we scatter, and push on along the road, and he comes clattering after us. The explanation is that nervousness, increased by darkness coming on, has sent the man a little off his head, and, ludicrous though it be, it is a little unpleasant for us. None of his comrades care to tackle him. 'It is a pity to shoot him,' 'His horse is tired and cannot catch us up,' and 'He'll be all right as soon as he has got over the first attack of fright'; and so we leave him to follow us, keeping a respectful distance. At length the fires twinkle ahead, and, tired and hungry, we get back to camp.

At dawn our missing man turned up—without his horse, it had dropped dead from fatigue. He had a wondrous tale of how he had pursued a host of enemies. The sole reward he got was a ducking in the *spruit*.

A small party such as that mentioned in this account of a scouting expedition is often necessary, as in this case, for ensuring the safety of the scouts in getting to and from their work through defiles and the like, where it might happen that the way would have to be forced past the enemy's outposts. But once on their ground, the escort should be carefully concealed. Their work is over for the time being, and the essential part of the expedition, that is, the scouting by one or two trained individuals, has commenced.

The scout must then be left with a perfectly free hand, and must not be tied to any certain hour for return. He can only judge for himself later on whether it is necessary to be away for two or three hours only, or for a whole night, before he comes back to the party. And that is one of the considerations which make me prefer to start from home or camp without escort in the original instance, as it leaves one altogether unfettered by considerations as to the feeding, resting, &c., of the patrol, or of necessarily making one's way back to the exact spot where it would be posted.

(P.S.—As will be seen in the following chapters, the rebel *impis* and their women and cattle were all found, when the troops came to attack them later on, in the exact positions assigned to them in the sketch map issued. Such "locating" would have been impossible had we tried to effect it by reconnaissances of the usual kind, that is, by parties of men. The natives would have gathered to oppose our coming, or—what is more likely—to prevent our getting away again; instead of gently stealing our honey bit by bit, we should have brought the whole swarm of bees about us, and the probability is that they would then have deserted that hive to take a new and more inaccessible one. Instead of being able to lead the troops straight to the enemy, we should merely have been able to say, "There is the spot where we fought them; they seemed to come from yonder; but it looks as if they had now gone somewhere else." And reconnoitring parties would again have had to follow them, with similar results, probably losing men every time, and gaining nothing.)

The value of solitary scouting does not seem to be sufficiently realised among us nowadays. One hears but little of its employment since the Peninsula days, when Marbot gave the English officers unqualified praise for their clever and daring enterprise in this line.

It is not only for savage warfare that I venture to think it is so important, but equally for modern civilized tactics. A reconnaissance in force in these days of long-range weapons and machine-guns can have very little chance of success, and yet for the same reasons an accurate knowledge of the enemy's position, strength, and movements is more than ever necessary to the officer commanding a force. One well-trained, capable scout, can see and report on an object just as well as fifty ordinary men of a patrol looking at the same thing. But he does so with this advantage, that he avoids attracting the attention of the enemy, and they do not alter their position or tactics on account of having been observed; and he can venture where a party would never be allowed to come, since the enemy, even if they see him, would hesitate to disturb their piquets, &c., by opening fire on a solitary individual, although they would have no such scruples were a reconnoitring party there instead.

It is difficult to find in history a battle in which the victory or defeat were not closely connected with good or deficient reconnaissance respectively. Good preliminary reconnaissance saves premature wearing out of men and horses through useless marches and counter-marches, and it simplifies the commander's difficulties, and he knows exactly when, where, and how to dispose his force to obtain the best results. But, as I have said above, such reconnaissance can often be carried out the most effectually by single reconnoitres or scouts. And a peace training of such men is very important.

Without special training a man cannot have a thorough confidence in himself as a scout, and without an absolute confidence in himself, it is not of the slightest use for a man to think of going out to scout.

Development of the habits of noting details and of reasoning inductively constitute the elements of the required training. This can be carried out equally in the most civilized as in the wildest countries,—although for its complete perfecting a wild country is preferable. It is to a large extent the development of the science of woodcraft in a man—that is, the art of noticing smallest details, and of connecting their meaning, and thus gaining a knowledge of the ways and doings of your quarry; the education of your "eye-for-a-country;" and the habit of looking out on your own account. Once these have become, from continual practice, a second nature to a man, he has but to learn the more artificial details of what he is required to report, and the best method of doing so, to become a full-fledged scout.

We English have the talent of woodcraft and the spirit of adventure and independence already inborn in our blood to an extent to which no other nationality can lay claim, and therefore among our soldiers we ought to find the best material in the world for scouts. Were we take this material and rightly train it m that art whose value has been denoted in the term "half the battle," we ought to make up in useful men much of our deficiency in numbers.

Houdini, the conjurer, educated the prehensibility of his son's mind by teaching him, in progressive lessons, to be able to recapitulate the contents of a shop window after a single look at it; there is the first stage of a scout's training, *viz*. the habit of noticing details. The second, "inductive reasoning," or the putting together of this and that detail so noticed, and deducing their correct meaning, is best illustrated in the memoirs of "Sherlock Holmes."

CHAPTER 5

The Rebels Decline to Surrender
14th July to 18th July

Meanwhile, during the first week in July, the three columns, which had been out clearing the country to the northward of Buluwayo, returned, having had a great amount of hard work with only a modicum of fighting. The rebels of that region had been effectually broken and dispersed in ,ill directions—except at one spot, near Inyati, some fifty miles north-east from the town.

Colonel Plumer accordingly took a column out there,—nearly 800 strong,—and, after a clever and most successful night-march, surprised the enemy, at dawn, on 5th July, in a desperate-looking *koppie* stronghold called Taba-si-ka-Mamba. There was some tough fighting, and the newly-arrived corps of "Cape Boys" (natives and half-castes from Cape Colony), much to everybody's surprise, showed themselves particularly plucky in storming the *koppies*; but, as in the case of most natives, their *élan* is greatly a matter of what sort of leaders they have, and in this case there was every reason for them to go well. Major Robertson, their commandant, an old Royal Dragoon, is a wonderfully cool, keen, and fearless leader under fire.

In the end the place and its many caves was taken. Our loss amounted to ten killed, twelve wounded. The enemy lost 150 killed, and we got some 600 prisoners, men, women, and children, 800 head of cattle, and a very large amount of goods which had been looted from stores and collected at this place as the property of the *M'limo*. It was a final smash to the enemy in the north, though M'qwati, the local priest of the *M'limo*, and M'tini, his *induna*, both escaped.

The *M'limo's* cave was found, a most curious place, which I visited later on: a sort of ante-room in which suppliants had to wait while the priest went away to invoke the *M'limo's* attention; then a narrow cleft

Caught in the act by a Cape Boy

by which they would walk deep into the rock, and which narrowed till it looked like a split just before the end of the cave. And through this crevice they made their requests and got their answer from the M'limo. In reality, another cave entered the hill from the opposite side and led up to this same crevice, and it was by this back entrance that the priest re-entered, and, sitting in the dark corner just behind the crevice, he was able to personate an invisible deity with full effect.

Of such caves there are three or four about the country, where the rebels just now get their orders as to their course of action.

Office work still very heavy—especially as we have broken up the original Buluwayo Volunteer Field Force as an unworkable and rather overpaid organisation (the troopers getting 10s. a day *and* their rations!), and are now busy organising it anew as a regularly enlisted armed police force at 5s. a day, under military law and discipline. Nicholson, 7th Hussars, is working this task, and is a first-rate man for it.

The office work, although exacting, is most interesting all the same; the only drawback is that there are not more than twenty-four hours in a day in which to get it done. I certainly do look forward, though, to the hour of luncheon; yes, it sounds greedy—but it is for the glimpse of sunlight that I look forward, not the lunch. That is scarcely pleasant either to look forward to or to look back on—consisting, as it generally does, of hashed leather, which has probably got rinderpest, no vegetables, and liquid nourishment at prohibitive prices,—e.g. local beer at 2s. a glass. I live on bread, jam, and coffee, *and* that costs 5s. a meal; and prices are rising! Eggs are 32s. a dozen, and not guaranteed fresh at that!

Many of the strongholds to which I had first learned the way with patrols, I have now visited again by myself at nights, in order to further locate the positions of their occupants. In this way I have actually got to know the country and the way through it better by night than by day, that is to say, by certain landmarks and leading stars whose respectively changed appearance or absence in daylight is apt to be misleading.

The enemy, of course, often see me, but are luckily very suspicious, and look upon me as a bait to some trap, and are therefore slow to come at me. They often shout to me; and yesterday my boy, who was with my horse, told me they were calling to each other that "*Impeesa*" was there—*i.e.* "the Wolf," or, as he translated it, "the beast that does not sleep, but sneaks about at night."

14th July.—Last night I was riding alone across the *veldt*; I came suddenly upon a Matabele driving a horse and a mule towards the Matopos. He turned and fled, and I galloped after him to give him a fright, and then returned to the beasts, which I drove before me safely to camp. They were our own branded animals, which had been looted.

On getting back to Buluwayo at 9.30 p.m., after having been away for some days' solitary scouting, varied by such patrols as that described in the last chapter, I found that reports had come in from the officer commanding Fig Tree Fort, saying that rebel *impis* were on the move there. Ferguson had at once been sent off by the General, with fifty men of the newly-formed police, and Laing's column of about 150, which had lately come in from the Belingwe District. No sooner had the troops got there (on the 13th) than they found that the Matabele *impis* were merely pictures in the mind's eye of the commandant, a Dutchman, who had been imbibing not wisely, but too well.

15th July.—"Well! of all the murkiest rot that ever I heard of, this is the murkiest!" These words, and others to the same effect, but, to use the speaker's term, "murkier," saluted my waking senses at an unseemly hour of this morning. For a moment I was inclined to reach for my gun, or at all events, to let fly my feelings at the two loafers who stood yarning at my window-sill (we live on the ground floor in Buluwayo, because there is not a second to our house, nor, indeed, to any house in the place except "Williams' Buildings," and they are "buildings" being not yet built); but presently a lazy feeling of curiosity got the better of my momentary irritation, and I played the eavesdropper. It was

"IMPEESA"—"THE BEAST THAT DOES NOT SLEEP
BUT SNEAKS ABOUT AT NIGNT.

merely a discussion of the situation between two late troopers of the Buluwayo Field Force, dealing more particularly with the "Proclamation to the Rebels," which had been issued last night.

Their review of it was remarkable, not only for the vigour, and—well—the originality of their language, but also because it covered exactly the ground over which all travelled again when they came to discuss it with me, or in my hearing, during the remainder of the day. One thing that struck them all was that this proclamation of clemency which was now to be published to the rebels was made in England and not in Rhodesia, and that "it was made by people who had no more conception of how things were in this part of the world than a boiled dumpling had of horse-racing;" at least, that was what they inferred from the tenor of its wording. I do not say that they had read and inwardly digested the exact literal meaning of the wording. I think, on the contrary, that they had only grasped a general idea of it all; the very heading of a "Proclamation of Clemency" at such a juncture having filled their thoughts with rage, and left them to read the rest with biased minds.

Unfortunately for the proclamation, within a few hours of its publication there came from Mashonaland another of the horrid telegrams with which we are only too familiar now. After telling of three different murders of friendly natives by rebels on the previous day, it went on to say; the wife and two daughters of Mobele, the native missionary, reached Salisbury from Marendellas this morning. They related how the missionary was killed by rebels while he was endeavouring to save the life of James White, who was lying wounded. White was also killed. Then three little children of the missionary were killed. And the women themselves were maltreated and left for dead. They did not know their way to Salisbury, so followed the telegraph line, and travelled by night only, suffering great privations."

It is a far cry from Mashonaland to England, and distance lessens the sharpness of the sympathy, but to men on the spot—men with an especially strong, manly, and chivalrous spirit in them, as is the case in this land of pioneers—to them such cases as these appeal in a manner which cannot be realised in dear, drowsy, after-lunch Old England. A man here does not mind carrying his own life in his hand—he likes it, and takes an attack on himself as a good bit of sport; but touch a woman or a child, and he is in a blind fury in a moment—and then he is gently advised to be mild, and to offer clemency to the poor benighted heathen, who is his brother after all. M', yes! And though woman is his first care, and can command his last drop of blood in her defence, woman is the first to assail him on his return, with venom-pointed pen, for his brutality!

Then my friends at the window went on to talk on the clause which permitted loyally-disposed natives to carry arms. "Loyal!"—as if any native could be loyal if it did not happen to suit his circumstances, and even then, why should he be allowed arms?

> He was not likely to be at war with his brothers and cousins, and the absence of arms would be a good assurance of peace; whereas, after the late bitter experience, how would confidence ever be instilled into farmers to induce them to come and re-build the blackened ruins of farmsteads whose owners had been murdered by the selfsame natives glowering yonder, *assegais* and gun in hand?

My friends were deploring the fact that their would-be rulers far away are quite out of touch with the circumstances of the case. Writers in the press, they said, gaily condemn the burning down of *kraals* and consequent destruction of the grain stores, which are all the natives now depend upon for food. But burning down a *kraal* is more or less a formal act, which has a deal of meaning for the native comprehension. That the store of grain is lost thereby is quite a fallacy. The grain is buried here in pits beneath the *kraal*; grain will not burn in pits, it can only be destroyed by drowning.

I was glad when at last my early arguers moved on to get their morning coffee. Had I been so minded, I might have soothed their feelings by telling them the latest news we had from captured rebels; that they need not vex their souls over the wording or the terms of the proclamation so thoughtfully provided for our use by those at home, for whether put in that or any other form, there was not the slightest chance of its being seriously accepted by the rebels. Our informants came from four different ways, and agreed like one in showing that although North-Western Matabeleland has thoroughly been cleared, the lower and more trappy part, in the Matopos, as well as the North-Eastern parts, remain the home of mutiny, and there, at least, the *impis* will not think of giving in until the white man comes to fight them, and they promise boastfully that he shall suffer then.

The proclamation offering terms to the rebels by which they may surrender has gone forth to them by the best messengers that could be got, that is, by men who have been captured in the field, or who have come in offering to give themselves up, and also by native policemen, who, having been disarmed on suspicion of rebellious tendencies, have been since retained in open arrest. But so far the result has not been entirely satisfactory, although it has done some good, and undoubtedly the thin edge of the wedge towards peace has been inserted, but it will yet need some driving to get it home and finally to split the log of rebellion.

Many of the rebels would probably give in if the leaders would but let them. They are tired of war, and sick of being hustled about. But then these leaders have a strong power over them, and they are fighting with the halter round their necks, for they know their crimes are far too great to be condoned, and thus they try to carry on until the bitter end.

In the north, where they have suffered most hard blows, the *impis* are much broken up, and there it is that some of the people are surrendering of their own accord; they are coming in, in driblets and small bodies it is true, but still this is a beginning. There are, so far, no chiefs among them. Then, on the other hand, there exists a large proportion who still have the idea that they yet may beat the whites, and drive them from the land, and they are encouraged in maintaining this idea by spies' reports, which tell them how the white men are daily going down-country to the Cape. Now that the road has been rendered safe and open by the operations in the Matopos, hired waggons, in addition to the bi-weekly coaches, are taking passengers in scores. The high cost of living at famine prices, and all business at a standstill, are the reasons for this exodus.

Then the *M'limo*, fearful for his own old skin, continues to issue most encouraging news and orders. He has revived with much success the story that disease is sweeping off the whites in Buluwayo, and promises that any warrior "doctored" by his charm is proof against the British bullets, which on his hide will turn to water. They only have to wait till all the whites are dead or fled, and then they will enjoy the good things of the town, and live in palaces of corrugated iron. All this they believe implicitly.

The rebels in the south have every reliance, and with reason, on the impregnability of their rock-strongholds; and their confidence is strengthened by their store of grain and cattle, which were being brought, long before the outbreak, into the hills by the *M'limo*'s orders. Of arms and ammunition they have plenty, although the puzzle is to say from whence they come. But there they are—Martinis, Lee-

Metfords, Winchesters, besides the blunderbusses and elephant guns, which at the close quarters of this fighting make very deadly practice. And then our so-called friendlies are known to be supplying them with information of our moves, as well as with such luxuries as *kaffir* beer and cartridges.

It is only, even now, internal jealousies among the rebel chiefs that save the whites from being blotted out. The attempt to make Nyamanda king, if ever seriously intended, fell through abortively; each of the great chiefs desires that honour for himself, and thus the different *impis* do not amalgamate to crush us, but they let our puny force go round and punch them all in turn, in such a way as breaks them daily smaller.

The proclamation has gone forth to these men too; but answer comes there none, except at times when scouting parties meet, and then the rebels shout to us, from their look-out rocks, such words as these: "And so you want to end the war, do you? Yes, it will be ended soon, for none of you will live to keep it on." And then they add a stream of highly-coloured threats of personal damage they will do to our nice white corpses. The tired, desponding tone of impending submission which one would hope to hear is altogether absent from their talk.

Then, even those who have surrendered have done it in a mere half-hearted way; that is to say, scarce one among them has produced his gun. Of course, the terms of their surrender include the giving up of their arms; but that is an extent to which they do not wish to yield. They cannot tell when they may want to break out again, and where

A HUMAN SALT-CELLAR

would they be then without their guns? That is the way they reason with themselves. It suits them, for the time, to come and *"konza"* to make peace, to save their skins and sow their crops; but, all the same, they stow away their guns and ammunition in their holes among the rocks, and hand up, as their "arms," their oldest *assegais* and shields. Thus, even when the present military force has broken up the *impis* in the field, and cleared their strongholds out, there will remain a tale of work for local police to do in carrying out disarmament. And it is then, and only then, that peace can settle firmly on the land.

The doses being given now may seem too bitter to our tender-hearted countrymen at home; but, "though bitter now, they're better then." It seems the only way to get these men to understand there is a greater power than their *M'limo*; and once the lesson has been unmistakably brought home to them, there is some hope that a time of peace *en permanence* may dawn for them. It is the end for which we all are striving here. And the present system of Sir Frederick Carrington is the most promising that could be devised to suit the circumstances. With his tiny force, he goes from point to point where *impis* are collected; in every case he strikes them hard, and promptly builds a fort there on the spot, and leaves a party in possession. The people round are told they may surrender. The forts are then to act as police posts in the future, to ensure the peace of every outside district, by standing as a sword of Damocles to all offenders, and a handy tower of refuge for friendlies who are oppressed.

We shall soon be in a position to judge the value of the rebels' threats, for all is now prepared for our campaign in the Matopos; Laing's column (200 strong) being encamped near the western end, Plumer's (of 800) at "Ushers' No 1," near the central part. This latter camp I visited late at night on the 15th.

16th July.—Early this morning I picked up Pyke and Taylor (the Native commissioner), and we rode on to inspect the country between the centre and west of the enemy's position. At Jozan's *kraal* (friendly), about four miles north of the enemy, we stopped to talk, get news, and lunch. Lunch was got for us by our host, Jozan, as follows:—A live sheep was brought, and laid before us on some leafy twigs; its throat was then gently cut, the liver taken out, and fried in an iron bowl. Off this we made our meal, without any bread or other concomitant, excepting salt, which was held by a human salt-cellar for us. We took our salt by dipping each his hunk of meat into the nigger's grimy palm.

PREPARING LUNCH

We had a good look at the enemy's position, and then we got thirty of Jozan's men, armed with *assegais* and shields, to go with us across the neutral valley and examine the great *kraal* that lay opposite, in which watch-fires had been burning the night before. As we got near to it, we spread out our little army into a crescent shape, with two horns advanced, and we attacked the village in style; but the only enemy there were two men and one ox, and these cleared out in a great hurry before we got in. We burned the *kraal*, and then reconnoitred into the *koppies* beyond, where we found another *kraal*, also deserted, which we burned. Among other odds and ends of loot in this *kraal*, we found a high-jump standard, evidently stolen from the Athletic Sports Ground near Buluwayo.

But my release from town and office life now came. As I knew the Matopos country and the enemy's whereabouts, I was sent to act as guide to Colonel Plumer, who was to have the immediate direction of operations in the Matopos, Vyvyan taking the office work off my hands.

17th July.—The general now took up his quarters in camp, to direct affairs against the Matopos. And the following day I took Pyke, Richardson (interpreter), and four native scouts into the Matopos, to get a view of Babyan's stronghold: Babyan's being the central and important *impi* of all, and in close communication with the westernmost *impi* at Inugu.

We approached the position through open, park-like country interspersed with piles of granite boulders a hundred feet in height; from these *koppies* we could hear the look-out men calling a warning cry to each other, and now and again we could see them, perched up on high, watching our movements. I was sorry then that we had brought natives with us, as, if the enemy were to come and have a try at us now, it would be easy enough for us three, had we been alone, to gallop away; but, having the boys on foot with us, we should now have to stick to them and help them away. So they hampered us somewhat. But still we didn't do badly.

The valley in which the enemy lay was surrounded by rugged *koppies*; one of these was a great, dome-shaped mass of granite; we went for it, as being easy to climb, and less trappy and liable to ambush. Upon its crest stood the ruins of a farm belonging to Usher, and a path led up a little gully to the huts. Instead of taking this path, we were sufficiently wily to go round the hill for a bit; then leaving our horses hidden in a clump of bushes, with two sharp-eyed boys in charge, we quickly scrambled on to the top of the *koppie*. Two or three of the enemy, who had been using this as a look-out place, bolted away before us. We had a very useful view from here of the lie of the ground, and of the position of the enemy, as shown by the smoke of his camp-fires.

One felt tempted to stay there, and drink in every detail and map it down; but suddenly I saw the head and shoulders of a crouching figure dash across the opening between two rocks at the foot of our position, followed by another, and another—not fifty yards from us. They were racing to cut us off in the glen! They had seen us on the top, and guessed that our horses would naturally have been left on the pathway. But they were sold—as were also another party, whom we could see hastening out into the bush to cut us off on our homeward path. We gave them a few shots, and then scuttled down the far side of the rock, got our horses, sent our boys trotting along ahead of us, and we quietly got away through the bush by a totally different route to that by which we came.

---

1. A more detailed account of the operations in the Matopos—together with a complete and interesting description of the organisation and work of the Matabeleland Relief Force—will be found in Lieut.-Colonel Plumer's book, *An Irregular Corps in Matabeleland*.

CHAPTER 6[1]

Campaign in the Matopos
19th July to 24th July.

19th July.—At last out time came. The order was given to the men in the morning, "Bake two days' bread, and sleep all you can this afternoon." At what was usually our bedtime the whole column paraded without noise or trumpet call, and at 10.30 we moved off in the moonlight into the Matopos. I was told off to guide the column, because I knew the way. I preferred to go alone in front of the column, for fear of having my attention distracted if anyone were with me, and of my thereby losing my bearings. And there was something of a weird and delightful feeling in mooching along alone, with a dark, silent square of men and horses looming along behind one.

Neither talking nor smoking was allowed—for the gleam of a match lighting a pipe shines a long way in the darkness. Except for the occasional cough of a man or snort of a horse, the column, nearly a thousand strong, moved in complete silence. Once a dog yelped with excitement after a buck started from its lair; the orders for the night expressly stated that no dog should go with the column, and accordingly this one was promptly caught and killed with an *assegai*.

Soon after midnight we were within a mile of the place; the square halted, and each man lay down to sleep just where he stood—and jolly cold it was!

An hour before dawn we were up and on our way again, moving quietly onwards until we were close to the pass among the *koppies* which led into ,the enemy's valley. Here, just as dawn was coming on, we left the ambulance and a reserve of men, together with our greatcoats and other impedimenta, and formed our column for attacking the stronghold.

First came an advance force comprising the two corps of Cape

Boys, Robertson's and Colenbrander's. Cape Boys are natives and half-castes from the Cape Colony, mostly English-speaking, and dressed and armed like Europeans. There were also 200 friendly Matabele under Taylor, the Native commissioner, twenty mounted white scouts under Coope, and a Hotchkiss and two Maxims under Llewellyn. This force was under my command.

Then came the main body of white troops under Colonel Plumer; this consisted of three troops of the newly-raised police under Nicholson, the M.R.F. (Plumer's corps), with two mountain battery guns. Also a detachment from the Belingwe column under Sir Frederick Frankland, which had volunteered to join in the fight (and had had to march all night from a distant camp to overtake us) and see the fun.

Sir Frederick Carrington was there also, though properly speaking he was on the sick-list with bronchitis,—not a thing to be trifled with when you have an old bullet-wound in your lung,—and with him were Lord Grey and Cecil Rhodes.

And so we advanced in the growing daylight into the broken, bushy valley, which was surrounded on every side by rough, rocky cliffs and *koppies*. Fresh paths and spoor showed that hundreds of rebels must be living here, and at last I jumped with joy when I spotted one thin streak of smoke after another rising among the crags on the eastern side of the valley. My telescope soon showed that there was a large camp with numerous fires, and crowds of natives moving among them. These presently formed into one dense brown mass, with their *assegai* blades glinting sharply in the rays of the morning sun. We soon got the guns up to the front from the main body, and in a few minutes they were banging their shells with beautiful accuracy over the startled rebel camp.

While they were at this game, I stole onwards with a few native scouts into the bottom of the valley, and soon saw another thin wisp of smoke not far from me in the bush; we crept cautiously down, and there found a small outpost of the enemy just leaving the spot where they had been camped for the night. At this point two valleys ran off from the main valley in which we were; one, running to the south, was merely a long narrow gorge, along which flowed the Tuli River; the other, on the opposite side of the river from us, ran to the eastward and formed a small open plateau surrounded by a circle of intricate *koppies*. While we were yet watching at this point, strings of natives suddenly appeared streaming across this open valley, retiring from the camp on the mountain above, which was being shelled by our guns. They were going very leisurely, and, thinking themselves unobserved, proceeded to take up their position among the encircling *koppies*. I sent back word of their movements, and calling together the Native Levy, proceeded at once to attack them. To do this more effectually, we worked round to the end of the main valley and got into some vast rock strongholds on the edge of the Tuli gorge.

These, though recently occupied by hundreds of men, were now vacated, and one had an opportunity of seeing what a rebel stronghold was like from the inside; all the paths were blocked and barricaded with rocks and small trees; the whole place was honeycombed with caves to which all entrances, save one or two, were blocked with stones; among these loopholes were left, such as to enable the occupants to fire in almost any direction. Looking from these loopholes to the opposite side of the gorge, we could see the enemy close on us in large numbers, taking up their position in a similar stronghold. Now and again two or three of them would come out of a cave on to a flat rock and dance a war-dance at our troops, which they could see in the distance, being quite unsuspicious of our near presence.

They were evidently rehearsing what they would do when they caught the white man among their rocks, and they were shouting all sorts of insults to the troops, more with a spirit of bravado than with any idea of their reaching their ears at that distance. Interesting as the performance was, we did not sit it out for long, but put an abrupt end to it by suddenly loosing a volley at them at short range and from this unexpected quarter.

Then, clambering down among the rocks, we crossed the Tuli River and commenced the ascent of the towering crags in which the enemy were located. Of course this had to be done on foot, and I left my horse tied to a tree, with my coat and all spare kit hung in the branches.

Our friendlies went very gaily at the work at first, with any amount of filing, but very little result; the enemy had now entirely disappeared into their caves and holes among the rocks, merely looking out to fire and then popping in again. Our own niggers climbed about, firing among the rocks, but presently did more firing than climbing, and began to take cover and to stick to it; finally, two of them were bowled over, and the rest of them got behind the rocks and there remained, and no efforts could get them to budge. I then called up the Cape Boys and the Maxims (in which Lord Grey assisted where it was difficult to move owing to the very bad ground); these reinforcements came up with no loss of time and went to work with a will. It was delightful to watch the cool, business-like way in which Robertson brought his Boys along. They floundered through the boggy stream and crawled up the smooth, dome-shaped rocks beyond, and soon were clambering up among the *koppies*, banging and cheering. Llewellyn, too, brought his guns along at equal speed, and soon had them in equal position on apparently inaccessible crags, where they came into action with full effect at every chance the enemy gave them.

The fight gradually moved along the eastern valley, in the centre of which was a convenient rock from which I was able to see all that was going on, and it formed a good centre for directing the attacks, as the enemy were in the rocks on every side of us. The Cape Boys, after making a long circle round through part of the stronghold, reassembled at this spot, and from it directed their further attacks on the different parts requiring them, and it became the most convenient position for the machine guns, as they were able to play in every direction in turn from this point. For the systematic attack on the stronghold a portion of it is assigned to each company, and it is a pleasing sight to see the calm and ready way in which they set to work. They crowd into the narrow, bushy paths between the *koppies*, and then swarm out over the rocks from whence the firing comes, and very soon the row begins.

A scattered shot here and there, and then a rattling volley; the boom of the elephant gun roaring dully from inside a cave is answered by the sharp crack of a Martini-Henry; the firing gradually wakes up on every side of us, the weird whisk of a bullet overhead is varied by the hum of a leaden-coated stone or the shriek of a pot-leg fired from a Matabele big-bore gun; and when these noises threaten to become monotonous, they are suddenly enlivened up by the hurried energetic "*tap, tap, tap*" of the Maxims or the deafening "*pong*" of the Hotchkiss. As you approach the *koppies*, excitement seems to be in the air; they stand so still and harmless-looking, and yet you know that from several at least of those holes and crannies the enemy are watching you, with finger on trigger, waiting for a fair chance. But it is from the least expected quarter that a roar comes forth and a cloud of smoke and the dust flies up at your feet.

It's laughable to watch a Cape Boy prying into a cave with his long bayonet held out before him, as if to pick some human form of winkle from his shell. Suddenly he fires into the smoke which spurts from

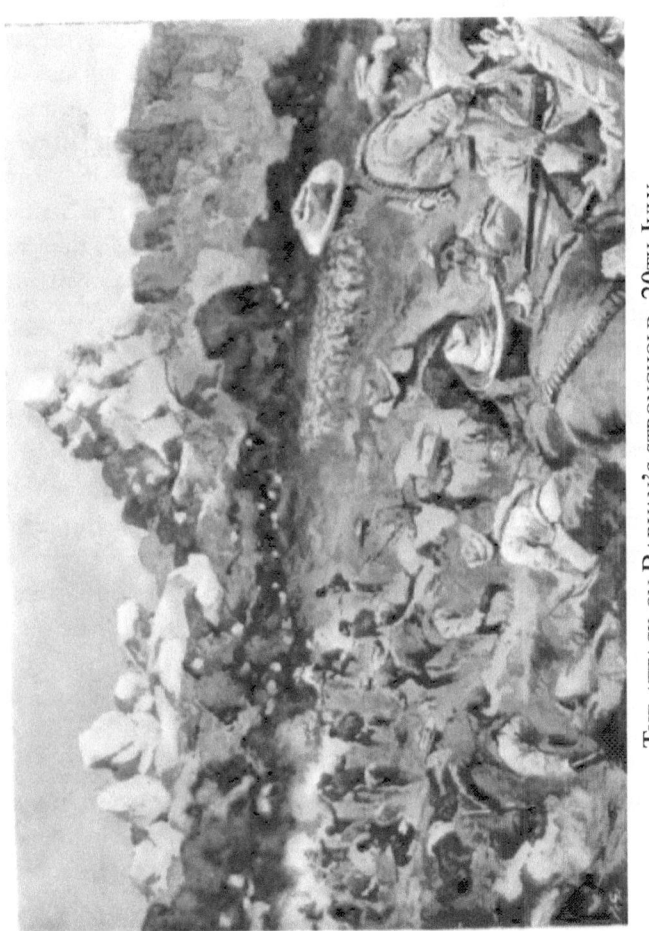

The attack on Babyan's stronghold, 20th July

the cave before him. Too late: he falls, and then tries to rise—his leg is shattered. A moment later, three of his comrades are round him; they dash past him and disappear into the hole, two dull, thud-like shots within, and presently they come out again, jabbering and gesticulating to each other; then they pick up the injured man by his arms and drag him out into the open, and, leaving him there for the doctor's party to find, they are quickly back again for further sport.

At one moment they appear like monkeys on unexpected points of rock, at another like stage assassins creeping round corners and shooting,—or being shot. As we turn the corner, going up one of the paths, we find ourselves face to face with a similar string of rebels trotting down the path. For a moment the thought crosses one's mind. Shall we stop to fire or go for them? but before the thought has time to fashion itself, we find ourselves going for them. Nor do they wait for their bayonets: they turn helter-skelter, rushing up the path, diving among the rocks and grass, for though fond of administering cold steel, it is the last thing they wish to meet with themselves, and so we treat them to the next best thing, a few well-aimed shots.

Out on our central rock again, we get reports from various detached attacking parties, showing that at every point the rebels are being cleared or killed in their dens; but plenty of individuals of them still are left, and of this we have practical demonstration in the frequent visitation of bullets and other missiles, and some of them do their shooting pretty accurately, the Maxim attracting the aim of many a marksman among them. One of these marksmen we have nicknamed "Old Potlegs," from the nature of the missile (the iron legs of *kaffir* cooking-pots) with which he treats us at intervals of ten minutes or so. Another on the other side we have christened "Rinderpest," because he is a plague to us with his Lee-Metford rifle.

Meantime, several of our men have got hit, and have been brought in to our central rock, some of them brought out at considerable risk, too, by their officers and other men. But there are no stretchers to put them on, our bearer corps of friendly natives, who had been detailed to accompany the force, having entirely disappeared during the advance. (We afterwards found that they had dropped the stretchers in the Tuli River, and had dispersed themselves into the safest hiding-places they could find.) Nor was our surgeon here at first, Surgeon-Captain Lunan, for wherever firing was the hottest, there he went—to try and make it hotter. So in the meantime we did the best amateur work we could on the wounded men brought in. Of these

Amateur Doctoring

there were six, all badly wounded, in addition to two more killed; and it is a pathetic comedy to watch the burly Royal Artillery sergeant transforming himself into a nurse for the occasion with a rough good-heartedness that does not stop to consider whether his patients are black or white.

At last the firing slackens off; our Maxim and our marksmen have stopped the fire of "Rinderpest," "Pot-legs" and Co. for good, and our parties return from their attacks in different directions, pretty tired, but cheerful; and now, having cleared the stronghold, we might well return to the main body, who are still in the main valley behind, but without stretchers we cannot carry the wounded, so, while we take a rest, our flag-waggers signal back for stretchers to be sent with white men to carry them, and not the useless friendlies.

But, from our apparent inaction, the Matabele, who still are watching us, gather that we are in some sort of distress; presently they are calling to one another among the rocks between us and the main body, and very soon we find that they are collecting in force in the Tuli River gorge, intent on cutting us off should we attempt to rejoin our friends.

(The above was written while we paused inactive on the field, waiting for the stretchers.)

A piquet, which we had posted in this direction, soon became pretty warmly engaged with them, but the only danger of the situation was the danger to the enemy themselves, for our main body, quickly realising the state of affairs, came down upon their rear, and in a few moments, finding themselves between two heavy fires, this wing of the rebels broke up in hurried flight, leaving some twenty of their dusky bodies huddled dead among the yellow grass. Very shortly afterwards a string of white men carrying stretchers, escorted by a squadron of the M.R.F. on foot, came up to our position, and soon we were comfortably on our way to rejoin headquarters.

During the return march I sent the Cape Boys skirmishing into the strongholds on either side of us, but they found them, in every case, completely clear of living enemies, though numerous bodies and blood-trials spoke to the success of the morning's attack.

On reaching the main body, we lunched and slept, while the surgeons got to work on the wounded; among these, unfortunately, a number of amputations were found necessary, on account of the terrible wounds inflicted by the Matabele missiles.

We learned with much regret of the death of Sergeant Warringham, who, while we were fighting in the stronghold, had been shot when scouting down the Tuli gorge, and had been brought in under a nasty fire by Colonel Bridge, Captain Vyvyan, and others, patrolling near him. The party. Colonel Frank Rhodes among them, had lost several horses shot, but, with the greatest luck, came out un wounded themselves, except Lieutenant Taylor, who was slightly hit. From daylight up till two o'clock we had been at it, and though practically only the advanced force had been engaged, the action was a complete success, and Babyan had been broken up in his own stronghold. And since he is the great leader among them, having been one of Lobengula's most trusted *indunas*, and also having visited the English in their own country, his defeat should have a great moral effect among the remaining rebel chiefs.

During the afternoon we returned to camp, arriving there after dark. A curious incident occurred on this march back, which might have had unpleasant effects on the man concerned. Lieutenant Lowther of Coope's Scouts was sent on ahead of the column to call up another ambulance from the camp, but in doing so he lost his way, and was missing for the next two days, eventually turning up at Fig Tree Fort, some five-and-twenty miles distant, having met with various adventures with small parties of the rebels on the way.

21st July.—It had been part of the General's plan that while we were attacking Babyan, Captain Laing with his column should also simultaneously attack the enemy's *impi* on the Inugu Mountain, some eight miles to the westward. During our attack yesterday morning we had heard Laing's guns banging away in a very, lively manner in the distance, so that we had expected, on returning to camp, to get some news from him, but none came. We accordingly sent off some native runners to go and find him, and to bring back information, in case he should yet be among the mountains, and we also sent a mounted patrol down to where his camp should be had he been successful, and returned into the main valley of the Malema River.

But we could learn nothing of him; the natives returned and reported that he was cut off by the enemy from all power of communication. Naturally this began to make us feel somewhat anxious, as I had already reported on the danger of the gorges in the neighbourhood of the Inugu, and of the knowledge the enemy had of their tactical strength. So this evening the general desired me to take a strong patrol of a hundred men, and go and find Laing.

We left camp soon after dark, and followed the Malema valley in the moonlight, until we were in the pass in the mountains which led down to the Inugu. My idea was to move through the outlying hills to strike the spoor which Laing had made in going into the hills, and simply to follow that track until I found him. Even to strike the spoor, one had to pass through some very nasty country, parts of which were in occupation of the enemy; but as their main strength would now be collected against Laing, and those that were left behind would probably be asleep, I did not expect much opposition on their part. At length we successfully struck the spoor, but, to my great surprise and delight, we found it was quite fresh spoor, leading *outward* away from the mountains, and it very soon brought us to within sight of his camp-fires; so, sounding a few trumpet-calls as we went, in order to show that we were no enemy, we made our way into his camp about eleven o'clock.

We found he had had a good fight, having been attacked in *laager* after he had got well inside the gorge; he had eventually driven off the enemy with the loss of nearly a hundred, his own losses being three whites killed and ten wounded, twenty-five friendlies killed or missing and eighteen wounded, and eighteen horses and mules killed. We did not wait longer than to hear the good news, but started back at once for our own camp, which we reached at three in the morning, and, needless to say, the general was delighted to be roused up to receive the news.

Captain Laing's column had left their camp in the Malema valley on the 19th, and had gone into the pass alongside the Inugu Mountain, but without seeing a sign of an enemy. They had gone on to the end of this pass, hoping to find a route by which they might come into Babyan's stronghold from the southward, and thus co-operate with us in our attack on the 20th. They *laagered* for the night with their waggons on the evening of the 19th in the widest part of the Inugu pass.

Just before dawn on the 20th, they had stood to arms, as usual, when suddenly a number of shots were fired close outside the *laager*, and the outlying piquet came running in, accompanied, rather than pursued, by a crowd of Matabele. No alarm could have been more sudden, but the men, being all at their places, were able to open fire on the moment, and their volley checked a rush that had evidently been carefully organised, when it was within twenty yards of the waggons. Although checked in their attempt, the enemy did not at once recoil, but kept up an irregular and hasty fire from what cover they could then gain among stones and grass; but, disheartened by the readiness with which they were received, and the telling fire of the defence, they began to get away by twos and threes into the better cover of the rocks which commanded the camp on all sides.

It was now that the column suffered most, for the enemy, firing at short range, with good rests and from safe cover, picked off men and mules with great frequency. At one place in particular a number of their best marksmen were collected together, and did great execution until the 7-pounder was turned on them, and, firing case at fifty yards, effectually stopped their fire. The Maxim gun had here, too, attracted the special attention of the enemy, and four successive men were struck down while firing it, until Captain Hopper himself finally took the saddle.

Then the friendly natives in the *laager* were sent out to make a diversion, either to draw the enemy on or to frighten him out of his position, in either of which cases he would give our Maxims and rifle fire a chance. The enemy, suspecting they were going to be cut off, took the latter course; they began to retire in large numbers, in consequence of which the defenders were enabled to inflict heavy loss upon them, and sent them flying scattered and disheartened. But in their short outing a large number of our Native Levy were killed, wounded, or became missing, probably, in the latter case, taking to caves on their own account.

The column now continued its original work, namely, that of endeavouring to get round to Babyan's stronghold, but, finding their course altogether barred by mountains, they turned back, and made their way out to the camp where I found them. Their action had, however, much simplified ours in Babyan's stronghold that day, for Babyan, having heard of the approach of Laing's column towards Inugu, while as yet he knew nothing of our moves, had sent part of his *impi* to assist the Inugu rebels; this force had come upon the scene of Laing's fight only to meet their friends in full flight, and had, therefore, taken no part in that battle; and in the meantime, during their absence, we had smashed up their own main body in their stronghold.

22nd July.—Forgot that I had been up all night, and went for a bit of solitary exercise into the hills, to investigate some signs I had noted two days before of an *impi* camped in a new place. After a tedious bit of work, I found that they had decamped. I then went to the neighbourhood of Babyan's stronghold, but could see no natives about there. Also, in accordance with the general's instructions, I selected a position in which to build a fort to command this portion of the Matopos. I chose a point where there was open, fairly flat ground for half a mile in every direction, close to a permanent stream, at a spot where there was a mighty thorn tree which would serve for a "crow's-nest" or raised platform from which a look-out man could see well in every direction, and where a Maxim gun would command the whole of the ground round the fort. On return to camp, I drew out the design and plan of the proposed fort, and in the evening again went out there, taking with me a portion of Robertson's Cape Boys to start work upon it the following morning. This fort was named Fort Usher, being near the site of one of Usher's farms.

24th July.—It is reported that the rebels have again returned to the Inugu gorge, so Nicholson was sent off today with a strong party to investigate. A second *impi* is reported to be about the Chabez valley about twelve miles westward of us in the Matopos; from Buluwayo they report that a third is near the town (Laing has been ordered to move in that direction); while a fourth is said to be thirty-five miles west of Buluwayo, and 500 of Gambo's friendly natives are to go against it, accompanied by Chief Native Commissioner Taylor. This makes things seem pretty lively, but so very often these reports end in nothing, especially when they emanate from Buluwayo.

One thing that adds to the excitement this evening, is that on seven hills around the camp we can see the signal fires of the enemy burning, which may mean that they are contemplating a big attack on us. We have withdrawn the party who were out building the fort, and concentrated them in camp, and I shall sleep with my pistol-belt on. (I generally only sleep with my pistol under my pillow and the lanyard round my neck—this latter precaution I never omit.)

We sleep soundly, yet very lightly, in camp. If anyone comes within ten yards of me,—however softly he may tread,—I wake up without fail. Bedtime is looked forward to with some zest here, for early rising and hard work all day make one pretty ready for rest by the evening, and very soon after supper one makes for one's blankets.

The bedroom is usually the lee-side of a bush or *scherm* of cut branches. The bed—if you are luxurious, and are marching with waggons—is a valise-roll, comprising waterproof sheet, cork mattress, blanket, and small feather pillow— but what is more usual, is just your blanket, and your saddle for pillow. One's toilet for the night is simple: doff hat, don nightcap, and loosen your boot-laces, or, if you have them, change your boots for shoes. Then you are ready to sleep, and to turn out on the moment if there is a night alarm.

If you have a fire at your feet, you place the butt of the longest log close to your hand, so that during the night you can keep it stoked without having to get up for the purpose.

And then you take a last look at the glorious star-spangled ceiling overhead, and, until all is blurred in sleep, you see in the dark mantle above you the veil of ignorance that shrouds the earth from heaven's light beyond—the starry points of brightness that tend to light us are holes made in that covering by the work of good men, whose example and whose teaching encourage us to try and take our little part in letting in the light in imitation of the greater radiant orb—to lighten up the darkness till the daylight dawns.

CHAPTER 7

Our Work in the Matopos
25th July to 2nd August.

25th July.—Today I have had a long day reconnoitring, taking Pyke, Jan Grootboom, and Tagili. Pyke, as I have before indicated, is one of the best among a very good lot of young colonial officers serving in Plumer's corps; and a very keen and useful scouting officer. Jan Grootboom is a Cape Boy of Zulu extraction, and is a man of exceptional courage and soldierly ability. As one of Grey's Scouts—and one who loathed the ordinary *kaffir*—said of him: "He is not a proper nigger; his skin is black, but he has a white man's heart. I will shake hands with him." He is a clever scout, and a daring spy—one who has no hesitation in disguising himself as a Matabele, on occasion, and going in among their women to gather information. And he is a first-rate man in a fight. So, altogether, he was of the greatest service to me. Tagili is a good native scout, and faithful, but not "in the same street" with Grootboom.

We went into the Matopos, to the gorge of the Chabez River, about fifteen miles east of camp. It is a very nasty bit of country, and we had to keep our eyes open as we went, for we knew the rebels were about, although we could see nothing of them. This is a particularly dangerous sign; if they see you are a strong party, too strong for them to attack or capture, they do not mind showing themselves, and they come out to get a better look at you; but if it is a small party, and one which they have hopes of, they will hide and lie low, in order to get you in their grasp. I think they had hopes of us, for we got pretty close to their stronghold, and saw where they ought to be, but not one of them showed up. As we prowled around, we came across frequent tracks not many minutes old; possibly they went and waited for us on the path by which we arrived, but if they did so, they were sold, for we came back by an entirely different route.

The Chabez River rises in the valley of the Umzingwane, and runs south through the Matopos. It enters the Matopos through an enormous gorge, in the cliffs and heights of which the rebels have numerous caves, while they keep their cattle in the thick bush jungle along the river banks.

We first approached the place by the upper ground among the mountains, then, making our way round, we got into the Umzingwane valley, from which we could look into the mouth of the gorge, and could see what an impossible country it was for working in. We spent some time guessing at the enemy's position, determining which would be the best way to attack them, and in mapping the ground; and then we retired a short distance across the valley to a *koppie*, from which we could watch the place without fear of anybody approaching us unseen.

But the way we had come was an impossible one for waggons, and I wanted to ascertain whether it was possible to bring them by a better route along the Umzingwane valley; so, leaving Pyke and Grootboom to watch the stronghold,—for we hoped that as evening came on, the enemy would light up their fires for cooking, and would thus betray their position,—I made my way back along the valley in the direction of our camp. Here I arrived after dark, having found this way also impossible for waggons. It would therefore seem necessary to organise some pack transport to take us to the Chabez stronghold, and afterwards, by the Umzingwane valley, towards the strongholds of the eastern end of the Matopos. Once here, we shall be on the Tuli-Buluwayo road, where the waggons, having gone round by Hope Fountain, or by Buluwayo, could rejoin us.

27th July.—Major Kershaw took out a strong patrol for a further reconnaissance of the Chabez position. He was able to get up to the high ground overlooking the river gorge, and found that it broke up into most difficult country, of *koppies* and bush and deep ravines leading down to the river. While he was there, a good number of the enemy showed themselves on the different *koppies*, evidently watching his moves, but not inclined to attack him. On his return march to camp, Major Kershaw, with one or two others, was riding at some distance from the main party, when he came across a large party of the enemy going towards the Chabez; he luckily saw them first, and was able to hide until they had passed by.

Out in camp here Press correspondents have to bring me their messages, in order to get them signed for transmission by the field telegraph, and it is most interesting to see what marvellous news some of them can manage to fake up out of very inadequate material. Anything to be different from his rival! but is it always certain whether the information sent is true or not? Poor old Mother Necessity is not "in it" with a budding war correspondent. Many of them do not seem to grasp the broader military features of what is going on; but the local pressmen, being often fighting men themselves, are much the best in this respect, and it is a great pity that it is not their news which is cabled home.

29th July.—Today, when out scouting by myself, being at some distance from my boy and the horses, I lay for a short rest and a quiet look-out among some rocks and grass overlooking a little stream; and I saw a charming picture. Presently there was a slight rattle of trinkets, and a swish of the tall yellow grass, followed by the sudden apparition of a naked Matabele warrior standing glistening among the rocks of the streamlet, within thirty yards of me. His white war ornaments— the ball of clipped feathers on his brow, and the long white cow's-tail plumes which depended from his arms and knees—contrasted strongly with his rich brown skin. His kilt of wild cat-skins and monkeys' tails swayed round his loins. His left hand bore his *assegais* and *knobkerrie* beneath the great dappled ox-hide shield; and, in his right, a yellow walking-staff.

A MATABELE WARRIOR

He stood for almost a minute perfectly motionless, like a statue cast in bronze, his head turned from me, listening for any suspicious sound. Then, with a swift and easy movement, he laid his arms and shield noiselessly upon the rocks, and, dropping on all fours beside a pool, he dipped his muzzle down and drank just like an animal. I could hear the thirsty sucking of his lips from where I lay. He drank and drank as though he never meant to stop, and when: at last his frame could hold no more, he rose with evident reluctance. He picked his weapons up, and then stood again to listen. Hearing nothing, he turned and sharply moved away. In three swift strides he disappeared within the grass as silently as he had come. I had been so taken with the spectacle that I felt no desire to shoot at him—especially as he was carrying no gun himself.

31st July.—We started on the war-path again. We broke up camp, sending the waggons round to go by Hope Fountain on to the Tuli road, there to meet us two days hence. Colonel Bridge had organised a packhorse train, and this now accompanied the column, carrying four days' supplies; but, as events proved, the horses, from overwork and want of food, are scarcely up to the job.

In the evening we started on our march to the eastward, past the fort which had been erected near Babyan's old stronghold, and a couple of miles beyond this we bivouacked, no fires nor lights being allowed. At 3 a.m. we were roused up and continued the march. There was no difficulty in finding the way, as I have got to know this ground pretty well. The only difficulty was to lead so that the column, which was marching in a big square, ready against an attack at any moment, should be incommoded as little as possible by the frequent thick patches of bush.

Just before dawn we arrived on Purser's Farm, one of the most delightful spots for a settler that I have seen in this country, but with its homestead and gardens now all ruthlessly destroyed.

Here we formed ready for the attack against the high ground overlooking the Chabez, which lay about a mile to our front. Kershaw, having already been on the ground, was detailed to command the attack, while I was sent round with Coope's Scouts to have a look in at the back of the position and to see whether a second effective attack could be delivered from that direction. We accordingly got away down to a rocky ridge which overlooked the entrance of the Chabez gorge; from this point we had an excellent view of the back cliffs and their caves which formed the enemy's lair. And we sent back word to Colonel Plumer that the guns would have a good opening here, and that the Cape Boys would probably be able to deliver an effective attack.

Presently we could hear Kershaw's men opening fire beyond the skyline of the ridge overlooking the gorge, and we could see the enemy swarming out of their caves to meet them. We accordingly worked our way nearer and nearer to them, and for a long time we were unnoticed, but when, after a time, the main body of our force began to appear in the valley, the alarm cry of the enemy could be heard echoing along the heights; still they seemed to consider us too distant to do them any harm, and they took no precaution to hide themselves from our view.

In an incredibly short space of time M'Culloch with his mule-guns was clambering up the rugged *koppie* on which we were posted, and the two 7-pounders were very soon fitted together and ready for action on the summit of the rocks.

Meantime we could hear heavy firing going on among the heights opposite, but could see very little of what was going on, as most of it was taking place just over the skyline.

But, seeing a small knot of niggers clustered on one of the nearer ridges, the artillery let fly a shell or two at them. It was very funny to note the effect of the first one through my telescope. I was watching three men sitting on the rock; one of them was talking eagerly to two others, gesticulating with his right hand and scratching himself with his left. "*Bang!*" went the gun close to my ear, but of course the little group before me did not hear it; the man talked on and scratched away, it seemed for well-nigh a minute. Suddenly the three of them were sprawling off the rock in different directions, throwing themselves down apparently head first, and then running for their lives! The shell had evidently just passed over their heads. The next two or three shells were similarly a little high, and burst out of sight on the other side of the ridge.

It afterwards turned out that they could not have been better sent, for, dropping well into the next valley, they had scattered their charge of shrapnel over the main force of rebels (four hundred men) who were gathered there, and who had not then been found by Major Kershaw's party. A very few shells were enough for them; they scattered and fled before they even came to blows with our men, merely given them a good target as they retired down into the deep gorges of the lower Chabez River. This ended the skirmish, and we made our way

THE THEORY AND PRACTICE OF WAR

down to the river and there bivouacked for breakfast.

Then, leaving the dismounted men and guns and baggage, the mounted part of the force went on for a raid towards the cattle valley near Inyanda's stronghold. We moved along the open valley close under the foot of the Matopo Mountains for about four or five miles, till we came on some cattle-paths leading from the grazing-grounds into the hills. Following up the main one, we (Coope's Scouts) found ourselves in a very nasty little gorge leading in between the mountains. Leaving our horses under a guard at the entrance, we clambered in amongst boulders and thick jungle that blocked the little path.

For about half a mile it was as nasty a place to be caught in as one could wish; then, getting on to rocks where the gorge opened out a little, we could hear the cattle lowing, dogs barking, women and boys yelling, as they evidently drove the herd from the farther end of the valley deeper into the mountains; and, at the same time, along the heights on either side we could see the Matabele gathering and moving to cut us off at the entrance. Seeing it was useless to try and follow the cattle in such a place, we amused ourselves in checking the boldness of the rebels moving on the heights by throwing in our shot among them. Then we made our way out again, and, remounting, continued our way along the foot of the hills.

Riding along by myself in the bush, my heart jumped with joy when I suddenly came upon the fresh spoor of cattle and of men leading into another small valley; I sounded my whistle and started along on the spoor, the scouts rounding up to me and taking up the trail just like a pack of hounds. After tearing through the bush for a short distance, we presently came upon a *kraal* in a secluded spot among the rocks; and there were the cattle right before us, with the men driving them! The men did not stop for us to catch them, but took refuge among the rocks, and while one part of the scouts dismounted to cover the operation with their fire if necessary, the remainder circled round the cattle and headed them back from the hills, through the bush, out into the open valley. One or two of the niggers in the rocks fired at us, and as we were advancing towards them to dislodge them,

I suddenly felt a blow on my thigh as though someone had struck me with a hammer; it knocked me down, and I turned round, thinking that I must have run against a tree stump, but none was there; and then I realised that I had been struck with a stone covered with lead, fired from one of these big bore guns. It did not even cut me, but my thigh is now a mighty bruise, black and blue all over and very stiff. Our only other casualty was Bodle's horse, which was struck with a Lee-Metford bullet through the hoof. In the course of the intermittent firing which was going on I had to use "Rodney" pretty freely, but it was for the last time, for, in helping the men to catch some goats among the rocks, I broke his stock, and he was useless to me for the rest of the campaign.

It was now getting late, and though part of our scouts had got among the outlying kraals of Inyanda's stronghold, we had now to make our way back to camp, some six miles, very pleased with ourselves and very tired.

2nd August.—Started at 5.30 from our bivouac on the Chabez. As we intended to camp the night on the Tuli road at the point where it passes the Umzingwane River (at Dawson's Store), we sent our pack train direct to the spot, some twelve miles across the valley, while our main body went on to complete yesterday's reconnaissance. We moved along to Inyanda's stronghold, which is a lofty mountain of great pinnacles of rock with jumbled boulders, caves, and bushy gorges. First, we shelled the front of it, where the main *kraal* was situated, until the rebels evacuated this point, and made their way to the back of the mountain. A flanking patrol of ours to the right was suddenly attacked by a strong party of the enemy, but the patrol held its own well, and extricated itself cleverly from the difficult ground it was in, without any casualties, having killed five of the enemy.

On the left we worked round through the bush to the rear face of the mountain. Here were the caves which formed the grain-stores of the rebels, and after shelling these for a short time, we sent up parties

A CHANCE SHOT

to capture them. The enemy made no attempt to hold the place, but had retired over the back of the mountain by the time our men had got up to the caves; but one of them, firing a parting shot, wounded Captain Lloyd, our signalling officer, through the lower part of the thigh. Once more my pocket-case of bandages came in useful, as there was no medical officer up there with us, but the wound was not a serious one.

We found very large stores of grain here, packed in immense neatly-woven grass baskets made with a small mouth which was sealed up with mortar; there were mealies (maize), *inyaooti* (Kaffir corn), monkey-nuts, rice, dried melons, and *mahoba-hoba* fruit, &c., these were all stored in large, dry caves, of which the entrances had been stockaded. We found many cooking-pots, shields, *assegais*, clothes, and even children's dolls; these latter were merely little clay models of bodies with short arms and legs, but no heads, and these are said to be of precisely the same pattern as the dolls of the ancients which have been excavated in some of the old ruins of the country.

From Inyanda's we moved on to the spot where I had formerly located Sikombo's *impi*. This we found deserted, but the size and extent

Our Field Telegraph

of the *scherms* still standing there showed that at least two thousand men must have been lately in camp in them. We burned these, and, continuing our march through the hills for another mile or two eastward, we came out on the Tuli road just at the spot where it enters the Matopo Pass.

It was here that Brand's patrol was attacked on the 10th April by overwhelming forces of rebels, and had a very tough fight of it before they succeeded in getting clear of their attackers and in making their way back to Buluwayo. Out of their party of a hundred and fifty, they had lost five killed and fifteen wounded, and some thirty horses killed; the dead had to be left on the ground, and there was only one two-wheeled cart and a Maxim gun on which the wounded could be carried. As no force had been out here since the fight, we halted for a space, went over the ground, and buried the remains of the killed. It was very easy to follow the course of the fight by the footprints and wheel-marks of the Maxim, which still remained, and by the carcasses of the horses which were lying about the *veldt*. In the evening we made our way back along the road to Dawson's Store (ten miles), where our pack-train had been joined by our waggons.

We have supped, and most of us are asleep, although it is not eight o'clock yet.

I have seen in the *Fortnightly* an article on "The Human Animal in Battle."

It is interesting, but it doesn't exactly tally with the impressions gleaned from experiences here. Allowance must be made, of course, for individual constitutions, but the author seems to imply that for the generality, "courage is a powerful exercise of will to overcome the more natural tendency to run away"; but it seems to me to be an exercise that is put into practice very promptly and automatically by some people.

He talks of the soldier as going into a fight with his mind full of the question as to whether he is going to be killed, and if so—why? That he then discovers that fighting is not pleasure, it is not sport; he merely gets dazed, and all his senses are blurred.

As far as I know, men going into action are, as a rule, thinking of anything but getting killed, and they are anything but dazed. If they happen to think at all about anybody being killed, they do so as in ordinary life—and death: they reckon on their neighbours dying, but not on themselves. There is naturally a sort of excitement which takes possession of one, and which, I think, works on you to the same extent as a couple of glasses of champagne. You forget all fatigue, and your wits are more than usually sharpened.

This brightening of the wits is similar to that which occurs in the case of an actor on the stage. Ask him in the wings, just before he goes on, what are his next few lines, and he probably could not tell you: he steps before the footlights, and at the same moment his mind, I suppose, concentrates itself on the matter in hand, the lines come to him without effort of memory, and his wits are about him to the extent that if one of the "gods" interrupts with a bit of chaff, the actor can rap back a *repartee* at him that would take him a month to work out in cold blood. In the same way, one's wits brighten in a fight: one seems to see clearly in every direction at once, to grasp what the enemy is at, and also what is wanted on one's own side, before, around, and behind one. The mind is clear and not confused, and is buoyed with a feeling of elation and cheery excitement, but with a cruel under-current, close below the surface, which the *kaffirs* so aptly describe as "seeing red."

A little instance in a fight two days ago will illustrate my meaning. A trooper coming back from the firing line with a message to the rear, saw, as he passed, one of our Cape Boys skulking under cover behind a rock. "For'ard on, Alexander!" he shouted cheerily, and picked up a stone to playfully enforce his command. At this moment a Matabele in a cave close by fired and just missed him; he merely altered the direction and the force of his throw, and hurled the stone hard at the cave instead of at the Cape Boy. Then with eager haste, mad with rage, and swearing volubly, he dashed up the rocks to "give the nigger snuff."

This sudden change from cheery light-heartedness to blood-thirsting rage is one of the peculiarities of the mind during a fight.

Another curious statement in the article is that in action fear plays some game with one's secretion of saliva, and that an intense thirst results. Speaking for myself, I have been in as great a funk as any man of my weight and years; but I do not recollect any particular thirst connected with it. I have for my part never seen much difference between the thirst of the battlefield and that of the polo-field, the cricket-field, or any other field, except perhaps one, the pig-sticking field, which certainly can produce a thirst peculiarly its own, and one which transcends that of any other pursuit—but even that thirst is not the result of fear.

Fraser, 7th Hrs.　R. Moncreiffe　Signaller　Baden-Powell, 13th Hrs.　Turner, 42nd
(lying down)　　　　　　　Col. Plumer, Y. & L. Rgt.　De Moleyns, 4th Hrs.

COLONEL PLUMER AND STAFF
Watching a fight in the Matopos

CHAPTER 8

Fighting in the Matopos
3rd August to 5th August,

4th August.—Today we had a delightful patrol. At one o'clock this morning I left camp (at Dawson's Store on the Umzingwane), with Richardson as interpreter, Jan Grootboom, Jonas, and three other native boys, and went across the valley eight miles to the foot of the Matopos. Our fighting against Babyan, and our subsequent raids along the Matopos, had evidently disturbed the rebels at the eastern end of the mountain. We knew that Sikombo, Inyanda, and Mnyakavulu had retired from their original positions, to a position a little more retired within the Matopos, but we were not sure whether Umlugulu had also joined them in their concentration, and I was now anxious to ascertain this, and at the same time to capture one or two prisoners, if possible, who might serve as guides, or give us information regarding the new positions taken up by the enemy.

As we got near to one of the hills, close to which I had already passed on one or two occasions, we saw the twinkle of a watch-fire, and just before dawn about half a dozen were lit there in succession, but apparently lit by one or two men only, probably as a lure or a blind to us. However, at dawn, we saw what they were, and we passed on *via* the Tuli road. At the point where this road passes through the end of the eastern hills was the scene of Brand's fight of the 10th of April. Jan Grootboom had been with this column, and gave us a most circumstantial account of the fight, taking special care to show us his own horse where it lay shot dead. Father Barthelemy, who is with our force now as chaplain, was also in this action, and did grand work, so they all say, in helping the wounded and giving the last rites to those who wanted it, whatever their creed.

As we went down the road through the pass, we found the road

My Boy preparing breakfast

barricaded with trees which had been felled in such a way as to lie across it; evidently a plan of the enemy's to prevent Brand's force from turning back and escaping by the way they came. Just beyond one of these barricades, we found the remains of a white man who had been killed in that fight, a young fellow with light curly hair. The other bodies had been buried during our visit of the 2nd inst.

We went on till we came to the ruins of a roadside hotel and store well in among the mountains. Here we began to find fresh spoor of natives moving about. After a short rest and breakfast, we went in closer to Umlugulu's stronghold, and by dint of careful climbing about the rocks, and by spying with a good glass, we were able to see not only that the enemy were there, but pretty well how they were located.

So that part of our work was accomplished; but I still wanted to catch a prisoner—though I did not at first see my way to doing it. However, in the course of our prowl, we presently came on fresh well-beaten tracks, evidently of women and children going to and from the outlying country, probably bringing in supplies. This seemed to offer us a chance of catching some of them coming in, although, as the sun was up, we had little hope of being very successful.

But luck was with us again, and we had hardly settled ourselves near the path when I saw a couple of women coming along with loads on their heads. The moment they saw us, they dropped their loads and ran, but Richardson and I galloped for them, and one, an elderly lady, gave herself up without any fuss; but the other, a lithe, and active young person, dived away at a tremendous pace into the long grass, and completely disappeared from view. We searched about, and kept a bright look-out for her, but in vain.

Then Richardson questioned the old lady, who proved to be very communicative; she was apparently superintending the supply department of Umlugulu's *impi*, and was now returning from a four days' visit of inspection to the supply base in some of his villages in the district. She was a lady of rank too, being a niece of Umzilikatze, and we should not have caught her, so she said, had her escort not been a pack of lazy dogs. She had four Matabele warriors with her, but they had dropped behind on the path, and should not now be far off. This was good news to us, and, calling up our Boys, we laid an ambush ready to catch the escort.

While this was being done, I happened to catch sight of our young lady stealing away in the distance. She was getting away at a great pace, her body bent double to the ground, taking advantage of every bit of

RUNNING AFTER A LADY

cover, more like an animal than a human being. Away I went after her as hard as I could go, and I had a grand gallop. When she found that concealment was no longer any use, she straightened herself and just started off like a deer, and at a pace equal to my own; it was a grand race through long grass and bush, the ground gradually getting more rough and broken as it approached the hills, and this told in her favour, for as her pace slackened for want of breath, my horse also was going slower owing to the bad ground. So she ran me right up to the stronghold, and just got away into the rocks ahead of me. I had, of course, then to haul off, as to go farther was to walk into the hands of the *impi*. The bad part of it was, that she had now got in there, and would spread the news of our being about, and they would probably come out and upset our little plan of catching the party on the road.

Then I made my way back to my patrol, but, finding that the enemy did not come along, we guessed that they must have seen us and were hiding themselves somewhere, and accordingly we spread ourselves out and proceeded along their route for some distance, examining the grass and bush as we went; but we failed to find them. (*P.S.*—One of our scouts in searching the bush actually came across them, but, being cut off by them, hid himself in the neighbouring *koppie* till nightfall, when he made his way back to camp and told us how the four Matabele were stalking us when we thought that we were stalking them.) Eventually we came out on to the plain by a different path than that which we used on entering, and got back to the main body about noon, having been out eleven hours.

The main body had now moved its camp to within a couple of miles of the mountains, preparatory to attacking this end of the Matopos.

THE BATTLE OF AUGUST 5TH

The sketch above will explain the nature of the operation which led to Colonel Plumer's victory on August 5th.

The old lady whom we had brought into camp, whose name is Umzava, is a charming old thing, and after a good feed of meat is very communicative.

This afternoon I went for a short ride into the hills with De Moleyns and Pyke; we got three shots at rebel scouts who were watching our camp from the neighbouring heights, and we saw a good number on the hills farther off; so they are evidently on the look-out for us.

Umzava, over a tin of meat this evening, confirms our idea that there are five *impis* collected in the position within the hills near us. Many of the rebels would like to give in, but their chiefs will not let them. They are all much disheartened by the rapid successive blows that they have had in the Matopos, especially as they have looked upon these mountains as impregnable strongholds. The defeat of Babyan especially had been a very severe blow; a large number of their best men had been killed here, including five chiefs; and Huntwani, their leading *induna*, had been severely wounded in the leg. The rebels are pretty well off for meat, food, and ammunition, but are getting tired of war, as it prevents the sowing of next year's crop, and they are beginning to lose faith in the *M'limo*, who had promised that all the whites should die of rinderpest, instead of which the whites seem to be increasing every day in numbers.

6th August.—The column paraded in the dark at half-past four in the morning, and moved off silently, without lighting fires or pipes, as we were close under the heights occupied by the enemy's look-outs. It fell to me to act as guide, since I knew something of the country to be traversed and the point where the enemy were posted. It meant passing through the two outer ranges of hills and through a wooden pass into a semicircular valley or amphitheatre, two sides of which were occupied by the rebel *impis*. At sunrise we arrived in the pass leading into this valley, where we were completely sheltered from view by the bush. The back of the valley was formed by a single high ridge of smooth granite, and from it five offshoots ran down into the valley like fingers from the ridge of knuckles. At the tips of each of these fingers rose rocky peaks among the bush and jungle of the lower valley; these peaks and the fingers themselves form the strongholds of the individual *impis*.

It was evident that if we could get our guns into the commanding position afforded by the knuckles, they would be able to bring an effective fire to bear on each of the strongholds in turn, and thus prepare the way for our storming them from the valley. Our force consisted of the M.R.F., some of the police, Coope's Scouts, Robertson's and Colenbrander's Cape Boys, two mountain guns, the Maxims, Hotchkiss, and rocket tubes, with friendly natives to carry them.

Colonel Plumer, who was commanding the force, now ordered the guns, with a strong escort of 130 men under Captain the Hon. J. Beresford, 7th Hussars, to endeavour to gain a position on the ridge, moving up that shoulder of it which might be termed the thumb. With Beresford I sent two of my boys as guides and scouts, and I told Beresford to keep a good look-out in going out, as he might find Inyanda's *impi* on the right of his path, while the remaining four were away to his left. At 7.30 this party moved off to our right front. The main body meantime were to remain concealed where they were until the guns got into position for shelling the strongholds, upon which it would move forward and attack them in succession.

While we were waiting, I climbed up on to a neighbouring *koppie* to have a look round with my telescope. On almost every hill I could see natives, and on one hill in particular, which overlooked the path where I had been scouting yesterday, and by which they evidently expected us to arrive, were collected a large number of their scouts. It was great fun watching them through the glass, as they seemed so close to one, and were entirely unconscious one's presence. One or two kept an anxious lookout to the eastward (we were due west of them), while the remainder, in a hidden position, were having their breakfast. Presently the glint of the arms of Beresford's party attracted their attention, and their consternation was almost ludicrous to watch; on all the other *koppies* one could see that the alarm had spread, and without noise or shouting the rebels were stealthily collecting together under arms.

Beresford had been gone for nearly an hour, when presently we heard him open fire; there was a rattle of a few shots, quickly followed by a roar of volleys and rapid sustained fire; this, echoing back from the hills around, developed into a continuous roar, which was added to by the roll of the Maxims and the booming of the bigger guns. This was a sound we had not expected to hear, as we thought there could not have been any very serious attack so early in the day in such an outlying portion of the field, but we had not reckoned upon the rapidity in which the enemy would move this day.

So soon as we recognised that serious fighting was on hand. Colonel Plumer sent Captain Coope with a patrol to see how Beresford was getting on. Coope worked his way round, and later on reappeared with the information that Beresford in the course of his march had been suddenly attacked by the enemy converging on him from three sides at once; he had formed his small party into a square on a convenient plateau, and there, for over an hour, remained hotly engaged, the enemy rushing up to within a few yards under the good protection afforded by the boulders and bush. It was a stiff and plucky fight on both sides. The enemy, rushing on in great numbers, seemed confident of overwhelming the little force opposed to them; but the whites were ready for them, and opened a steady, destructive fire on them, which checked them time after time.

Some natives having effected a lodgement in some rocks commanding the position, Lieutenant Hervey was ordered to dislodge them with a few of his men, and it was while dashing forward to do so that his sergeant-major was shot dead, and he himself fell mortally wounded through the body. His place was at once gallantly taken by Mr. Weston Jarvis, who had sauntered out with a gun to look at the fun, but proved himself a cool and able leader in a tight place.

At one moment, seeing a volley from the enemy was imminent, the order was given by one of the officers to his men to take cover. The men in charge of the Maxim by mistake took this order as applying to them and left the Maxim, in order to take cover as directed; in an instant the rebels saw their chance, and made a rush to get the gun. Llewellyn, the officer in charge, saw their move, and jumped forward himself and alone to counteract it. It was a race for the gun; Llewellyn was there first, and, jumping on to the saddle, turned its stream of fire on to the natives, who were within a few yards of him, and they turned and fled, falling to the fire.

The native muleteers behaved very pluckily, taking their carbines and assisting in the defence; the friendly natives who had been employed in carrying the Maxims and Hotchkiss showed very little heart; they crept in and took cover under the back of the mules, excepting one or two, who, when the enemy were close up, got away and joined their ranks. The guns were excellently served, firing case into the enemy at fifty yards; both the officers in charge of the guns—Lieutenant M'Culloch, R.A., and Lieutenant Fraser, West Riding Regiment—were wounded, but both continued to work with the battery.

At one time a war rocket was fired, partly as a signal and partly to obtain a moral effect, and it certainly succeeded in the latter respect, for after its unearthly bang a dead silence seemed to come over the scene, both sides ceased firing as if by common consent, and then the

AFTER THE FIGHT

weird notes were heard of Sikombo's war-horn reverberating through the mountains with a sound like that of a steam siren, calling up reinforcements for the fight.

But meantime, hearing what was going on there, Plumer ordered an immediate advance of his main body. Coope's Scouts were to lead the way, supported by the two corps of Cape Boys, backed up by the M.R.F. As we came out into the valley from our position, we could see the enemy collected in front of Beresford; they were not then actively attacking him, but they were evidently ready and awaiting further reinforcements, but our appearance soon changed their plans. Retreating hastily from the immediate neighbourhood of Beresford's position, under fire of his Maxims, they retired on to the next ridge (or fore-finger) to him, many of them getting into position at the *koppie* at the end of it. This ridge we at once attacked; pressing on with Coope's Scouts, we were at the foot of the ridge almost as soon as the enemy were on to the upper part of it, and here the fun began.

Dismounting and leaving our horses under cover of the rocks, we commenced to clamber up the hill, firing whenever we got a chance. They were firing back at us, but, as a rule, well over our heads; we were in much greater danger from our friends behind. The Cape Boys, who were supporting us, came swarming across the open at the double, every man firing as he ran; men 100 yards in rear as gaily as those who were leading the rush, none of them stopping to take much aim. However, the moral effect on the enemy was all that could be desired. He had not settled himself into position on this ridge before he found the swarm of whites and Cape Boys assailing it, and it required very little pressure to make him quit and take up a better position with the supporting *impi* on the next ridge.

But those of the enemy who had succeeded in getting into the *koppie* at the end of the first ridge were evidently determined to hold their own there, and they opened an unpleasantly accurate fire upon us from this coign of advantage. During a pause for breath in the course of the rush, I was talking to Schroeder, the war correspondent, when a fellow had a crack at us from the *koppie* and cut up the sand between our feet; we then adjourned our conversation to the lee side of a big rock.

Kershaw's squadron was now called up to assault this *koppie*, while I was recalled to take Coope's Scouts round by Beresford's position, and, if possible, to work round the flank and rear of the enemy, to observe and report what was going on in that direction. I gathered my party and rode off accordingly, and a parting salute from the defenders of the *koppie* whistled harmlessly over our heads as we went. It was shortly afterwards, in carrying out the storming of this *koppie*, that poor Kershaw was shot with two bullets through him at the entrance of the main cave, and his sergeant was shot through the head at the spot where I had been talking to Shroeder, probably by the same man who had fired at us.

On passing through Beresford's party, I only stopped a few moments to hear his report and to say a word to the wounded, and then rode on, after a handshake with one or two friends. The curious look in the eyes of some of these men who had been near to death haunted one for some time after.

After leaving him, for about half a mile we began the ascent of the ridge, and a very nasty place it was. It was a single narrow track going diagonally up the face of the cliff, very steep and rocky, so that we had to go in single file, leading our horses. We were completely at the mercy of any enemy who liked to come and fire down upon us from above, or who liked to cut in on the path after we had passed up it. In order to prevent this as far as possible, and also to guide supporting parties on to our track, we left one or two men at points along the path.

Finally, on nearing the top, we halted and concealed our horses in the bush. Coope went on ahead as leading scout, and had a look over the crest, and returned to say that the enemy in long strings were retreating across the ridge about half a mile beyond, and that if we could get a few men up to assist us—we did not number more than half a dozen at this point—we should have a grand chance at them. He also said that there were some goats close by, and he thought he had heard

THE DEATH OF KERSHAW

men's voices.

I then went up with him to have a look, and could see the enemy getting away as he described. To get up here we had quitted the path for the last forty yards, and had climbed on to some rocks overlooking it; and now, when Coope went back to bring up the men, I came in for a little fun on my own account.

The bleating of goats was continuous close by, and then I saw the reason: two goats had been tied up, twenty yards apart from each other, in order to make, them bleat. Close by, behind a rock, were seated eight niggers, evidently lying in ambush waiting for us to come up the path, following the attractive sound of the goats' voices, and here was I in a position where they did not expect me! Suddenly one of them saw me, and they took the alarm and dived down to the other side of the rock, but one with a gun stood for a moment looking for me, and gave me a very good chance; he did not join the others behind the rock, but dropped were he was.

They then opened fire on me, but I was in long grass, and merely had to lie down to be quite safe, shifting my position a few yards each time before I returned their shots. I was very quickly joined by half a dozen men, and we had quite a little duel with this piquet of the enemy; but it had the bad effect of bringing more of them upon the scene, and although they had not the pluck to come out and drive us back, they effectively barred us from getting any farther forward.

However, from where we were, on the summit of the ridge, we had a splendid bird's-eye view of the whole of the battlefield, and a good view also of those parties of the enemy who were already in retreat. Too good a view, in fact; it was like a bad dream to see this beautiful opportunity for a pursuit, and yet to find oneself tied by the leg from want of men.

I now began to signal down to Plumer, telling him the state of affairs up here, and asking for more men to come and join in the pursuit, but the reply came back that every man was now employed in making a final attack on the *koppies* in the valley below; and from where we stood we had a beautiful view of what was going on.

The Cape Boys had worked their way round to the enemy's right as far as the third and fourth ridges, and did some pretty hard fighting as they went. In one place they found the rocks so steep that they had to take off their boots in order to obtain sufficient foothold, and at one point a counter attack on the part of the enemy in overwhelming numbers pressed them back for a bit. Robertson, Serjeant, and Hubert

CAPE BOYS BARING THEIR FEET FOR THE ATTACK

Howard led this attack, the latter getting wounded in the foot.

The M.R.F. and the police attacked the central portion of the enemy's position with great steadiness and determination, and drove him out of one position after another, until at last the enemy seemed to give up all hope of continuing the struggle, and strings and parties of them could be seen making off over the hills in all directions, followed wherever they made a good target by the fire of the Maxims and the 7-pounders. Had we had more men where I was, we could have carried out a most effective pursuit; but after all, the smashing they got was sufficient in itself, and after a time the firing died down, and we could hear the trumpet sounding the recall.

Making my way down to Plumer in response to a signal from him, I found him on the knoll where Beresford's party had been attacked. Although naturally satisfied with the result of the day's work, Plumer was evidently affected by the loss of his friend and right-hand man, Kershaw.

We now found that out of our force of seven hundred, five had been killed and fifteen wounded, and among the latter was Lieutenant Hervey, for whom there is little hope. The enemy's force was estimated at from four to five thousand men, and of these we killed between two and three hundred.

To our great surprise, we found that it was already three o'clock; the day had flown by very quickly. We then re-formed the column for marching back to camp, the wounded being taken on stretchers carried by Cape Boys; and I was placed in command of a strong party to act as a rearguard to prevent any attacks from the enemy when moving through the defiles. As we moved slowly away, burning everything inflammable as we went, in the way of huts or long grass, we could see small parties of the enemy going about the field picking up the dead and wounded, and at one point one of our parties engaged in the same work was fired upon by some of the enemy in a *koppie*, and the rearguard went to their assistance; we found they were bringing out the body of Sergeant M'Loskie laid across the saddle of a spare horse.

Just as we were leaving the hills, a fairly large party of the enemy appeared, following us up and jeering at us. Our boys shouted back at them, and discovered that they were part of Umlugulu's *impi*, who had been detached early in the morning to a distant point in another direction where they had expected our attack to come from, and they only arrived on the scene now, to find it was all over. We gave them a parting long-range volley, which effectually stopped them from following us any farther, and just as darkness was coming on, we got out on to the open beyond the mountains.

It was long after dark before we got back into camp. And it was then a curious contrast to see the men being cheered into camp by those who had been left as camp guards, as they marched in singing "The Man who broke the Bank at Monte Carlo," while here and there between the flickering camp fires the heavy stretchers could be seen slipping quietly past to the hospital.

The following was our roll of casualties in this fight. It is curious what a large proportion of them are officers and non-commissioned officers. Seven officers, eight non-commissioned officers, and three troopers.

Killed, 5.—Major F. Kershaw, 2nd Battalion York and Lancaster Regiment; Sergeant Oswald M'Loskie, Sergeant William Gibb, Sergeant Innes Kerr (all of the Matabele Relief Force); and Battalion Sergeant-Major Alexander Winstree, Matabele Mounted Police.

Wounded, 15.—Sergeant-Major W. M. Josephs, M.R.F., slightly; Sergeant Arthur E. Brabant, M.R.F., slightly; Trooper W. M. Currie, M.R.F., severely; Troop Sergeant-Major Rawlings Dumeresque, M.R.F.; Trooper Alfred John Evelyn Holmes, M.R.F., severely; Trooper Thomas Gordon, M.M.P.; Captain Windley, B.F.F.; Lieutenant the Hon. Hubert Howard, of Robertson's Cape Boys; Lieutenant Robert H. M'Culloch, Royal Artillery; Lieutenant Norman Warden Fraser, 2nd Battalion Duke of Wellington's West Riding Regiment; Captain Charles H. Fowler, M.R.F.; Corporal Richard Turnbull, M.R.F., and two Cape Boys, slightly; Lieutenant H. J. Hervey, M.R.F., dangerously (since dead).

IN THE MIDST OF LIFE

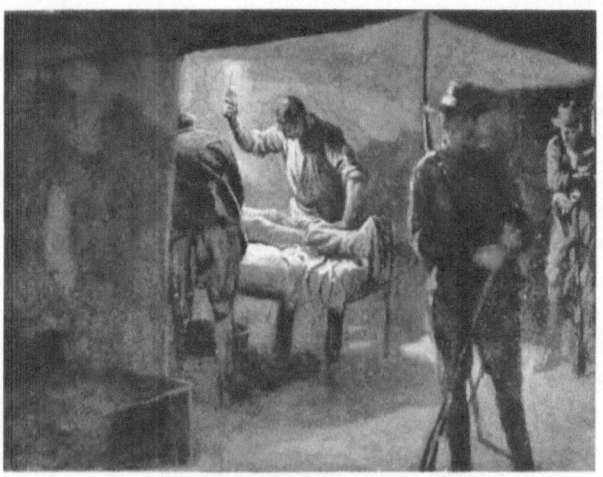

THE OPERATING TENT

CHAPTER 9

The Final Operations in the Matopos
6th August to 10th August.

6th August.—It is a sad shock to sit in one's little mess of half a dozen comrades once more, and to find two of them are missing from the meal. Poor Kershaw and Hervey! Now and then one is on the point of calling to the usual sleeping-place of one or other of them to bid him come and eat, when suddenly the grim, cold recollection strikes you—"He is yonder—dead."

Poor Hervey took his mortal wound as though it were but a cut finger, yet knowing that he was fast passing away. Now and then he sent for those he knew to come and see him and to say goodbye. He was perfectly possessed and cheery to the last, and happily without much pain.

Poor chap, this was his first fight. He had been the paymaster to the forces, and had asked me to get him some appointment in the field. When he joined us in camp, I could not for the moment find a billet for him, till it occurred to me that there was a small company of men who had come up from Kimberley without an officer. They were so deficient in belts and bayonet scabbards that they always went with bayonets "fixed," and had thus gained for themselves the nickname of "The Forlorn Hope."

On suggesting "The Forlorn Hope" to Hervey, he was delighted, and it was at their head he so gallantly met his death.

His death is to me like the snatching away of a pleasing book half read.

And Kershaw was the very type of a cool, brave, energetic officer. His loss to our little force is irreparable.

BRINGING AWAY THE DEAD
AFTER SIKOMBO'S ACTION, 5TH AUGUST

Colonel Plumer sent me today in command of a patrol of a hundred mounted men, to go round by a new way to the back of the position occupied by Umlugulu; to burn *kraals*, &c.; to ascertain whether the rebels were still there, and if so, to show them that we were none the worse for yesterday's fight. As soon as we got round the end of this mountain, we found numerous tracks of people going in there, fresh that morning, and we could see smoke rising from several parts of the stronghold; and presently the appearance of scouts on various points of the ridge showed us that the rebels were still there.

At one point I climbed a small mountain to have a look round, while the men dismounted, and rested their horses at the bottom. A few minutes after I had started to go up, De Moleyns followed me. I did not know till afterwards that we formed quite a little procession. First I came; then came one Matabele, followed by a second, assisting him,—they were stalking me from rock to rock; after the Matabele came De Moleyns, similarly stalking them. Near the top I suddenly changed my course, and came back unexpectedly on the flank of the two Matabele, who thereupon took to their heels in another direction.

From my look-out place I could see a gorge leading into the mountains at the back of Umlugulu's stronghold; I accordingly mounted the men and proceeded warily, under cover of the bush, to this valley. On arriving near the entrance of it, two or three of us dismounted, and climbed to the top of a small *koppie* which commanded a view of the stronghold. Here we could see a good number of Matabele collecting on the heights as well as on the lower slopes. Taking a few mounted men, we made a show of entering the valley, whereupon those of the enemy who were on the heights proceeded to show themselves conspicuously, evidently hoping to draw us on to attack them, while those in the bottom of the valley took cover and concealed themselves in the bush to form an ambuscade, to catch us on the one path which we should have to follow. So we played with them for a bit.

Suddenly De Moleyns, who had been scouting farther along the range, came galloping in, to tell us that a herd of cattle were being driven in from the plains towards the mountain at racing pace. Leaving one troop to keep the attention of the enemy engaged in the valley, I made a dash with the remainder of the squadron to intercept the cattle. Such a yelling from the women on the hill-tops, and counter-yelling from the men in charge of the cattle! For some little time we could not see the cattle, owing to the thickness of the bush, and fearing lest it might only be a ruse to draw us on, I kept part of the squadron back as a reserve; but this yelling of the ladies persuaded me that they were really alarmed for their cattle, when a bit of open ground showed us that it was a good herd of mixed cattle and sheep, I saw that no trap was intended, and that we really were on the track of their meat supply.

In a few minutes more, after an exciting race, our leading troop succeeded in heading the cattle, just as they were entering a small hidden gorge in the mountain, and we brought them triumphantly away. Then, withdrawing the remainder of my force, which had continued to toy with the enemy in the main valley, we made our way home.

This loss of their cattle had evidently violently enraged the rebels, and they ran along the heights parallel to our march, calling us all sorts of names and yelling dire threats. This practice of shouting defiance and insult is very common with the *kaffirs*; but their wit is not, as a rule, of a brilliant order, and we can generally produce something better on our side, which effectually silences the enemy. One remark which never fails to make them squirm, and which we therefore generally reserve for a telling "last word," is the following pertinent question:—"Why are your crops not sown yet? Are your prospects of a harvest very gaudy, now that you are living shut up among the rocks like "*dassies*" (rock-rabbits), and dare not show your faces in the fields?"

Today, again, the enemy recognised me individually, and saluted me with threats, yelling my name, "*Impeesa*," with savage intensity.

As we should have to traverse a somewhat dangerous path before we could arrive at our camp,—the same pass, in fact, in which Brand had been attacked, and so nearly done for,—I sent on a message to Plumer, asking for a few men to be sent there to cover our passage through it. Meantime, as we went along, we destroyed seven of the enemy's *kraals*, and added to the picture by burning much of the long grass *en route*. Although the enemy gathered in some numbers about the pass, having seen that we were reinforced, they did not venture to attack us, and we got back into camp all safely with our loot shortly after dark. The cattle formed a very welcome addition to our commissariat.

8th August.—I was sent to find a good road by which the column could gain a commanding central position among the strongholds of the enemy. I had with me Captain Coope and several of his scouts. We made our way by various tracks and gorges to a *koppie* near to where Captain Beresford had his fight on the 5th. From the top of this *koppie* we were able to see the line of country the column would have to take; and from it I could see the spot where the enemy's piquet had laid their trap for us in the fight of the 5th. Through my glasses I could see that the piquet was still posted there, and that among their number was a Cape Boy dressed in European clothes. While watching them, I noticed ten Matabele sneaking down towards the foot of our *koppie* from another direction, and we did all we could to entice them to come at us; but they were too suspicious, and gave no chance to our hidden escort of capturing them. So, having seen for ourselves all that we wanted, and having taken the necessary bearings, we made our way back to camp.

That night reveille was whispered at 11.30. It was a curious time for reveille, and utterly puzzled our cook; we had supped at seven, and it was not time for morning coffee; however, Rose (Rose was not a clean white-capped and aproned maid, but a horny-handed pioneer) was equal to the occasion, and hatched us out some Bovril in a pile of embers (for no fires were allowed). Taking with us two days' rations, we moved off silently, on foot for the most part, only the scouts taking their horses, and these, for the present, were led in rear of the column. So silent was our departure that my two native trackers did not awake to accompany us, and I presently found that the task of guiding fell on my shoulders alone, which is all very well for a bit, but becomes tiring when carried on for some hours; the strain of constant attention is very great, and the want of trustworthy assistance to confer with at doubtful points becomes much felt.

I was finding my way chiefly by the stars, and, during the first part of the march, by our old spoor. But now and again men would come up to advise me, with the comforting assurance that we were going wrong, and would endeavour to put me on the right line,—one, indeed, had his advice prevailed, would have taken us directly into a camp of the enemy.

Nothing is more distracting than such interruption, and nothing is more calculated to make one really lose one's bearings.

The maxim, "*Do not speak to the man at the wheel*," should ever be borne in mind, and acted up to, by those with a column who think they know better than the guide. If they think that he is going wrong, they should hold their tongues, but should also note every mark by which they may find their way back on to the right line, should he eventually have to confess himself lost.

But no interference with him should be allowed by word or move. This applies equally by day as by night. Over and over again I have found myself confused or harassed by amateur scouts and guides crowding on to one, and sometimes even going ahead, talking and joking, not the least recognising the state of mind of the man responsible for the direction of the column.

However, we got along all right, over villainous ground; but the way was not hard to find, because I had merely to follow our own spoor of the morning, and this I did by feeling it through my thin-soled shoes, rather than by finding it with my eyes, for which the night was very dark.

The column came along in the following order: first, Coope's troop of scouts, then a squadron of the armed police, the corps of Cape Boys, the screw-guns on mules, four squadrons of Plumer's corps, followed by the led horses of the scouts and the rearguard.

The pace, as is always the case in a night march, was exceedingly slow; every small stream, or ridge of rocks, or piece of tangled bush caused long delays, and the head of the column had continually to halt, or to move at a very slow pace, in order to enable the rear to close up. In Ashanti, where, similarly, we had to move in long strings in single file, I have found it necessary to halt the head of the column for as much as an hour after getting over a fallen tree with a small brook alongside, so long did it take the column to get over the obstacle in the dark and to close up to its proper distance again. Similarly, in this case we came to a small rocky pass, of less than fifty yards, which delayed us for an hour. Much of the delay was caused by horses losing their footing and getting down among the rocks; the battery mules, wonderful beasts that they are, came over without a mishap, but the horses seemed perfectly helpless in the dark, and eventually got so far behind that they lost touch with the column.

The officer in charge of them, finding himself hopelessly detached, made all snug for the night, and eventually got back to camp in the early dawn. Luckily, my orderly, Parsons, who had charge of my horse, and consequently of my two days' food, managed to keep touch with the column, as did also the leaders of four or five other horses. The difficulties of keeping up connection were increased by our having to maintain absolute silence, and not showing lights of any description. Close above our path we could see the smouldering watch-fires of the enemy, and it speaks well for the order of the force that it passed so near to them without arousing their suspicion.

At length, after struggling on through thorny bush and over broken, hilly ground for six hours, we found ourselves, an hour before dawn, at the foot of the ridge which commands this part of the Matopos. Here we rested a while, hoping that the horses might rejoin us. I was but lightly equipped for this night march,—a flannel shirt and breeches well ventilated by wear and tear; as long as we were moving, I was all the better for it, but when it came to lying about in the chill of the early morning, I began to feel the cold, and as I lay in the long grass, I wrapped it round me to form a kind of blanket. As the dawn came on, we proceeded to ascend the ridge by the narrow path along the face of the cliff, which my party had taken in the fight of the 5th.

We approached the top with all precaution, and surrounded the spot where we expected to find the Cape Boy and his piquet, but to our regret we found they were not there; this evidently was their post by day, whereas their night quarters were somewhere farther back. And shortly afterwards we found them. There was a lively ten minutes between them and our Cape Boys among the rocks, and just as we were about to send reinforcements, our boys returned jubilant, having driven out the Matabele, killing four and getting one of their number wounded,—the bullet having struck his *bandolier* and glanced through his arm.

From our position on the top of the ridge we had a splendid view of jumbled mountain-tops and rocky, bush-grown gorges stretching in every direction,—a brutal country for military operations, but a splendid one from a rebel's point of view. The ridge itself forms a kind of backbone or watershed through the mountains, and is passable throughout its length for troops and mule-guns.

Passing round the scene of the fight of the 5th, we came to the mountain which formed Mnyakavula's stronghold, a place covered with huts among the bush and boulders, and evidently full of caves. It was practically deserted, but still one or two niggers were to be seen about, so we fired a few shells into it to show there was no ill-feeling, and then sent some Cape Boys to examine it to destroy the *kraal*. In going over it we found innumerable fresh bloodstains about the rocks, showing where wounded men had been brought in, and in two of the caves we found a number of dead bodies,—all showing how heavily the garrison of even this one small stronghold had suffered on the 5th.

Here we halted for breakfast, each of us boiling our own "billy," but having to share our eatables to a certain extent with those unfortunates whose horses had been lost during the night.

Then we pushed on again towards Umlugulu's stronghold, the same which we had reconnoitred from the rear the day before yesterday. Here we hoped to find some enemy, because this *impi* was one which took no real part in the fight of the 5th, and had therefore not been broken up by us. As we approached the place, we could see numbers of men gathering both on the right and on the left of our mountain; dogs were barking to the left, and women yelling. The guns were quickly unlimbered, and were soon sending their shells crashing into the gullies of the opposite mountain. A futile fire was returned, the distance was too great, and presently the enemy could be seen creeping away by twos and threes to safer and more distant retreats.

Once more my telescope did me a good turn. I saw a very suspicious-looking stone deep down in the canyon below us. I aimed the glass for it, and my heart jumped when I saw it was what I had hoped for, a cow looking out of a hole in the rocks. I could then see that there were others in the cave behind it, and sending down a party of Cape Boys, they soon were in possession of a herd of thirty head.

Then I went on with three others to find a fresh position for the guns, and to reconnoitre a neighbouring valley. We found a place for the guns, and sat there admiring the view, while De Moleyns went

Shelling the enemy out of the Matopos

off about 200 yards from us to find a way down between the rocks into the valley. We saw him coming back towards us, and just as he got within fifty yards there was a yell, two shots, and De Moleyns, hatless, came galloping in like mad. Some half a dozen Matabele were stalking up to us among the rocks; he had come unexpectedly among them, and they had missed him at about ten yards. We banged away at where we saw their smoke, and they replied, but very soon their firing ceased, and we saw them streaking away over the next hill. We then went to have a look at this valley, and while studying the far side with our glasses, we saw a number of Matabele creeping down to lie for us among the rocks.

A very pretty sight they were, lithe and active, bounding down from rock to rock, their dark skins shining in the setting sun and showing off their white war-ornaments. But we did not admire for very long, for, noting that they seemed to gather in one particular spot among the rocks, we put a few well-directed shots into it at 900 yards, and they quickly scuttled out again and went back the way they came, one dropping in his tracks to a shot from Coope. After this we stood up boldly on a rock to admire the view at leisure, till suddenly there was a ragged volley and the *"phit-phit"* of bullets overhead; these came from some niggers we could not see, but we fired back at the *koppie* which we suspected, and then gracefully retired to a less exposed position.

We took a circuit round and burnt a hut or two, and then went down to the water in a bog about 400 yards from the camp: here we watered and grazed our horses, bathed ourselves, filled up our billies, and cut a lot of glass to make our beds with on the hard rock platform that was to form our bivouac for the night. Suddenly our peaceful operations were interrupted by first one shot and then another fired up at the camp. These shots were soon followed by a more regular rattle of musketry, then came volleys in which the jolly Maxims joined, and finally the solid bang of the 7-pounders swelled the chorus. We were missing all the fun; we soon got mounted, gathered up our grass and our billies, and made our way up to the camp.

What I call a camp is hardly what the ordinary mind would picture: there are, of course, no tents or other such luxuries; the force is merely formed in an extended square with guns and Maxims at each of the corners, and where each man happens to stand in the ranks, there is his place to cook his food, to eat, and to spread his blanket for the night.

The spot we were camped on was a huge, open, flat rock, closely approached on three sides by broken rocks and bush, and in this broken ground a small but daring party of the enemy had crept up and were endeavouring to exact satisfaction for the loss of their cattle. It was curious to see how calmly the men in the square took it all; only that side of the square on which the enemy appeared bothered themselves to notice him, the other three sides went on with their cooking and suppers just as if the bullets whizzing over their heads were swallows flying through the air at sunset. After five or ten minutes the enemy retired and the firing died away. Half an hour later, just after dark, it suddenly broke out again; the enemy had crept up once more within fifty yards, and were firing at our fires.

They seemed to become accustomed to the fire of the Maxims, but when we let them have it with the 7-pounder, loaded with case, at fifty yards, they did not like it, and when the Cape Boys made a sortie round their flank, they fled for good, leaving four dead on the ground; but as they went, they found time to shout "goodnight" to us, telling us to sleep well, since that night would be our last—they "would have our livers fried for breakfast in the morning."

This was not quite the last we had of them that night, for a party went down with an escort to get water at the bog, but there they met with a pretty warm reception, and soon came back to camp swearing, with water-bottles empty, but luckily with no one killed. Then we coiled down to sleep, and did pretty well till midnight, when a storm of wind arose, accompanied by thunder and a sprinkling of rain, and we got the full benefit of it in our exposed position. Personally, I was very comfortable in my bed of broom-bush and grass, with my saddle as a protection against the wind, so that I did not feel the cold to the extent that some poor fellows did.

10th August.—We hoped to be attacked at daybreak, but it never came, and as we marched back during the day, we never saw another nigger. They had cleared out altogether, and we got back to our standing camp outside the hills about mid-day.

And then I rode thirty miles into Buluwayo during the night, in order to report to the general that the enemy in the Matopos were now completely broken up, and probably willing to surrender if we gave them a chance.

12th August.—Instead of starting for grouse-shooting or any other form of shooting, I am, on the contrary, settling down to office work today, but I find it more irksome than usual, as I have a slight touch of fever and dysentery, and a certain feeling of over-tiredness which keeps me lying up during my spare moments, and yet I don't feel inclined to sleep at all; and I find my temper a little short today, as the following extract of a letter which I have sent to one of the patrolling column will show:—

> If you want to catch the niggers, you will have to move more quickly and more secretly, that is, by night. It is no time now to save horses, but to make use of their condition; do not think that because you cannot see an enemy, there is no enemy there. We had our *laager* fired into three times the other night when there was not an enemy to be seen, so take care that your *laager* is guarded, and do not leave it to chance. If you let the men smoke on a night march, you might as well let the band play too.

A COMFOTABLE CORNER
ON AN UNCOMFORTABLE EVENT

The Peace Indaba with the Matopo Rebels.

Mr. Cecil Rhodes carried out the peace negotiations with the Matabele chiefs. He was assisted by Dr. Saner (on his left) and Capt. Colenbrander (on his right), and accompanied by Mr. Stent (war correspondent of the *Cape Times*).

CHAPTER 10

The Situation in Matabeleland and Mashonaland

16th June to 28th August.

I said that when I left camp to come into Buluwayo, on the 10th, it seemed a good opportunity of accepting the surrender of the rebels, if they liked to come in. They had suffered a succession of severe blows, and, while still in a state of disruption consequent upon them, would probably be only too glad to surrender. But if they were left to themselves for a short time, they might reorganise their forces and continue to give endless trouble in the Matopos, which might mean a great deal more expense to us of time and men.

So, before leaving camp, I had made a few preliminary arrangements, in order that no time should be lost in opening communication with the rebels. We had, as a prisoner, Inyanda's mother, and I sent her with a few men to the site of his *kraal*, which was close under the mountain where his people still hung out. There the men built a small hut for her, gave her a supply of corn and meat, and an old half-witted woman to grind the corn for her and, hoisting a big white flag on the tree above her hut, they left her to be called for. As they came away, they shouted to the rebels up on the hill, telling them that if they wanted peace, they might come down and talk to the old lady, as she would give them all information about it.

It was necessary to do something of this kind to induce the natives to believe anything we said on the subject of peace; they were too suspicious of a trap if we went and tried to talk to them ourselves. This plan eventually succeeded; her people came down to talk to the old woman, took her away with them to consult with the chief, and finally sent messengers, carrying the white flag, to our camp, to say that they were ready to talk.

Unfortunately, I was not able to have any say in the matter myself, as I was now down with dysentery, and on the sick-list. But, eventually, on the 22nd August, Cecil Rhodes, with Dr. Sauer, and Captain Colenbrander, went into the Matopos to meet the rebel leaders, near the *koppie* where Kershaw was killed on the 5th.

Jan Grootboom, the native scout, was sent on into the hills to summon the *indunas*, and presently they appeared, following Grootboom, who carried the white flag at their head, with an air of immense importance. Among the chiefs were Umlugulu, Sikombo, Somabulana, Hliso, Manyoba, Malevu, Inyanda, Babyan, and over thirty other *indunas*. Rhodes sat on an ant-heap, with Dr. Sauer on his left, Colenbrander on his right, and Stent, of the *Cape Times*, just behind him.

Rhodes got up to salute the chiefs in their own language, and stood out in the centre to do so; all were in silence awaiting his opening word. He stood, and paused, and, smiling, had to turn and ask, "What is that word?" (It was "*Umhlope,*" which is the usual salutation of peace after war.) Somabulana then opened the *indaba* (conference), and, as spokesman for the Matabele, said that they had been driven to rebellion chiefly by the official bullying on the part of the Native Police. When he had done, Sikombo went on to charge five of the Native commissioners with abuse of their powers. The chiefs wound up by saying they merely wanted justice, and would be glad to end the war. Rhodes promised there would be an alteration as regards the Native Police, and said that if they intended now to lay down their arms, their complaints would all be taken into consideration. Sikombo laid down his gun and *assegai* at Rhodes' feet, and said that this indaba represented the nation "as its eyes and ears," and all that they wanted was to live at peace with the whites.

Then he was asked why it was that the Matabele, in breaking out, had exceeded the usual rules of war, and had murdered women and children? And he said it was because white men had been reported to be doing the same thing. It was then pointed out to the chiefs that nothing could be done unless they and all their people laid down their arms; and the chiefs agreed to bring all their people out of the hills within the next few days, and so that conference ended.

(P.S.—It was not till 13th October, after many further conferences, that a final settlement was come to.)

A squadron of the 7th Hussars now arrived at Buluwayo, under Major Ridley, having completed a long patrol through the Guai district, finally breaking up such small parties of rebels as remained there, and bringing about their general surrender.

The situation in Matabeleland now is as follows:—

The whole of the north of the country is clear and peaceful; in the south the rebels are treating for peace in the Matopos; but, in the east and the north-east, bodies of them are still massed in the outlying districts. In the east, in the Belingwe district, about a 100 miles from Buluwayo, Wedza still remains in active rebellion, supported by various small chiefs occupying mountain strongholds. In the Selukwe district, just south of Gwelo, two chiefs, Monogola and Indema, still resist all efforts to reduce them. To the north-east of Gwelo, in the Maven district, at least one strong *impi* is collected; and the Somabula forest, north-west of Gwelo, and a 100 miles north-east of Buluwayo, is reported to be full of rebels.

On the borders of this forest is the great grain district belonging to Uwini, who has several different tribes dependent on him for their supply and direction. Moreover, M'tini, who had been defeated in July at Taba-si-ka-Mamba, has retreated on to the Shangani, and now has his *impi* in full work there, under the orders of M'qwati, the local *M'limo*, and it maintains small posts on all the chief paths to prevent well-disposed natives from coming in to surrender or to take refuge with us.

Colonel Paget, with a column of Imperial troops (7th Hussars and Mounted Infantry), is moving through South Matabeleland, *via* Tuli and Victoria, to Gwelo. Such is the situation today (22nd August); and Ridley's column of 7th Hussars and Mounted Infantry, having completed their work in the Guai district, are at Buluwayo, and will now be sent against the Somabula. And, were I well enough, it is probable that I should be sent in command; but here I am on my back, limp and washed-out, and really thin this time! And only a short time ago I was thinking that I had never been so fit in my life, and certainly never burnt so brown a colour! I am having a poor time of it, but it is not so bad as it might be; Sir Frederick is more than kind to me, and spends all his leisure alongside my bed, at all times of the day and at odd hours of the night, telling me how things are going on, and soothing my disappointment at not being able to get out into the field.

Then, I am wonderfully lucky in having an excellent doctor. Dr. Strong, and a most excellent cook—not that I require much, but that little has to be of the right kind. This is not a very large world, and the lady who runs the neighbouring restaurant, being told to supply me with invalid food, came in to see me, to inquire into my symptoms herself, as she had formerly been a hospital nurse, and therefore thoroughly understood what one ought to take; but before becoming a hospital nurse, she had learned the art of cooking in the kitchen of the Powells of Dorking, our cousins. Having made this discovery, and having thereby gained a personal interest in me, she has exerted herself to the utmost, and has fully succeeded in supplying me with the most appetizing food possible under the circumstances.

26th August.—Ridley's column started today for the Shangani, and though I am now feeling quite well, the doctor would not allow me even to think of going with it. I have seldom felt so down about my luck before. Meantime, in the Matopos, negotiations are still going on about the surrender, but the rebels do not seem over anxious to give in. At an *indaba* today, a hundred young warriors, with two chiefs, met Cecil Rhodes and party, and talked to them pretty cheekily. They said that unless they had their rights they had no desire to come in. All these men carried rifles and *bandoliers* full of cartridges.

One of them, named Karle Kamarlo, had been captured by us in the early days of the outbreak, had been tried and been sentenced to be shot; he was taken outside the town by two troopers, and was there shot by them. One shot struck him in the forehead and apparently came out at the back of his head, and the other struck him through the shoulder and he was left lying on the ground. When the burying party came out for him, they could not find him. It appears that the bullet which struck him on the head was not strong enough for his skull, and merely glanced round under his scalp without breaking the bone, and came out through the skin at the back, giving the appearance of a shot clean through his head.

By this wound the man was merely stunned, and when his executioners had retired, having, as they thought, carried out the penalty of the law, he got up and walked off in the other direction. It is now said that he intends to sue the company for assault and personal injury! Another man present at the *indaba* asked if our doctor could do anything for him, as in the fight of the 5th he had been standing almost in the line of fire of the Maxim, and in one instant had received nine wounds in his side and leg, most of them very slight; he had been practically crimped as if with an iron rake.

There seem to be various opinions here as regards the surrender. One says that the rebels should be made to surrender entirely unconditionally, and should only be allowed to do so on condition of their giving up their arms and such of their number as are guilty of murder. Others say that that is right enough in theory, but if the rebels refuse, as they very probably would, it means part of the force trying to fight them during the rainy season, while the other part will have to be withdrawn from the country owing to inability to supply them. Sickness and reverses will probably result, and in the end the murderers will not have been caught; whereas, if told that they can now surrender, and reoccupy their *kraals* and sow their crops, the capture of the murderers and the thorough disarmament can afterwards be effectually carried out by the police. And the police, by occupying fortified posts in all the grain-growing districts, will thus have the whip hand of the natives, as they can prevent them from sowing or from reaping any crops at will.

This question of supply and transport is very pressing. We are using all the transport we can lay our hands on, and yet we can only manage to keep our present wants fairly well supplied; while the reserve which we want to lay down, ready for the rainy season, is only being formed at a very slow rate. Towards the end of November the rains will set in, the roads then become impassable, and the mules die of horsesickness. We therefore want to lay down a sufficient reserve of food in the meantime to carry us through the four months at least of rains; but we cannot get contractors to tender for the transport, and it is very difficult to purchase even in Cape Colony. The oxen up here are all dead, and ox waggons coming up from the Cape are not allowed to return thither, for fear of spreading the rinderpest. The Transvaal border touches ours near Tuli, and we might get supplies in that way, but the Boer Government will not allow the export of food-stuffs from their country, fearing famine for themselves.

Meanwhile, great events have been going on in Mashonaland. Rebellion, as I said before, broke out there on the 16th June. Bands of Matabele rebels had made their way to Mashonaland after the first defeats near Buluwayo. They spread reports among Mashonas that the whites had all been killed in Matabeleland, and that now was the time to rise and similarly put an end to their rule in Mashonaland; and they threatened that, in the event of the Mashonas not rising, the whole of the Matabele nation under Lobengula *redivivus* would shortly be down on them. A few Native commissioners in touch with their people might have counteracted these reports, but none did so, and consequently rebellion broke out, as it had done in Matebeleland,

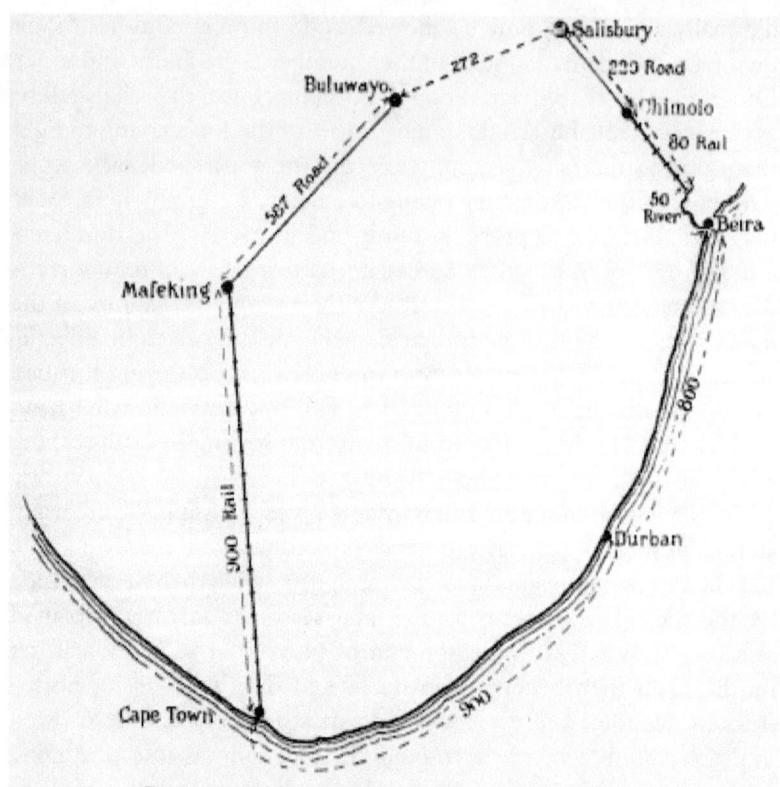

ROUTES TO MATABELELAND AND MASHONALAND

The above sketch shows the approximate distances that supplies had to travel from Cape Town in order to reach the respective centres at Buluwayo and Salisbury—Cape Town to Buluwayo, 1487 miles; Cape Town to Salisbury, 2050 miles.

with the sudden and brutal murders of whites—men, women, and little children—in all parts of the country.

Townships went into *laager*, local defence forces were organised to the number of eight hundred men. Judge Vintcent being commandant-general. Rescue patrols went out to bring in outlying settlers and miners. But here again arose the insurmountable difficulty of transport. There was only one road, namely, that *via* Umtali to the coast at Beira, by which food would come. This road extended for over 200 miles across the *veldt*, and then met the railway in Portuguese territory which partially connected it with the coast; thus the whole distance for Mashonaland supplies to come was: Cape Town to Beira, 1700 miles; by river, 50 miles; by rail, 100 miles; by road, 200 miles; total, 2050. This road was intercepted near Umtali, and held by a powerful tribe of rebels under Makoni.

Reserve supplies in the country did not amount to anything dependable, and could only last the defenders for a few weeks at most.

The rebels in Mashonaland occupied chiefly the districts round Salisbury and the Salisbury Umtali road, and the district east and south-east of Charter. They are by nature far less warlike than the Matabele, and are not given to attacking in the open, but content themselves with murdering helpless farmers, waggon and other small parties, and then retire to their fortified *kraals* and cave strongholds if attacked.

On the 18th June, Captain Turner, who was on his way through Mashonaland with a troop of fifty Natal volunteers for Matabeleland when the Mashonas broke out, went to the rescue of White at the Beatrice Mine, but was attacked in some narrow gorges by masses of rebels, and compelled to retire with a loss of three killed and three wounded.

On the 19th June, Captain Nesbit made a very plucky dash with thirteen men to rescue some white settlers, including two women at Mazoe, thirty miles north of Salisbury. He had to fight his way through the rebels to get there, and the party had a running fight of it for nearly the whole way back against heavy odds, the enemy rushing up to within a few yards at the time. Gallant work was done on this occasion by Messrs. Ogilvy and Harbord, who acted as advanced guard to the party. The waggonette in which the women were conveyed had been "armour-plated" with sheets of corrugated iron, but nearly all the mules were killed or wounded. Five men were killed and five wounded, and eight horses killed. But in the end the gallant little band got into Salisbury.

Captain Bremner, 20th Hussars, whose services had been placed at the general's disposal, was, in accordance with Sir Frederick's directions, making his way to Salisbury to act as staff officer there. He was caught by the rebels *en route* and killed, together with one or two settlers at whose house he was resting. The loss of this useful officer was a great blow to us, especially at this juncture, when things wanted organising in Mashonaland.

Towards the end of June the following relief parties arrived in Mashonaland from Matabeleland: namely, Beal with 133 men, Watts 100, White 65 (Grey's and Gifford's Scouts); the latter column especially made a wonderfully rapid march, and did some dashing work. And from the Cape there arrived, *via* Beira, 600 Imperial troops under Colonel Alderson. These consisted of 240 mounted infantry, 100 R.E. and R.A. and M.S.C., 150 West Riding Regiment, 50 York and Lancaster Regiment.

Their disembarkation and transport by rail was effected under great difficulties, owing to want of proper tugs, lighters, wharves, rolling stock, &c. One lot stuck in the mud in the Pungwe River for twenty-four hours; a train ran off the line and killed several of the horses, another train collided with the wreckage, and Colonel Alderson and others on the engine had to jump for their lives. But in spite of all obstacles the force made its way rapidly into Mashonaland. It turned and attacked Makoni's position, defeating him and taking his fortified *kraal*; 200 of the enemy were killed, 350 head of cattle and a number of prisoners taken, our losses being four killed and five wounded.

Among the killed was Captain Haynes, shot while escalading the wall of Makoni's head *kraal*. The force then went on attacking various other tribes along the road, establishing frequent fortified posts as it went, and in this way secured the safety of the supply route to Salisbury, and brought much-needed supplies into that place.

Alderson is now in local command of all the forces in Mashonaland, receiving his instructions from the general here by telegraph. By means of strong columns he is now breaking up the rebels in various directions, and forcing them out of their strongholds. But this latter is a particularly dangerous and unpleasant work, since the strongholds in Mashonaland consist, as a rule, of *koppies* undermined in all directions with caves and crannies, in which a very few determined men can hold their own against almost any number. But Tommy Atkins is reported to be quite equal to the occasion, and apparently delights in the novel form of getting killed. Alderson's total force amounts to 2200 men and 580 horses.

Sir Frederick Carrington's management of this extended force operating in a country which is equal in size to Spain, France, and Italy put together, is like a man playing on a small piano to a large room full of people. Our room is over 600 miles in length, and the piano a very small one, because the doorway (the transport and supply) is too small to admit a larger one. The piano's notes are eight small field columns, seven laagered towns, and twenty-four fortified posts. He plays them by telegraph from his music stool at Buluwayo, and has to make them reach every corner of the room. He burns to be out himself with one or other of the columns, but it cannot be; he has to sit here to read the music and to play the notes accordingly, to pull the ropes, to consult with the other heads who have to be consulted, and to be at the end of the wire for communication with the High Commissioner at the Cape.

Extract from a Letter Home.

28th August.—Your two letters of 17th and 24th July just received. Yes, you are quite right. We would do much better here if we had three times the number of men. But—we could not by any possibility feed them if they were here. Even to feed our present force through the approaching wet season, when roads will become impassable, requires four million pounds of food extra to what we have got here and on the road—*i.e.* 600 extra waggons; and we cannot get anybody to tender for the job. There are so few oxen left in South Africa. That is why we have to go on as best we can with this little force.

★★★★★★

You ask about our climate here. Well, what is your ideal of a perfect climate? Because that would about express it. Bright sun always, breeze all day, thermometer 70° in the shade at midday, cool nights. Doors and windows always open. In town the dust is the only drawback to it all. In camp there is not a tent or any shelter, except a few branches to keep off the wind. We all live entirely in the open, and it is delightful.

★★★★★★

I am keeping an illustrated diary for you.

It may be of use, in case of future expeditions of this kind, to jot down what kit I have found best for the work.

1. On yourself.

Hat.—A "cowboy" "broad-brimmed felt hat with ventilating holes punched in the crown, and a brown silk *puggree*. The hat is better than a helmet, because it shades the whole of the face, and so prevents the awful infliction, veldt sores on the face, cracked lips, and burned nose; and it protects the nape of the neck and temples from the sun; can be slept in, and suffers no damage from rough usage, and does not interfere with the aim when shooting; it is light, and so does not cause weariness or headache as the helmet often does; it protects the face and ears better than the helmet does in going through thick bush, the brim turning down with the pressure of the branches.

Neckerchief.—A grey-coloured handkerchief loosely tied round

Our working kit

the neck prevents sunburn, and can be tightened up at night as a comforter.

Shirt.—Brown or light-grey flannel.

Cummerbund.—Grey or brown flannel cummerbund saves dysentery, chills, &c., especially at night.

Breeches.—Khaki cord, with back pocket to hold notebook and field bandage.

Gaiters.—Brown soft leather (some men prefer *putties*, but I think gaiters best for coolness, ease in taking on and off, and for circulation of the blood). Instead of breeches and gaiters, many men wear trousers of moleskin or other strong material.

Boots.—Shooting boots, strong well-dubbed. In wet weather india-rubber soles are very slippery, but in dry weather, on rocks, they are perfect. Rubber-soled shoes should he carried on the wallets.

Spurs.—The colonial fashion of wearing one spur only is not a bad one where mounted infantry work is to be done. The spur should be very short, so as not to trip you when on foot.

Coat.—Burberry khaki gabardine, carried by day rolled up on the pommel of the saddle. Nightcap in one of the pockets, also a warm muffler.

Waistcoat.—A cardigan waistcoat or a sweater (grey or brown) is a very great comfort—can be carried rolled inside coat during the heat of the day.

Watch.—Wristwatch, with very thick hands, and lever action, as made by Dent (Charing Cross).

Belt.—Brown leather, with rings or dees to hang things on. These include—

Revolver.—Service pattern in an open "cowboy" holster, with cord lanyard round your neck.

Whistle.—Secured to the belt (or round the neck) by a cord suffiiently long to allow it to reach your mouth.

Knife.—Comprising tin-opener, turn-screw, corkscrew, skinning blade, borer, tweezers, &c.

In a pouch on the belt:
Flint and Steel.
Compass.
Revolver Cartridges.

Pipe and Tobacco

2. On your horse.

Saddle.—The colonial military saddle.

Wallets.—Slung across the cantle, where they are far more handy than in front.

In near Wallet.—Spare flannel shirt; socks; spat gaiters; toothbrush; toothpowder, soap, hair-brush (wrapped in a towel).

In off Wallet.—Sketch-book; map; quinine; camera; housewife; tin of cocoa; tin of Bovril or potted meat; bread; knife, fork, and spoon.

Much of the above can be carried in the pockets of the coat if more room is wanted in the wallets for rations.

Cooking "Billy" in leather case on the cantle. The Bechuanaland Border Police pattern of "billy" is very good, and carries its own drinking-cup. Your ration of meat can be carried in the "billy."

Water-bottle, Telescope, Nosebag, on near side of saddle; Field-glasses, Axe, Carbine Bucket, on off-side of saddle.

Shoes with india-rubber soles strapped on outside the wallets.

Carbine.—Lee-Metford Sporting Magazine Rifle, or the cavalry L.-M. carbine are very good, but involve carrying a *bandolier*. A Colt's repeater carries its own fourteen rounds, but if it jams or gets out of order, is difficult to repair on the *veldt*. The carbine bucket is merely a shoe in which the "butt of the rifle rests, while the barrel is kept near the side under your arm or attached to the arm by a loop of cord.

The carbine should' be fitted with a brown leather sling by which it can be carried across the back when climbing or when riding (where there is no possibility of meeting an enemy or a buck), or it can be hung from the point of the shoulder, ready for immediate use.

Blanket is worn under the saddle, with a numnah between it and the horse's back to prevent its becoming wet and sour with sweat.

Bridle.—Ordinary military head-collar with a "9th Lancer" or "Pelham" bit, and a "reim" (thong) for tying up or knee-haltering the horse.

Chapter 11

The Downfall of Uwini
8th September to 14th September.

6th September.—I am now back at work again in the office, but only doing it indifferently well; Vyvyan is away with Ridley's column, and meantime Nicholson is helping me in the office. He has been marvellously quick at picking up the threads of the office work, and consequently is of the greatest assistance.

7th September.—Sir Frederick has today given me a better tonic than any which the combined medical faculty of Buluwayo could devise. He has told me that he is anxious for me to go and take charge of the column which is now under Ridley in the Somabula Forest. He has privately consulted Dr. Strong, who has been looking after me, and he considers that I may now safely go. After hearing this, it did not take long for me to get ready. Packing my kit on one horse and riding another, I said goodbye to Buluwayo, and with my nigger Diamond riding a third horse and leading a fourth, I started this afternoon, and am now camped for the night on the Umguza River, where some of Plumer's men are stationed.

8th September.—Took with me three of Plumer's men as escort, *viz*. Troopers Abrahamson, White, and Parkin, each with two horses and three days' rations. We started at sunrise to follow up Ridley's column. I could picture nothing more to my taste than a ride of from eighty to one hundred miles in a wild country, with three good men, and plenty of excitement in having to keep a good look-out for the enemy, enjoying splendid weather, shirt-sleeves, and a reviving feeling of health and freedom. Everything promised to make it one of the delightful times of my life. But before we had gone ten miles, I found I wasn't very fit; at sixteen miles we off-saddled, and a cup of tea refreshed me,

GIANTS' PLAYTHINGS
Specimens of fantastic granite rocks seen in Matabeleland
and Mashonaland

but I could not eat. I began to have thoughts of sending back for a cart to bring me ignominiously home again. However, after an hour's rest, I reflected that it was only a natural weakness after being so long on the sick-list.

So we went on for nine miles, to where Mr. Fynn was camped on a farm belonging to Arthur Rhodes (better known as "the *M'limo*"). Fynn is here collecting together native prisoners and refugees, and giving them ground on which to sow their crops. My thanks to you, Fynn, for that armchair where I slept most happily, and then the excellent tea and boiled rice, followed by another spell in the arm-chair! While resting here, three rebels came in to surrender, and they told us how the white troops, meaning Ridley's column, were several days on ahead, and that two days ago they had surrounded the rebels and had kept firing on them for the whole of one day and part of the next; one of the niggers went through a pantomime descriptive of the battle, and showed us how, during the fight, he himself lay low in a *donga*, and heard first the single shots of the white men replied to by the deeper bang of the native muskets, then the increasing rattle and roar of musketry, then the rapid *tap, tap, tap* of the Maxim, mingled with the crack of volleys and the roar of 7-pounders.

He imitated all the sounds beautifully, as well as the crouching attack of the skirmishers, the falling of the wounded rebels, and the flight of the remainder. His action was perfect, but I eventually discovered it was all a lie from beginning to end. No such fight had taken place—he merely made it up, as he hoped to please us; but meantime I was miserable at the thought that the action had come off and I was too late for it. At the same time, it aroused my impatience, and we pressed on that evening eight miles farther to the Bembezi River. There we off-saddled and coiled down in the dark, taking turns to keep watch. It was a lovely night, but was rather spoilt during my watch by a beastly hyena coming and sniffing around, and growling and snarling at us every now and then.

9th September.—Started at daybreak, and got to Inyati (fourteen miles) by eight o'clock. Here we found Terry of the 7th Hussars with six men occupying a small fort. Their life did not seem too cheery; small fort, open flat, blazing sun, and flies innumerable. Rudyard Kipling would well describe this young sprig, fresh from Charterhouse, accepting the surrender of numbers of Lobengula's trusted old warriors. He had under his charge in the fort stores of food and grain, for the better protection of which he had drawn largely on the roof of the mission church across the flat. After breakfasting here, we pressed on again under a blazing sun, hoping for water, but finding none. On and on over yellow, grassy, bush-grown flats for fourteen miles, till we struck a river-bed in which were a few pools of water. Here I lay down utterly done up, but after a wash in a pool and some tea, I soon got all right, and in the cool of the evening we went on another four miles to the Longwe River. Like nearly all the so-called rivers here, it was but a riverbed of sand, in which one had to dig for water.

We found here a convoy of four waggons with supplies for Ridley's column, but they could give us no information as to where he was camped, or how far ahead he might be; they were merely following along on his track. They had a strong escort, and were quite prepared to take care of themselves in the event of an attack. Among the troopers on escort was one Madden, an old Swaziland acquaintance. Our two days' journey had brought us respectively thirty-three and thirty-two miles from Buluwayo,—a total of sixty-five.

10th September.—Again we started at daybreak, and passed by Taba-si-ka-Mamba, a mass of jumbled-up *koppies*, six miles by three, which had formed one of the chief rebel strongholds in this part of the country, until Plumer's force had stormed the place, and driven the enemy out, on the 6th July last. The rocks and *koppies* here, like those in the Matopos, are piles of granite boulders, and in many cases assume most fantastic forms. Here and there they look like castles on the top of peaks; in other places, like gigantic loaves of bread, and in one place there was a tower of five of them placed one on top of the other for a height of nearly a hundred feet. We rode on until we came to the next river, the Umsangwe, a distance of ten miles; it was blazing hot, and I now began to feel a very poor creature. It was too far to go back again, and we could only hope that the column was not very far ahead, especially as we had not too much quantity or variety of food with us.

I lay up during the heat of the day with a waterproof sheet spread over a thorn-bush as a shelter from the sun. The men dug water in the sand, washed, and baked bread. To bake bread, lay your coat on the ground, inside upwards, mix the flour and water in it (it doesn't show when you put the coat on again); for yeast or baking powder use the juice of the toddy palm or Eno's Fruit Salt to make a light dough; scrape a circle in the ashes of the fire, flop your lump of dough, spread fine sand all round and all over it, then heap the embers of the fire on to it; in half an hour an excellent flat loaf of bread results. It requires scrubbing with a horse-brush before you eat it. At half-past three we saddled up and trekked on to the Shangani Paver, which was only four miles farther on. It is a mighty river on the map, but is nothing more in nature than the usual sand river-bed with occasional pools, the sand being about a hundred and fifty yards wide, with reed-grown banks on either side. To get water, you have to scrape out a hole of two feet deep, and fairly good water comes immediately. We had brought a nigger guide with us from Inyati, and he said that Ridley's column would be found on the Uvunkwe River, and that this was only a short distance on from the Shangani; so we pressed on.

But as night closed in, our nigger got frightened, and he told us that there were Matabele about. We replied that that was exactly the reason why we had come there. Then he said that the next water was so far off, that if we trotted the whole night, we should not get there till long after sunrise next day. We tried for a bit to get on in the dark, but rain had fallen since Ridley's column had passed along and had destroyed the spoor; we had no water, and only two days' food; our nigger guide was evidently unreliable: so we turned back to the Shangani, and there bivouacked for the night, taking it in turns, as usual, to keep watch.

11th September.—My anniversary of joining Her Majesty's Service, 1876-1896—twenty years. I always think more of this anniversary than of that of my birth, and I could not picture a more enjoyable way of spending it. I am here, out in the wilds, with three troopers. They are all Afrikanders, that is, Colonial born, one an ex-policeman, another a mining engineer (went to England with me in 1889 on board the *Mexican*), the third an electrical engineer from Johannesburg,—all of them good men on the *veldt*, and good fighting men. We are nearly eighty miles from Buluwayo and thirty from the nearest troops. I have rigged up a shelter from the sun with my blanket, a rock, and a thorn-bush; thirteen thousand flies are unfortunately staying with me, and are awfully attentive. One of us is always on the look-out by night and by day. Our stock of food, crockery, cooking utensils, and bedding does not amount to anything much, as we carry it all on our saddles.

Once, not very long ago, at an afternoon "At Home," I was handing a cup of tea to an old dowager, who bridled up in a mantle with bugles and beads, and some one noticed that in doing so my face wore an absent look, and I was afterwards asked where my thoughts were at that time. I could only reply that "My mind was a blank, with a single vision in it, lower half yellow, upper half blue," in other words, the yellow *veldt* of South Africa, topped with the blue South African sky. Possibly the scent of the tea had touched some memory chord which connected it with my black tin billy, steaming among the embers of a wood fire; but whatever it was then, my vision is today a reality.

I am looking out on the yellow *veldt* and the blue sky; the *veldt* with its grey, hazy clumps of thorn-bush is shimmering in the heat, and its vast expanse is only broken by the gleaming white sand of the river-bed and the green reeds and bushes which fringe its banks. (Interruption: Stand to the tent! a "Devil," with its roaring pillar of dust and leaves, comes tearing by.) I used to think that the novelty of the thing would wear off, that these visions of the *veldt* would fade away as civilized life grew upon me. But they didn't. They came again at most inopportune moments: just when I ought to be talking "The World," or "Truth," or "Modern Society" (with the cover removed), and making my reputation as a "sensible, well-informed man, my dear," with the lady in the mantle, somebody in the next room has mentioned the word saddle, or rifle, or billy, or some other attribute of camp life, and off goes my mind at a tangent to play with its toys.

Old Oliver Wendell Holmes is only too true when he says that most of us are "boys all our lives;" we have our toys, and will play with them with as much zest at eighty as at eight, that in their company we can never grow old. I can't help it if my toys take the form of all that has to do with *veldt* life, and if they remain my toys till I drop—

COLD AND HUNGRY
Clothing a rebel prisoner

Then here's to our boyhood, its gold and its grey,
The stars of its winter, the dews of its May;
And when we have done with our life-lasting toys,
Dear Father, take care of Thy children, the boys.

May it not be that our toys are the various media adapted to individual tastes through which men may know their God? As Ramakrishna Paramahansa writes:

"Many are the names of God and infinite the forms that lead us to know of Him. In whatsoever name or form you desire to know Him, in that very name and form you will know Him."

In the afternoon I rode out with one of the men some ten miles down the Shangani River, to see if we could find any spoor of the enemy crossing the sandy bed or coming to get water there, but we only found the separate tracks of three men at all fresh, though we found hundreds of old tracks. As we came in sight of our bivouac on our return, my man said, "There is a strange horse grazing with ours; someone has come to the camp;" and it was true enough—we had a visitor. Vyvyan, who was acting as staff officer to Ridley, had received my note which I had sent on by runners, saying that I was coming out to take command of the column, and that he was to return to Buluwayo to act as chief staff officer.

From him I ascertained that the column was only twenty-five miles away, and had not yet had a big fight, although it had lost a few men in taking some of the innumerable *koppies* in which the rebels of that part had taken refuge. So towards evening we saddled up and moved on, Vyvyan going on to Buluwayo with one man as escort, and I and my little party continuing our way eastward. We went on for three hours until the moon set, and then bivouacked for the night.

12th September.—On again at daybreak, through thick bush country, in which were numerous granite boulder *koppies*. Everywhere we found more or less recent tracks of natives, and the wheel-marks of Ridley's waggons once more became pretty well defined. Our horses were now beginning to get done—indeed, one of mine was doing his best to die; so, knowing that we must be near Ridley's camp, I pressed on ahead of the party leaving them to follow more leisurely. Presently I came across two niggers hiding in the bush, but evidently unarmed and afraid to run away. From them I managed to elicit that the camp was not far off, and they soon put me on the right path to it, and I got in in time for a late breakfast. The *laager* was formed in an open spot, surrounded on all sides at a short distance by eight *koppies* which formed the strongholds of the enemy.

One of these *koppies* had been attacked and taken two days previously, and the chief of the tribe had been there captured. But we had lost one man killed and four wounded, and there still remained seven *koppies* to be taken. One of my first acts in camp, after taking over command of the column, was to visit the hospital, where I found one man with his hand amputated; he bore it very well, and, being one of the best football players of the 7th Hussars, he was in good training, and therefore but little affected by it. When I said I hoped it would not spoil his football in the future, he laughed and said that as he played the Association game, he would be all the better without a hand. Another poor chap had a great double wound in his thigh (all unbandaged for my edification); and another, who was yesterday a particularly handsome young hussar, has today a horrible caricature of a face, with the whole of his lower jaw shot away.

And with what object? Merely to get half a dozen frightened niggers out of their holes in the rocks. Then I was shown the chief who had been captured—Uwini by name. He was badly wounded in the shoulder, but, enraged at being a prisoner, he would allow nothing to be done for him; no sooner had the surgeon bandaged him than he tore the dressings off again. He was a fine, truculent-looking savage, and boasted that he had always been able to hold his own against any enemies in this stronghold of his, but now that he was captured he only wished to die.

His capture had been most pluckily effected by Captain van Niekerk and two of his men. When his *kraal* was taken by troops, Uwini had scrambled down into the labyrinth of caves which ran through the rocks on which the *kraal* was built. Trooper Halifax and another crawled in after him, and followed him from one point to another of his refuge, often firing and being fired at by him. After some hours of this game of hide-and-seek, Halifax had managed to wound the chief; they then followed him up with a lighted candle, tracking him by his blood spoor, until they finally cornered him in a cleft of the rocks from which he could not escape. He was so disabled by his wound as to be unable to fire on them, and they made him a prisoner.

It now rested with me to decide what should be our next step. We had lost five men killed and wounded in taking one *koppie*, and there still remained seven to be taken, which were just as strongly held as

WARM AND COMFORTABLE

The little prisoner shows appreciation (with his right hanr) of the late contents of the jam-pot in his left

the first one; consequently we must expect to lose a number of men before we finally effected our purpose, and the probability was that we should not do this before we had first killed a large number of the rebels. The Native commissioner of this part had been murdered by the rebels and his police had joined them, so that civil power in the district had ceased to exist. There was in camp, however, an acting Native commissioner, Mr. V. Gielgud, who was to assume the post of commissioner so soon as the rebels could be induced to surrender.

This officer was most anxious that I should try Uwini by court-martial, for the following reasons:—Uwini was not only the leading chief of that part of the country, but was one of the four chiefs of the whole of Matabeleland who were supposed to be specially endowed by the *M'limo*, the god of the people; he was therefore in their eyes sacred, invulnerable, and infallible. He was well known to be the instigator of rebellion, and of several specific murders of whites in the district. His immediate punishment, then and there, would do more than anything else to restore our prestige and bring about the surrender of rebels, not only of his own tribe, but probably of the neighbouring tribes as well.

The chief, when asked by us to call upon his people to surrender, now that he was captured, absolutely declined to make any such proposition to them. He said that he had ordered them into rebellion, and had told them to fight to the last, and he was not now going to go back on his orders. He is a plucky and stubborn old villain. Time is very pressing, as we are getting constant information of rebels massing in three directions within reach of us, and to catch them we ought to be on the move at once; so I have determined to try him by court-martial, as any deserved punishment would certainly save much bloodshed on both sides, would save much valuable time that would otherwise be lost in operations against the stronghold, and should bring about the rapid pacification of the whole district and the restoration of our prestige in these parts.

There is no civil power to refer the case to, and by military law Uwini is a prisoner of war, and liable to trial by a military court; we are over a hundred miles from the general's headquarters, so that I could not refer the case with any certainty of getting an answer within reasonable time; and also, I know of several other similar cases having been tried lately by court-martial (P.S.—I had not then heard of any exception having been taken to this course), and I have therefore given the order for his immediate trial by Field General Court-Martial.

Uwini's *kraal*, like most others in this part of the country, was a large collection of thatched circular huts built on inaccessible crags of a small mountain; and above the *kraal*, on points of rocks, so as to be well out of the reach of thieves and marauders, were perched numerous corn-bins. These latter we could only reach by hoisting men up with ropes, but we were lucky in obtaining from them very large supplies of grain. Much of this we have used for feeding the women and children whom we had captured from this *kraal*, and these, spreading the news to others in other parts of the stronghold, have induced a good many of them to come and give themselves up to us.

In order to help the rebels to make up their minds about surrendering, I have ordered piquets to be posted at all places from which they draw their water supply; these are generally small wells in the neighbourhood of the *koppies* occupied by them, and their usual time for getting water is during the dark hours of the night, so I hope that tonight we shall considerably astonish them when they come to get their supply tomorrow.

My force here consists of a squadron of the 7th Hussars under Captain Agnew, a company of the York and Lancaster Mounted Infantry under Captain Kekewich, a strong troop of the Afrikander Corps under Captain van Niekerk, three Maxims, a 7-pounder under Captain Boggie, field hospital under Surgeon Lieutenant-Colonel Gormley, ambulance, and waggons carrying about a month's stores, a total of 360 men and horses.

13th September.—During the night a lot of shots were fired by our piquet on the stronghold. I visited them at dawn and found they had killed two rebels who had come out to get water. I had a long talk with the prisoners and refugees who were in camp, and learned from them that the mass of the Matabele were now spread about in the Somabula Forest. This forest extends in a semicircle for a distance of over a hundred and fifty miles from Gwelo down to the Shangani, and varies in width from fifteen to thirty miles. It is not, as a rule, inhabited, owing to the dearth of water, but the enemy had now taken to it, hoping to find a safer refuge there.

Our present camp is close to the edge of the forest, and is on the bank of the Uvunkwe River. This river runs along the side of the forest until it joins the Shangani some fifty miles from here. It seems to me that, by following down the Uvunkwe River for a short distance, and then striking through the forest to the Gwelo River, we should be able to come upon a large mass of the rebels who are said to be occupying a strong position in the hills.

The court-martial assembled on Uwini this morning, and tried him on charges of armed rebellion, for ordering his people to murder whites, and for instigating rebellion in this part of the country. The court-martial gave him a long hearing, in which he practically confessed to what was charged against him, and they found him guilty, and sentenced him to be shot. I was sorry for him, he was a fine old savage; but I signed his warrant, directing that he should be shot at sundown.

During the day I went over the *koppie* that had formed Uwini's main stronghold. It is a wonderfully strong mass of boulders about half a mile long and six hundred feet high. The approaches to it were strengthened by breastworks of stone and timber, and the mountain itself is honeycombed with caves. The cave in which Uwini was captured runs all through the mountain with innumerable ramifications. It is so narrow that in many places we had to crawl, now and then climbing up on our hands and knees, and sometimes having to creep down rough ladders made of tree-trunks. It was only then that we realised the difficulty that the men had had in effecting his capture, and their pluck in following up an armed and desperate man in such a very nasty place.

On my arrival in camp yesterday, it had been reported to me that one man of the Mounted Infantry, while out on patrol in the forest, had become separated from his party and was missing. Additional patrols had been sent out to search for him, and though they had followed up his spoor for some distance, they had been unable to find him. Today, again, patrols had gone out accompanied by native trackers, but towards evening they returned, having again been unsuccessful in finding him; they reported that his spoor led back in the direction of the camp, and so they had hoped he would have returned before them, but he has not yet returned. Luckily, he was carrying on his saddle the day's rations for the other. three men of his section, so that if he can only keep his head, and not overwork his horse, there is every hope that he will turn up again.

But that is the worst of these men when they get lost,—they seem to lose their heads, and tear off in all directions, until they exhaust themselves and their horses, when they become a prey to the enemy or go out of their mind. At night we send up rockets and fire guns in order to show the wanderer whereabouts the camp lies.

At sunset all the natives in camp, both friendlies, refugees, and prisoners, were paraded to witness the execution of Uwini. He was taken out to an open place in the centre of his stronghold, where all his people who were still holding out could see what was being done, and he was there shot by a firing party from the troops.

I have great hopes that the moral effect of this will be particularly good among the rebels, as he was the head and centre of revolution in these parts, and had come to be looked upon by them as a god. No doubt, when they have realised that he is after all but a mortal, that he has succumbed to our power, and that they have no other had to take his place, they won't delay long to surrender.

Indeed, I sent one old lady out to the rebel stronghold today to advise them to give themselves up, and to assure them that they could do so with perfect safety, but the old girl returned from her mission without bringing any of them with her. As she came back into camp, carrying her pass in a cleft stick, I was amused to hear one of the men say to her as she passed, "Hullo, old girl, are you back off furlough already?"

I had proposed to start off some of my column to the northward this evening, but in the afternoon a small boy came into camp and reported that there was a party of Matabele camped about fifteen miles away to the southward, on the Uvunkwe River, so I got Ridley to take fifty men and make a night march to attack them. The patrol started after dark, at seven o'clock, and very soon after they had left camp, we heard rapid firing in their direction. On sending out to ascertain the cause, we found that Ridley's party, in passing near to the piquet which was guarding the enemy's water-supply, had been mistaken by them for Matabele, and had been fired on, but luckily no one was hurt. I ran in the officer of the piquet, and after hearing his explanation of how the mistake arose, I abused him roundly, not for making the mistake, for we are all of us liable to do that at times, but because, when he opened fire, his men were not able to hit the hussars. This hurt him more than the most violent reprimand, because he prided himself on the good shooting of his men.

14th September.—Firing was kept up during the night by this piquet at frequent intervals. It was evident that the rebels were getting very thirsty; for two days and nights now they had not been allowed to get any water. During the few hours of darkness, just before dawn, numbers of them slipped away, and the remainder came and gave themselves up, many of them bringing in their arms. Thus, within a very few hours of his execution, the death of Uwini began to have its effect.

Through the breakup of Uwini's stronghold, large stores of grain fell into our hands, and as we have over a thousand prisoners and refugees now in camp, we have plenty of assistance in gathering it into a central store.

Early in the morning Ridley and his patrol returned from their night march. They had found the enemy's *scherms* deserted, the spoor showing that the *kaffirs* had cleared into the forest; they had had their long ride for nothing, and the only excitement they had encountered was that of being fired upon by our own piquet just after starting.

Again the search party, which had been sent out to look for the missing man, returned unsuccessful; no further signs of him had been found, and I fear that he must have fallen into the hands of the enemy.

No respecter of persons

"Hulloh, old gal! Back again off furlo'?" is the greeting of Tommy Atkins to an aged princess returning from a mission to the rebels.

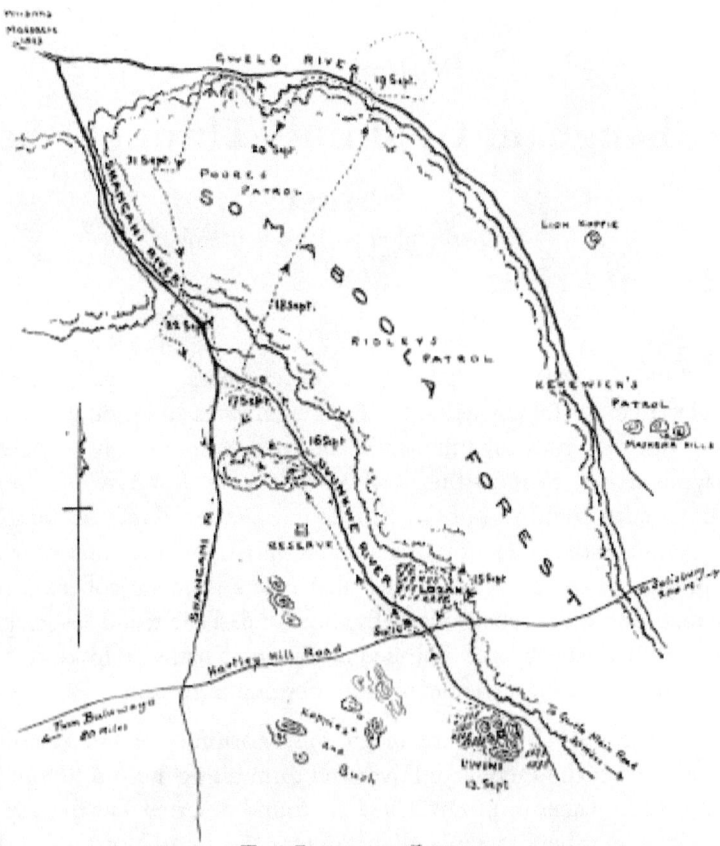

THE SHANGANI COLUMN

Sketch map showing the country visited by this column. The dotted line shows the route of that patrol of the column which I accompanied, Kekewich's and Ridley's patrols working to our right rear, through the forest. Scale approximately 20 miles to 1 inch.

CHAPTER 12

Shanghani Column—Through the Forest
14th September to 19th September.

14th September.—Today we have started operations against the Somabula Forest. Taking with me 160 men, hussars and mounted infantry, with two guns, an ambulance, and four waggons lightly loaded, I have marched away to the northward, leaving near Uwini's stronghold, under command of Captain Agnew, the remainder of the force, to complete the collection of grain and obtain the surrender of rebels. I propose now to break up the rebel *impi* said to be collected near here; to drive the rebels out of the Somabula Forest; and to break up posts which have been established on the main paths in this district, to prevent would-be surrenderers from coming in to us.

15th September.—Before dawn this morning we made a rapid march across the Uvunkwe River and through the bush to the grain-fields and villages of Lozan. These we found deserted, but fresh spoor of a large number of people, all making for the forest, showed that they had been there the previous day, but had got wind of our movements in time to make their escape. We managed to capture a few women, some of whom had come from the *impi* in the Mashene Hills, which I had proposed to attack, and they saved me much trouble by telling me that that *impi* was already on the move north-westwards, because of a strong column of white troops which was approaching it from the eastward, with the evident intention of attacking it.

This, I concluded, was Colonel Paget's column, which had been coming up from Victoria, *via* Gwelo, into the Maven district; so my obvious course was now to make for the north with all speed, and cut off this *impi* in its flight. But in doing so, I should have to pass through the most occupied part of the Somabula Forest, and I consider the most effective way of doing this will be to divide my force into three patrols, to move rapidly on parallel courses through the forest, as lightly equipped as possible, leaving the waggons with another party to follow along a central route in rear, to form, as it were, a supporting depot and reserve.

At Lozan's *kraal* we found ourselves well in the Somabula Forest, but it is scarcely a forest in the usual sense of the word. The trees are quite small and growing close together, more like a pheasant cover in England than a great forest, but without much undergrowth, and with sandy soil under foot; an easy place to lose your way in, and an unpleasant one on account of the want of water. But this same want of water should very much simplify matters when we are searching for the rebels, as we have simply to go to the few existing water-places to find their tracks, which we can then follow up with the certainty of discovering their hiding-place.

Our camping place for the middle of the day is on the drift where the Hartley Hill road crosses the Uvunkwe River, and the Native commissioner (Gielgud), my orderly, and I were making our way back from Lozan's to this camp by a roundabout route through the bush, in the hopes of picking up more prisoners, when we suddenly came on a couple of *koodoo*, splendid great brindled buck. I had a hasty shot at one with my Lee-Metford, and luckily struck him through the upper part of the forelegs, breaking both of them, and so disabling him. I was thus able to go up to him and finish him with another bullet, which, however, passed clean through him, making but a very small hole. The probability is that, had I hit him through the body in a non-vital spot, he would have gone on his way rejoicing.

We soon had him cut up and slung over my horse for conveyance to camp. On getting to our out-span near the drift, we came on the remains of three white people, who had been murdered here by rebels. One poor chap had evidently made a hard fight for his life, being at some distance from the others under a tree. There was not much by which to identify the bodies, but one had his teeth peculiarly stopped with gold, and a half-sovereign was picked up with some markings on it.

This evening I started off my patrols to operate through the forest; the right-hand patrol, consisting of about thirty mounted infantry under Captain Kekewich, is to go through the forest and follow the course of the Gwelo River, which forms the right-hand boundary of the forest. He is to gain touch, if possible, with Colonel Paget, and also to work out that side of the forest as much as possible, getting his water in the Gwelo River. The second patrol, forty men under Major Ridley, is to keep along the Uvunkwe River, which forms the left-hand boundary of the forest. His duty will be to patrol into the forest from this side, follow up and drive out all rebels, getting his water-supply in the Uvunkwe.

The third patrol, of forty of the 7th Hussars under Captain Poore, with which I am going, will press on at a rapid pace down the Uvunk-we and through the forest on to the lower part of the Gwelo River, where we shall be in a position to cut off all parties of rebels who may be retreating before Colonel Paget's attack and those of our other two patrols, and we shall there be able also to get on to the path which leads to the one great refuge in the north, the grain-bearing district of Inyoka. Meanwhile, the waggons, guns, and ambulance, with a sufficient guard, will follow leisurely along the Uvunkwe River, so as to be at hand with further supplies or assistance if required by any of the patrols. Each patrol takes with it as much food as the men can carry on their saddles, which, however, does not amount to more than four days' supply.

I started after dark with my patrol, and we did eleven miles in the moonlight before we off-saddled for our first bivouac.

16th September.—This morning by dawn we were rushing our way along the Uvunkwe, but could find no sign of the recent presence of the natives. The river holds plenty of water, and is a very pretty one, full of long reaches and pools fringed with green reeds and overhanging trees; the scenery round is generally undulating yellow grass *veldt*, thickly dotted with grey thorn-bush; it is all parched and dry as a bone. As we got farther on our way, the thorn-bush became thicker, and at last we got into a forest of thorns which defeated us. We had to lead our horses and to struggle at a very slow pace through this dense, prickly bush, and finally had to give it up as a bad job. We then made our way with difficulty down into the river-bed, where the going was more open.

Just as we were crossing the sandy bank, I saw that which made my heart stand still. A path of perfectly fresh tracks leading from the water up into another part of the same bush from which we had just emerged; so fresh were they that the water in some or the shallower puddles was still muddy, and a dog was quietly trotting along the path towards the bush. We did not wait one instant; Poore and I tore up the path, followed by the hussars, as fast as we could go. Dashing along the spoor like a pack of hounds, we very soon found ourselves in the bush, and among a lot of huts and *scherms*; but too late! We could hear the crackling of twigs as the niggers bolted in front of us into the deep, thick bush.

All their fires were left burning, and cooking pots full of pumpkins and mealies were boiling merrily on the fires; their clothes and clubs, *assegais* and loot, were lying about in heaps; there were army greatcoats, white men's and women's clothes, axes, saws, tinned provisions, and other articles, evidently spoils of murdered whites; and among other things I picked up a trinket which had its meaning for us, and that was a small necklace of peculiar black beads; this necklace was of the kind which only a certain regiment of Matabele were allowed to wear, namely, M'tini's regiment, which acted as the bodyguard of M'qwati (M'qwati is the high priest of the *M'limo* in these parts).

We were in luck indeed if we could but catch these men; it is this

FOLLOWING UP THE SPOOR

Spooring or tracking the enemy was our usual way of getting to him. With a little practice spooring can be carried out with great certainty, and at good pace.

impi which provides posts in different parts of the country with orders to kill any of the natives who desire to make peace with the whites, or to come in to surrender. I brought away with me a rhinoceros-hide *sjambok* (whip) and an *induna's* staff. From these evidences, and from the appearance of the huts, we guessed that this camp was the headquarters of M'tini, the leader of the regiment; but we knew from reports of prisoners that M'qwati usually lived at some little distance from M'tini, in a safer spot, so we hoped that with a little searching we might find him. Therefore, leaving Poore with his men to destroy the halts, I took two or three hussars with me, and followed the spoor for nearly another three miles alongside the thick bush. But by this time the sun had set, it was getting dark, and I could see no further sign of the rebels.

I therefore reluctantly abandoned the chase for the time being, and returned to Poore, who had now gone into bivouac on the river bank. Knowing that the rebels would probably remain in the thickness of the bush, but would have to come to the river to get their water, we lit up a line of fires after dark all along the river bank for nearly a mile opposite the spot where the bush came down to the river. This was to frighten the enemy from trying to get water, as they would think we had a number of men near each fire. As a matter of fact, so soon as we had finished supper we continued our march in the darkness down the river, and bivouacked again when we had got below the junction of the Uvunkwe with the Shangani River.

17th September.—I started before dawn this morning with a patrol of a dozen men to resume my hunt for M'qwati, going back to the spot where I had broken off yesterday evening. Poore meanwhile took another patrol up the Shangani, in order to intercept these rebels, should they think of retiring in that direction. On my way back I saw Ridley's patrol in the distance, and accordingly went across to him and arranged that he should further investigate this patch of bush, and cut off its water supply again that night, both from the Uvunkwe and from the Shangani. Then I went on and struck yesterday's spoor, and followed it into the bush; as this got too thick for the horses we dismounted, and pressed along on foot. Fresh spoor struck in on to the old, and every minute the scent, as it were, seemed to get hotter and hotter. We shoved along faster and faster, tearing along and being torn.

Suddenly I see smoke through the bushes, then the yellow thatch of huts. I jump forward, leaving my hat in a *Wacht-een Beetche* thornbush. I don't care—can't stop. There they are! I can see two men at any rate dodging about—there may be more. One fine big fellow in European clothes dashes out of a hut and makes off with a gun in his hand. I yell to him, "*Imana, andi bulali!*" (Stop, I am not going to kill you!) But he does not stop, and I try not to keep my promise, but unfortunately I have one of the newfangled guns that I do not understand—slipperty-slip, *click-clack and tick!*—but there's no report; three times I cover him with my sights, aiming nice and low, just about the small of his back, but each time my gun refuses to go off. I have forgotten to turn on or off some little gadget or other, and the man escapes. Curious that the momentary failure of a spring to act should spare a man to live to enjoy many years of domestic bliss or—to murder a few more fellow-creatures!

And that was the last we saw of these rebels. Of course we burnt their huts and followed on the spoor, and twice again we came upon others of their camps, but in each case they had suspicion of our coming, and managed to get out of the way as we arrived upon the scene, and it was impossible to pursue them with any hope of success in that impenetrable bush. However, I sent back a further message to Ridley by my orderly, informing him that the enemy were still in this track of bush, and telling him how best to deal with them. (The orderly who took this note came across a lion on the way, and had a shot, but missed him.)

I then went on with my patrol, back along the Uvunkwe, to meet a party who had been sent after us from the waggons with additional supplies of flour and coffee on pack-horses, and we met them at the place agreed upon. During our midday halt for lunch and *siesta*, I found a snake had had the impertinence to come and lie alongside of me for his afternoon nap, and so I killed him. Later on I strolled down to the river, to bathe in a large and tempting pool, in which several of the men had already been having a swim. The first object that met my view on arriving there was a leery-looking crocodile, who seemed to be winking at me with one eye; I had a shot at him (which missed) and then I sought another pool to bathe in; this one happened to be close to the enemy's watering-place, so, while undressed, I took care to leave my boots and rifle very ready for use in case of a surprise. Bathing became interesting when one had to keep a look-out with one eye for Matabele creeping through the reeds, and with the other for crocodiles rising from the water.

The horse guard

Vedettes are invariably posted in different directions while the horses are grazing, to ensure their not straying, and to guard against their surprise and capture by the enemy.

"A Merciful Man," &c.

Our horses gave put from want of food and overwork, though the men cared for them in every way, walking in their holey boots, and sharing with them their small rations of bread.

In the afternoon we started again with our newly-received supplies, to overtake Poore and the rest of our party, the men who had brought the supplies meanwhile returning to the waggons. Before leaving the neighbourhood, however, we got up a grand sham fight, and we fired volleys and independent firing. This was done with the idea of alarming the rebels in the bush, and of letting them know that we were here in some force, and probably firing on their friends; they would therefore probably not venture out at this end of the bush, and the other end was meantime being taken care of by Ridley and his party. Late that night we rejoined Poore, tired out, and heartily glad to turn in to sleep.

18th September.—Our usual daily march goes thus: Reveille and stand to arms at 4.30, when Orion's belt is overhead. (The natives call this "*Ingolobu*," the pig, the three big stars being three pigs, and the three little ones being the dogs running after them; this shows that *kaffirs*, like other nations, see pictures in the constellations.) We then feed horses—if we have anything to feed them with, which is not often; light fires and boil coffee; saddle up, and march off at 5.15. We go on marching till about 9.30 or 10, when we off-saddle, and lie up for the heat of the day, during which the horses are grazed, with a guard to look after them, and we go on breakfasting, bathing, and in theory writing and sketching, but in practice sleeping, at least so far as the flies will allow.

At 3.30 saddle-up and march till 5.30, offsaddle and supper; then we march on again, as far as necessary, in the cool hours of the early night. On arriving at the end of our march, we form our little *laager*; to do this we put our saddles down in a square, each man sleeping with his head in the saddle, and the horses inside the square, fastened in two lines on their "built-up" ropes. To go to bed, we dig a small hole for our hip-joints to rest in, roll ourselves in our horse-blanket, with our head comfortably ensconced in the inside of the saddle, and we would not then exchange our couch for anything that Maple could try and tempt us with.

This morning we started as usual at 5.15, and continued our way northward down the Shangani. We were now getting into a more tropical climate, and slender palm trees began to vary the woodland scenery, and dwarf palms and ferns abounded among the smaller bush. Everywhere we found spoor of big buck, and also of lions.

At last we came to the spot where we considered it desirable to leave the Shangani and strike across through the forest to get to the Gwelo River, where we should be in a position to cut off the retreating enemy. The map showed this to be a distance of about twenty-five miles; but the maps of this district are naturally not to be relied upon, since it has only been very sketchily surveyed, if surveyed at all. We had not left the Shangani a mile behind us before we came across a small affluent stream, and here we came on the spoor of natives not twenty-four hours old. As we were rising the bank of this stream, we saw a woman on the path.

She was too frightened to move, or even to speak, when we had captured her; but she had a baby on her back, and, seeing that I began to play with the child instead of eating it, as she had probably expected, she found her tongue, and was able to answer our inquiries. She told us that she belonged to a party of M'tini's *impi*, which was camped a short distance farther on in the bush; and she told us that the party that we had already surprised in the thick bush on the Uvunkwe was also the other portion and headquarters of that *impi*. While we were talking, one of the men said he saw a native running across the *veldt*. Galloping in that direction, I came across the spoor of a boy, which I followed till I ran him to earth in a thick bunch of grass, where he was lying completely hidden.

On questioning him, he corroborated what the woman had said. He was a plucky youngster, and faithless to his friends, for he at once volunteered to guide us to the spot where they were camped, and showed but little alarm on being hoicked up on to the front of one of the hussars' saddles. Dividing ourselves into two parties, we went forward in the direction indicated, and, passing a ruined farmstead on our way, we presently got into a tract of thick bush, and suddenly came upon a *kraal* in the heart of it. The people in the *kraal* were taken completely by surprise; they had not time to take up their arms, but dashed into the jungle, eager to make their escape. The hussars were, however, too quick for them, and, diving through the bush at a splendid pace with drawn swords, they succeeded in surrounding them before they could get away, and brought them all back into the *kraal*. Our detached party, in making a wider movement round this *kraal*, came upon a second, and similarly captured it and its occupants, together with a goodly flock of goats.

We then took our prisoners back to the water-place, and, as our horses were rather tired with their morning gallop, we halted there to take our mid-day rest. Our prisoners showed no signs of being sorry at their capture; in fact, they appeared rather glad than otherwise. The women built us shelters from the sun with branches and palm leaves, the men killed and cut up goats for us to eat, the children lit the fires and boiled the kettles; and so we made a peaceful, friendly-looking party.

In talking things over with the leading man among them, we found that they were tired of war, and were only anxious to surrender, but were kept from doing so by the orders of their chiefs, backed up by piquets placed on all their paths. They told us, too, that the path on which their encampment was, was a new one lately made by their co-rebels for getting to the northward to Inyoka; and that if we followed this path that night, it would bring us by the morning to the Gwelo River, and that there large parties of them were massed. Naturally, we determined to push on that evening, taking two men with us to act as guides; and we ordered the remainder to go down to our waggons, and there report themselves as prisoners, which they were quite willing to do. The two men we took with us were Umtenti and Umbalena.

Before starting on our evening march, we went and examined the homestead that we had passed in the morning, and found it was that of a white man, whose remains were lying in the garden. He had evidently been murdered there, and the place ransacked by rebels. We buried him, and put up a roughly made cross above his head, and then started on our way into the Somabula Forest. But now the horses were beginning to feel the effect of hard work and want of proper food. We had no grain for them, nor could we carry it if we had—their only forage was the withered, parched-up grass, which had no sustenance in it; watering places were few and far between; the atmosphere was hot, the sand was soft and heavy under foot; so that, after we had been marching for some hours, I was not surprised to hear that one of the horses had given out, and could go no more; and several of the men, finding that their horses were but staggering on under them, got off to walk.

Our pace was very slow, and the way was dark amongst the trees; the spoor was very hard to follow, and thus it took us a long time to get over any distance. At last we called a halt in a slightly open spot where there was grass, the horses got a bite of food, and we lay down and slept in our tracks for about an hour. Then on again till long past midnight. I was hoping all the time that we might arrive at dawn upon the Gwelo River, and thus surprise the enemy encamped there; but I now saw that the horses were too done for any active work unless they had a rest; and so we halted, off-saddled, and bivouacked, having done about forty miles today.

19th September.—Starting before dawn, we pressed on again through the forest, and emerged after about three miles on the bank of the Gwelo, passing through numerous deserted *scherms* of the enemy, but without seeing any signs of his recent presence there. Our guide now told us that if the enemy were not here, they would be at a little stream about a day's march the other side of the Gwelo; but while we were examining the drift, where the track of the Matabele crossed the river, we found a fresh spoor of two men going north, and our guides immediately said it would be no use to follow up the enemy along that path, because these tracks meant that two men had made their escape from the *kraals* we had captured yesterday, and had gone on ahead to put the remainder on the *qui vive;* and with our horses in their present state, I saw it would be useless to go farther away from our base on so doubtful a venture.

The Gwelo River itself is not a pleasing one; it is chiefly a bed of hard, black mud, lying between black, shiny rocks, with a few pools here and there, with an unpleasant smell about it. The sun, too, is now very powerful, and we are all feeling tired.

It has been an immense disappointment to all of us not to find the enemy here, but the hussars are first-rate fellows, and are cheery in spite of all their hard work and absence of reward. Most of them walked the greater part of the march on foot, in order to save their horses. They all work so well and quietly, no order even in daytime or in camp is given above the ordinary tone of voice, but it is always heard and obeyed at once; naturally it is a great comfort to have such men with one, for things are looking a bit more difficult now. We have placed twenty miles of waterless forest behind us, we have only three days' groceries with us and no meat, and our horses are very weak.

But though we have not encountered the enemy, they know of our presence in this out-of-the-way part of the world, and our spoor on their main path to the north will deter any more fugitives from coming up this way. Our next course will be to move down the Gwelo River until we come to the one other path which leads to Inyoka. This path is somewhere near the junction of the Gwelo and Shangani, and not far from the place where Wilson's patrol was massacred in the first Matabele war. By getting on to this, we shall be enabled to stop any other northward movement of the rebels, and it should bring us

FRESH HORSE-BEEF

We eventually had to take to horseflesh. the farrier and the squadron butcher did the necessary preparation, and it was very cheering to hear their cry, "Now boys, roll up for your rations."

back on to the Shangani in the direction of our waggons.

The only drawback is that our horses are giving out, and we have no meat, therefore we are now going on half rations, though I hope we shall manage to get some game to eat, as this is a celebrated game country. Nevertheless, I realise that there is some responsibility in having sole charge and guidance of so large a party of men, deep in an enemy's country, and one which is practically a desert, with no water except in the one river, and our maps cannot be depended upon as reliable to guide one. Our two natives, never having been in this country themselves, can only guess at our whereabouts.

CHAPTER 13

Shangani Patrol—Return March
20th September to 1st October.

20th September.—Woke up this morning much refreshed, after a good rest all yesterday and last night. Owing to the amount of lions' spoor about the place, we kept fires going all night as a precaution against them.

This morning we marched at five, after destroying large numbers of old *scherms* which had been occupied by the enemy, and we followed the course of the river for some miles, intending then to strike across country and make a short cut to the Shangani, as all maps, though differing in other details, showed this to be possible. However, we did not find it possible. We struck boldly out into the forest, and marched along at our best speed, which was not very great. Gradually, the heat of the day began to affect the horses; again, we were on foot leading and driving them through the heavy sand; but after going about six miles, we saw it would be impossible to reach the Shangani that day. We had already abandoned two horses, and several others seemed quite done up; our only chance now was to hark back to the Gwelo.

Another unpleasant item had been added to our experiences this morning, and that was the finding of several carcases of *koodoo* which had evidently died from rinderpest, so that there was little hope of our getting any fresh meat by shooting game in this district. I therefore gave orders that one of the horses should be shot, cut up, and issued as rations for the men, and it was quite a cheering sight to see the squadron butcher get to work in a professional way on that horse, and to hear him sing out when all was ready, "Now, boys, roll up for your rations."

I now wrote a note to the officer in command of the waggons, telling him that we should make our way to the Shangani, and should proceed along its bank towards him, but that, being short of food, we should hope for him to send a few pack-horses with fresh supplies to meet us. Then, loading up the two native guides with as much horse-flesh as they could carry, and filling up a tin biscuit-box with water from our water-bottles for them, we sent them off, taking their direction by the sun, to find the waggons and deliver the note.

Then we ourselves turned again and made our way back to the Gwelo, and there halted for our midday meal and rest. This was our menu: weak tea (can't afford it strong), no sugar (we are out of it), a little bread (we have half a pound a day), Irish stew (consisting of slab of horse boiled in muddy water with a pinch of rice and half a pinch of pea-flour), salt, none. For a plate I use one of my gaiters: it is marked "Tautz & Sons, No. 3031;" it is a far cry from *veldt* and horseflesh to Tautz and Oxford Street!

Our great difficulty is topographical information. Our two prisoners, whom we had now sent away, had been worse than useless as guides, because they had no idea of distance; our two maps differ widely as to the relative positions of the two rivers, and our view of the country is limited in all directions by bush. The natives, before they left us, told us that if we kept along the bank of the Gwelo until we came to a path turning off southwards at the foot of a tall fruit tree, it would bring us in a very short walk to the Shangani River, and we hope to strike that path tonight. We are all right so long as nobody gets sick or wounded, if we manage to get a tussle with the niggers (and I am in great hopes that when we strike the path, we may just drop on to them coming up it). Another difficulty is that our messengers may not prove faithful in taking our note to the waggons. Nothing like looking at the cheery side of things!

In the evening, we moved on again along the bank of the Gwelo, and soon after sunset we came across a path leading southwards from the river, and near the path was a tall palm tree, which we took to be the tall fruit tree spoken of by our two natives. This path was to take us in a very few miles to the Shangani, so, after supping at this spot, we started with light hearts to follow the track as it turned deep into the forest again. Every man was now walking, and either leading or driving his horse, and as we formed a long single string in the narrow path, our progress was extremely slow. On and on till past midnight, and by one in the morning we reckoned we had done about eight miles; but we ought, according to our guide's report, to have struck the Shangani long ere this. But no Shangani nor any sign of it was in sight; so, calling a halt, I told Poore to rest the men and horses, while Gielgud—who was an old American scout—and I went on ahead, to see if we could find the river within a reasonable distance.

We two were mounted on ponies, which seem to stand the hard work far better than the horses of the hussars, and having bright moonlight to show us the track, we pressed along at a fairly good pace. The sameness of the forest scenery was very tiring and very depressing, and we only longed to come upon the enemy, or for them to come upon us, to give a little variety to the monotony.

On and on we went, until we calculated we had done another nine miles, but never a sign of water. The moon was then getting low, and we agreed the only thing to be done was to turn back while there was yet sufficient light to see the track to rejoin the patrol, and to turn them back once more for a second time to the Gwelo River. My idea then, was that one of us should take the two best horses and ride for the direction of the waggons to try and get help, while the patrol should keep along the river bank, so as to be sure of its water, and simply live on horse until relieved. Gielgud very kindly volunteered to make the attempt to ride for the waggons. We had not gone very far on our way back towards the patrol, when the moon went down, and left us in the dark; but it only wanted a quarter of an hour to dawn, so we made a fire, and boiled our cocoa, in the course of which operation I fell fast asleep.

21st September.—As the dawn came on, I climbed a neighbouring tree and looked all round to see if there were any signs of the river, but nothing but an unbroken line of tree-tops met my gaze. As I was coming down from the tree, a jingling in the bush a short distance away attracted my attention, and there, to my horror, I saw the whole of my patrol had followed after us. This settled the question of whether to go forward or to go back; we must now press forward, even if it meant losing horses.

Again halting the party to give them a rest, Gielgud and I resolved to make one more effort to find water, not by going on along the path, but by striking off to one side where the ground appeared to slope downwards. It was heart-breaking work: every rise seemed to promise a valley on the other side, but we only topped it to find an ordinary dry, baked, grass *vley* beyond. After going some miles without success, we sorrowfully allowed that no more could be done; our ponies were getting fagged out, and we must try and get back to the patrol, with every prospect of having a bad day pushing on for water. Poor Gielgud was now asleep on his horse. I was leading the way back, and his horse following mine wearily, when I chanced to notice on the ground the place where a buck had been scratching in the sand. I thought to myself that he would not scratch there for nothing, so, dismounting, I continued the scratching with my hand, and after digging for some little time, I came to damp ground, and a little deeper the water began to ooze in.

Then I saw two pigeons fly up from behind a rock a short distance from me, and, going there, I found a little pool of water. You may guess how much we were relieved; it reversed the whole of the dilemma. An hour later we had got the party off-saddled there, watered and camped for the day, and here I am under my blanket shelter, scorching hot day, flies innumerable stopping all our efforts to sleep, and the prospect of another night march before us, which we sincerely hope will bring us out of this beastly forest to the river. We have now got only one pound of bread left for each man, a little tea, a spoonful of rice, and plenty of horseflesh; no salt, sugar, or coffee—these luxuries are past; and we expect nothing more for the next three days. Yet the men are singing and chaffing away as cheerfully as possible while they scoop the muddy water from the sand-hole for their tea.

I am mounting Gielgud and Corporal Spicer of the 7th on my ponies, and they are going to start to ride for the waggons as soon as the heat of the day is over. I shall not leave the men myself, but shall probably have to walk on foot; this I would not mind, but my boots are already very holey, and only the ankles of my socks remain, the feet have become most delicate lace.

At 4 p.m. we again moved on, having bid goodbye to Gielgud and his man, who have gone on ahead. Gielgud is a fine young fellow, Native commissioner by occupation, American by birth, cowboy by education, and gentleman by nature.

We held on steadily to the south and eastward till long after dark, and again a brilliant moon helped us on our way. In fact we do far more marching by night than by daytime. At last a halt was called, because two more horses had given out, and we had to transfer their saddles to other horses, which in some cases were already carrying two or three saddles on their backs, for we may as well try to save what government property we can I took the opportunity of this halt to go forward again to look for water, and I was not out of sound of the men's voices when I came on the wide expanse of river-bed lying in the moonlight before me. I *was* glad.

All my anxiety was now over. We camped then and there on a tree-shaded, rocky knoll overlooking the river. Poore and I have a splendid log fire between us. I boiled up my last spoonful of cocoa which I had been husbanding for a great occasion like this, and after a nugget of rock-like bread and a fid of horse, I am going to bed with my boots off! I do not care for Matabele now; I am going to try for a good sleep, and I will "see that I get it."

22nd September.—We had what in India would be called "a Europe morning," that is to say, we lay in bed longer than usual by half an hour, and did not get up till five. Then we marched for two hours along the Shangani: we were now out of the forest, but in pretty thick thorn-bush country. We now kept a good look-out for the enemy, hoping to catch them about the river, and patrolled into all likely-looking country on both sides of the river, as this was a part of the country in which Forbes' column in '93 met with several attacks from the enemy on their way back after the Shangani disaster. But we could not even find a sign of the rebels, although we saw what was also very interesting, and that was the spoor of lion. I had taken a patrol of three men across the river to examine some bush, and in coming back on to the river bank, one of my men cried out, "There is a lion!" and sure enough there was a fine great dark-coloured lion strolling along on a small island in the middle of the river-bed, about a hundred yards away.

I thought he would like to have some notice taken of him, so jumped off my horse to salute him, and the corporal with me did the same, and we both fired almost simultaneously. One bullet struck the ground under him and the other struck him in the ribs, rather far back, as for a moment he sank on his haunches, and then sprang forward among some rocks and was immediately lost to sight. I put my hussars up on different rocks to keep a look-out for him, and the main body of the patrol on the other bank of the river kept the look-out there, and I went down among the rocks of the riverbed to look for him, but could not find him. Poore joined me there, and also his sergeant-major, and the farrier, who came armed with a revolver only. But though we searched every corner of the rocks, we never saw the beast again. But we heard of him, for later on, when I resumed the search in the afternoon, one of the men whom I had posted on the look-out asked how many lions I expected to find there, as the one I had shot at in the morning had gone away up the river dragging his hindquarters after him. The man had supposed that I saw him too, and so said nothing!

We killed another horse today, and I took in my belt another hole. I seldom measured less round the waist than I do now.

Had a delicious bathe in the river. The only drawback to bathing is the difficulty of getting back into one's soleless socks again; next time I bathe I shall not take them off, but will bathe in them. The river is a big sandy bed with piles and ledges of grey granite rock, low banks covered with thorn jungle, occasional pools among the rocks. Some of the hussars, fishing in these pools, have managed to catch some good-sized barbel. It is wonderful what soldiers manage to carry as part of their kit,—here is a man carrying fish-hooks with him in this wilderness, just as in India, I remember, a man had a pair of skates among his things, which, however, came in useful when he got up to Kandahar in the winter-time. The men are certainly thin, but very healthy and hungry. When a man is hungry, it is curious to see how he furtively watches his neighbour eating, especially if he (the watcher) has already finished his meal.

I know you will ask, what is horseflesh like? Well, it is not so bad when you have got accustomed to it, and especially if you have a little salt, mustard, vegetables, &c., to go with it, and also if you did not happen to know the deceased personally. None of these conditions were present in our case. It is one thing to say, "I'll trouble you to pass the horse, please," but quite another to say, "Give me another chunk of D 15."

During the afternoon march I again took a patrol away to the flank of my main party, and had not rejoined it when darkness set in, consequently, in the main party, they began to fire some signal shots, to show me where they were, and I replied to these. For signal shots we generally fired three shots in rapid succession, but, to my great surprise, my signal was not only replied to by the patrol, but also by a volley fired in the darkness some distance ahead of us. The volley was immediately followed by the bright flare of a signal fire. I very soon rejoined my patrol, and together we pressed on in the direction of the fire. More shots were fired, to which we replied, and, on reaching the place, we were delighted to find our relief party, which had been sent out, under De Moleyns, to meet us. Here were camp-fires ready lit, bully-beef, sugar, flour, cocoa, laid out all ready for issue, and nosebags, stuffed with mealies, standing ready for the horses. It was a goodly sight, and what a meal we all made! The luxury of bully-beef!

And while we ate, De Moleyns gave us all the news of the other patrols which had gone out; the one which Kekewich had taken away to our right had communicated with Paget beyond the Gwelo River, and had then made a dash for a rebel *impi*, which was camped near the "Lion Koppie," some forty miles down the river, and had totally surprised them. The Mounted Infantry had charged as cavalry, fixing their bayonets, and using their arms as lances; they had killed some twenty of the enemy, and taken many prisoners, corn, and cattle. The prisoners whom our patrol had captured had duly given themselves up at the waggons, and our two native messengers had faithfully carried out their mission, and brought in the note asking for supplies.

All the patrols had met with lion adventures, one small party from Ridley's lot having walked into a family party of nine lions lying down; when the lions got up and stretched themselves and yawned, the scouts thought it time to retire. Another lion visited the waggons, and was wounded by a sentry firing on him at five yards' distance, but he got away; and even here, where we now were camped, the lions were round about; big fires were therefore kept going all night by the sentries. But we did not sit up late to talk over lion stories; all anxiety being at an end, we coiled down, put our feet to the fire, and slept like logs.

23rd September.—Leaving Poore and the patrol to rest and feed, and to follow on by slow stages, I got a fresh pony from De Moleyns, and, accompanied by him and by the party of men who had brought the food to us, I rode back to the waggons, twenty-two miles. There I got in touch again with the whole of my command; it seemed quite a peaceful change. I now sent orders for the whole force, including the waggons, which had been left near Uwini's, to rejoin me on the Hartley Hill road; my intention was to return along this road towards Inyati, as an *impi* was reported to be collected in that neighbourhood, and several parties of rebels occupied *koppies* near the road. Moreover, the country lying north of the Hartley Hill road had not been, so far, patrolled west of the Shangani. Leaving orders, therefore, for Poore to move by easy stages through that country down to Inyati, I determined to go there with my main body by the main road, having also a strong patrol moving parallel to the road, on the south side of it, clearing the *koppies* in that country.

28th September.—After sending off the waggons at 3.45 in the morning, I went with the mounted part of the column to the southward of the road, and at dawn surrounded a *koppie* occupied by rebels. They were too quick for us; having drawn a cordon round the *koppie*, we ascended it, and found their fires burning, food cooking, and their blankets lying about, just vacated, but not a soul to be seen, except a dog or two; the people had all bolted into the caves, with which the hill was undermined. We found the entrance to the caves near the top of the hill; it was merely a small hole under a huge rock, into which you had to let yourself down feet first. It led into a ramification of small passages and tunnels underground.

Deep down in this dark hole you came to a perpendicular shaft, thirty feet deep, leading, by a tree-stem as a ladder, into a deeper level of similar caves (I say *you* could do it, as I couldn't, for, in climbing about the *koppie*, I had sprained my ankle slightly, and I had to sit nursing it, while the others did the exploration of the caves). We called down into the caves, for anybody who might be there to come out, as we were going to use dynamite, and after getting out a large supply of grain and *kaffir* food, and sending it off to the waggons by gangs of prisoners, we blew up the cave with three charges of dynamite.

29th September.—On leaving our camp-ground this morning, which was on the Shangani River, Gielgud, following behind the column, saw two Matabele spies peeping at us from among the reeds in the river-bed, and he cleverly effected their capture with the assistance of some of his boys; one of the men carried a Martini-Henry rifle. When we got into camp that night, a man of the police, who was ill in the hospital-waggon, died suddenly of pneumonia. As we should have to start at 3.45 next morning, we had his funeral then and there, as soon as the grave could be dug. It was an impressive ceremony, the military funeral in the dark, among gleams of camp-fires and lanterns, with a storm of thunder and lightning gathering round.

1st October.—We had at last reached Inyati, only to find a letter from the general to say that the *impi* that we had come for has sent in to say that they wish to surrender, so that our last few days of hurried marching with weary mules and horses had again been thrown away. The general's letter goes on to say that the rebels are submitting in every direction, the war is practically over in Matabeleland, and that a court of inquiry is to assemble at Gwelo to hear my reasons for trying Uwini by court-martial instead of handing him over for civil power to try. That this is by direction of the High Commission at Cape Town, who, on hearing that Uwini had been tried and executed, had telegraphed ordering my arrest; but this in effect the general had respectfully declined to carry out.

In his letter the general says a court can assemble "as soon as Paget and you have finished your operations against Wedza." This was the first I had heard of my column being required to cooperate against Wedza, but a hint is as good as a nod, or whatever the phrase is, and I am losing no time about acting upon it. I have picked out all the best horses of the Hussars and the Mounted Infantry, amounting to 115, and these, together with a 7-pounder and two Maxims, I am going to take to Wedza's, with waggons carrying three weeks' provisions. Wedza's is about a hundred miles to the south-east of this. I am leaving all the sick and worn-out horses here at Inyati, where Poore will take charge of them when he arrives about two days hence.

The Afrikander corps under Captain van Niekerk belong to the temporary Matabeleland Police, and their engagement shortly expires, so I shall not take them with me, but shall send them back to Buluwayo ready for disbandment, and with them will go the ambulance, taking such men as are sick. These, happily, do not amount to many, but unfortunately include two officers of the Mounted Infantry, namely, Kekewich, who has both hands disabled from *veldt* sores, and Armstrong ill with dysentery. I am also losing the services of De Moleyns, who has been detailed to organise the new police force in Mashonaland.

Prince Alexander of Teck has taken his place as my staff officer, and is hard at work in arranging matters, so that we may get away to-morrow morning. Gielgud, too, is leaving us, as Inyati is his headquarters, and, peace having been restored in his district, he has now to settle down and arrange for the settlement of the natives, and for the receipt of further surrenders of rebels and their arms. Van Niekerk, who commands the Afrikander corps, will be a great loss to me, he is so very keen, and a most resourceful and helpful officer, and his men, too, have got on wonderfully well with Tommy Atkins both in camp as well as in the field.

Tonight we have had a camp-fire concert, by way of a farewell entertainment, and in honour of Her Majesty's record reign. We just had sufficient "*dop*" (Dutch brandy) to give everybody a tot in which to drink her health, and it was a pleasing sight to see, not only her own soldiers, but Colonials and Afrikanders as well, joining with all their hearts in singing "God Save the Queen," and in the cheers that greeted the proposal of her health.

CHAPTER 14

In the Belingwe District
2nd October to 13th October.

2nd October.—Early in the morning our diminished column started off from Inyati across the *veldt*, not following any road, but making its own way, south-eastward towards the Belingwe district. The column consisted of half a squadron of the 7th Hussars and the York and Lancaster Mounted Infantry, together with the 7-pounder and machine guns manned by police under Captain Boggie. About 160 men altogether, with ambulance, and waggons carrying stores and three weeks' supplies.

5th October.—We have been going steadily on over open, undulating country, with a range of blue hills beyond a wooded plain on our left, and rolling downs of yellow *veldt* on our right. All the anxiety of conducting a column, which I felt of late, is now off my mind, since water is to be found in every river-bed; but our horses and mules are very tired and worn-out, the grass is all parched and practically useless as food, and yet there is no other to give them; the sun is powerful, and by eight o'clock the heat of the day is already beginning, the thermometer going up to 98° and 100° in the shade at midday. All the country through which we are now passing has surrendered, and it is quite a new sensation to see natives walking across the *veldt* and not to go for them, to see fresh spoor and not to let your heart jump with joy.

Today we struck the Belingwe-Buluwayo road, and, following along it, we are passing through the Insiza Hills. This is a range of stony, thinly-bushed hills, where gold-reef claims are pegged out in every direction. Our night out-span is on the top of a hill among the burnt ruins of Stevenson's Store; it does make one feel a little badly disposed towards our black brothers when one sees a comfortable home like this wantonly destroyed, its little household knickknacks scattered, broken, and burnt about the *veldt*. It was near one such ruined homestead as that I found a poor little white chap of three years old, with his head battered, as these savages are fond of doing. After burying him, I kept one of his little shoes as a keepsake.

6th October.—We are once again in a country where an enemy is possible, which I much prefer to a half-and-half country, because here all ranks are apt to become slack in the precautionary duties of the line of march and camp. It is curious how new-comers fail to appreciate the necessity of precautions until they have been bitten or nearly bitten, and this they do in spite of all the teachings of history, such as Isandhlwana, the Prince Imperial, Bronker's Spruit, and a half a hundred narrow shaves that have never become public. They look casually round the wide, bare horizon—not a soul in sight; ergo, they argue, not a soul is there. They do not know how a nigger hides; even the best troop of scouts in Matabeleland have been taken in in this way.

An onlooker on a neighbouring hill, from which he commanded a bird's-eye view of the scene, saw this body of scouts approaching a rise, and on the other side of the rise there was similarly a body of the enemy coming up towards the scouts, each party unseen by the other. The natives were first to see their enemy: they dropped like one man in their tracks, and lay low in the thick grass. The scouts came on over the rise without having seen them, and rode right past them, within fifty yards. So soon as they had been lost to sight over the next ridge, the natives rose to their feet and went on their way rejoicing. I myself once marked down a Matabele in a patch of grass; I walked through it, and had passed within a foot or two of him before I saw his heel, Achilles-like, left outside the tunnel which he had wriggled for himself in the grass.

Newcomers take time to learn the value of spoor. Show them fresh spoor, and they will scarcely believe that it is that of the enemy, who should be somewhere in sight; if he were not hiding, and, seeing nothing to be alarmed at themselves, they are apt to mistake discretion for funk, and foolhardiness for pluck; they think that precautions, to say the least, are derogatory; to see them saunter into danger, is as it were to watch a child playing on the edge of a cliff. It is that same foolhardiness that stands in the way of many men becoming good scouts; there are plenty who are ready, if asked, to go and look into hell's mouth; but what one wants is a man who will not only go there, but who can see his way to getting back again to tell you what he saw. And to do this successfully he must be wary, and must notice all signs, however small, and be able to read their meaning.

A small incident which occurred to me the other day will give an example. I was out with a boy reconnoitring a hill occupied by enemy. In order to get a better view of it, we had to cross a difficult river, which lay between high, steep banks, and consisted of a chain of deep-water reaches and rocks, with only one practicable "*drift*," or crossing. It was not a very safe proceeding to commit ourselves to one single line of retreat, but in this case there was no alternative.

So we crossed over, but kept, if possible, a more than usually bright look-out for enemy, while moving as far as we could under concealment of the bush ourselves. As we went, we took special note of guiding marks, such as would serve to direct us back to our crossing-place should we be obliged to make for it in a hurry. (This use of guiding marks, such as peculiar trees, noticeable rocks, &c., is too often neglected, and yet may often be invaluable.)

We went on for about a quarter of a mile beyond the *drift*, and then, leaving the horses with the boy, I climbed up a *koppie* and got a view of the place.

So far, we had seen no niggers about, but presently, glancing back towards the *drift*, I saw three buck suddenly appear, coming as hard as they could away from the bush near the river and towards us. Presently they stopped, and, without noticing us, wheeled up and faced the way they had come, staring hard with pricked ears. For a moment or two they stood, and then, springing round, they dashed past us, evidently fully alarmed. We did not wait to see what had startled them, but, clambering down the rocks, I mounted my horse, and we shoved back for the *drift* as fast as we were able, keeping our eyes "skinned" the while.

We got to the bank all right, and, looking into the gully that formed the river-bed, were relieved to find it all clear; but, on looking back, we could now see a number of black heads and shoulders of niggers bobbing along among the rocks and bush, evidently hastening down to occupy the *drift* and to cut us off. Luckily, by acting on the hint given by the buck, we were before them, and were not long in getting across to the open ground on the other bank of the river.

The hint, as seen in the open, was but a very small one, and would probably mean nothing to the man who declines to accept hints;

Strolling home in the morning

"Halt! who comes there?"

and were he always acting alone it would not matter much, except to himself,—for he would not live long to carry on his neglectful course,—and there is no objection to his being rash at times—in fact, for successful scouting, some risks *have* to be run; but when he has command of others, for whose safety he is responsible, it is another thing, and nothing may then be left to chance.

9th October.—At last, after trekking with weary, half-starved animals for eighty-seven miles from Inyati, we are in sight of our goal. Wedza's Mountain, a noble-looking peak, can be seen peering over the intermediate range, at a distance of some twelve or fifteen miles from us. We are camped at Posselt's cattle farm, where there is a certain amount of grazing for our beasts; but Posselt's cattle are all in the hands of the rebels. The Native commissioner of this district, Mr. Jackson,—eager and helpful,—has joined us, and also Lieutenant Yonge, with twenty men of the Belingwe garrison and a Nordenfeldt gun.

But, to our great disappointment, they had no news of Paget's column, with which we are expected to operate. Before leaving Inyati, I had sent runners to Buluwayo to report my departure on this expedition, and asking that Paget should be informed, by telegraph, that I should be about here this day (9th October), and I had hoped to find an answer from him awaiting us. On the other hand, we are much cheered to learn that the rebels in this district are still unsubdued and cheeky.

10th October (to be marked with a red mark when I can get a red pencil).—Jackson and a native boy accompanied me scouting this morning; we three started off at three in the morning, so that by dawn we were in sight of one of the hills we expected might be occupied by Paget, and where we hoped to see his fires. We saw none there; but on our way, in moving round the hill which overlooks our camp, we saw a match struck high up near the top of the mountain. This one little spark told us a good deal. It showed that the enemy were there; that they were awake and alert (I say "they," because one nigger would not be up there by himself in the dark); and that they were aware of our force being at Posselt's (as, otherwise, they would not be occupying that hill).

However, they could not see anything of us, as it was then quite dark; and we went farther on among the mountains. In the early morning light we crossed the deep river-bed of the Umchingwe River, and, in doing so, we noticed the fresh spoor of a lion in the sand. We went on, and had a good look at the enemy's stronghold; and on our way back, as we approached this river-bed, we agreed to go quietly, in case the lion should be moving about in it.

On looking down over the bank, my heart jumped into my mouth, when I saw a grand old brute just walking in behind a bush. Jackson could not see him but was off his horse as quick as I was, and ready with his gun; too ready, indeed, for the moment that the lion appeared, walking majestically out from behind the bush that had hidden him, Jackson fired hurriedly, striking the ground under his foot, and, as we afterwards discovered, knocking off one of his claws. The lion tossed up his shaggy head and looked at us in dignified surprise. Then I fired, and hit him in the ribs with a leaden bullet from my Lee-Metford. He reeled, sprang round, and staggered a few paces, when Jackson, who was firing a Martini-Henry, let him have one in the shoulder; this knocked him over sideways, and he turned about, growling savagely.

I could scarcely believe that we had actually got a lion at last, but resolved to make sure of it; so, telling Jackson not to fire unless it was necessary (for fear of spoiling the skin with the larger bullet of the Martini), I got down closer to the beast, and fired a shot at the back of his neck as he turned his head away from me. This went through his spine, and came out through the lower jaw, killing him dead. We were pretty delighted at our success, but our nigger was mad with happiness, for a dead lion—provided he is not a man-eater—has many invaluable gifts for a *kaffir*, in the shape of love-philtres, charms against disease or injury, and medicines that produce bravery. It was quite delightful to shake hands with the mighty paws of the dead lion, and to pull at his magnificent tawny mane, and to look into his great deep yellow eyes.

And then we set to work to skin him; two skinning, while the other kept watch in case of the enemy sneaking up to catch us while we were thus occupied. In skinning him, we found that he was very fat, and also that he had been much wounded by porcupines, portions of whose quills had pierced the skin and lodged in his flesh in several places. Our nigger cut out the eyes, gall-bladder, and various bits of the lion's anatomy, as fetish medicine. I filled my carbine bucket with some of the fat, as I knew my two boys. Diamond and M'tini, would very greatly value it. Then, after hiding the head in a neighbouring bush, we packed the skin on to one of the ponies, and returned to camp mightily pleased with ourselves.

On arrival there, the excitement among the boys was very great, for, as we rode into camp, we pretended we had merely shot a buck; but when Diamond turned out to take my horse from me, he suddenly recognised the skin, and his eyes almost started from his head as he put his hand over his mouth and ejaculated, "*Ow! Ingonyama!*" ("Great Scott! a lion!") Then, grinning with excitement, he asked leave to go and get some more of it. In vain I told him that it was eight miles away, and close under the enemy's stronghold. He seized up an *assegai* and started off at a steady trot along our back-spoor.

And very soon one nigger after another was doubling out of camp after him, to get a share of the booty. In the evening they came back quite happy with various tit-bits, and also the head. The heart was boiled and made into soup, which was greedily partaken of by every boy in camp, with a view to gaining courage. Diamond assured me that the bits of fat, &c., of which he was now the proud possessor, would buy him several cattle when he got back to Natal. Alas! I am afraid he may be reckoning without his rinderpest!

12th October.—No news yet from Paget, although Jackson has sent some runners to get round past the enemy's country to communicate with him, and to tell him that we are waiting for his orders here. In the meantime, I do not intend to waste time, but shall go for one or two of the minor chiefs round about here; and shall also reconnoitre Wedza's stronghold, so as to have, if possible, a map and report of it ready for Paget's use when he comes.

Today we have marched to the Umchingwe River, and our camp is close to where I shot the lion yesterday. We got there at midday, and our arrival was at once signalled by the rebels to each other by means of smoke-fires, lasting for about three minutes, on the two mountains which forms the strongholds of Monti and Matzetetza. I had sent some native spies to find out where Wedza is now keeping his cattle, as, if they are grazed away from the stronghold, we might be able to make a raid on them, but the scouts have not yet returned; nor has Jackson come back yet with some friendly natives whom he went away to collect. But since the warning has been given to the various strongholds by these smoke-fires, I thought it useless to wait any further, and have ordered that this night, at sundown, all available mounted men (numbering about 120), should go to reconnoitre Wedza's stronghold, taking two days' rations with them.

Meantime I started in the afternoon myself, with Parkyn, my orderly, to act as interpreter, to go to Matzetetza's, to see if we could get his people to talk with us, and if so, to advise them to surrender. They had already been attacked some weeks before by Laing's column, which had driven them from their *kraals* for the time being, but they had since reoccupied them. But when Parkyn and I, got there, we found the *kraal* apparently completely deserted, and though we shouted for anybody who might be in the caves to come out and talk, explaining to them that we were harmless individuals, merely coming to talk of peace, no one appeared; so we got nothing by our ten-mile ride, except the mild excitement of keeping our eyes open all the time, Parkyn being a little apprehensive of some attempt to cut us off.

So about sundown we rode back and got on to the path which would be followed by our party on its way to Wedza's, and very soon we saw them coming along in the moonlight, or rather, we heard them long before we saw them, for the air was so clear and still, that though the column was supposed to be moving in silence, we could hear the men muttering to each other for seven minutes before they came up to us, that is, over half a mile. We ourselves, to test their eyesight, sat quite still, and found that we were not noticed until they were within twenty yards of us, although the moon was bright and our horses were grazing near.

As we went on past one of the strongholds, a signal-fire flared up above us, which was quickly answered by another one from the very hill to which Parkyn and I had been addressing ourselves in the afternoon, so that there had been natives there listening all the time. These signal-fires merely flashed up for a minute or two and were extinguished again; but it was very annoying to have one's moves thus published. For a good part of the way it was very bad going, and we had to do much of it on foot, leading our horses across rivers, rocks, and bog; but at last, in the middle of the night, we arrived in the valley formed on one side by Wedza's mountain, and on the other by a parallel ridge of bush-grown hills. On both Wedza's and the opposite mountain we could see fires twinkling at various points, which showed that both were fully occupied by the enemy, who at the same time did not seem to suspect our presence between them. We formed square and bivouacked.

13th October.—Rousing up the men at half-past two, and leaving the horses with a guard of fifty men, we went on foot close under Wedza's mountain, with the idea of lying in ambush there to catch some of his people getting water in the morning, and from them to get such information as we required as to the strength and disposition of the forces, the whereabouts of the cattle, and other interesting items. Along the foot of the mountain and parallel to it flows the Chingweze River, and we had to cross this to get to the foot of the mountain, and we found it a worse job than we anticipated, for the river was wide and deep except at one spot, where it was passable through a tumbled mass of great smooth rocks and boulders extending for about three hundred yards. On these the men with their nailed boots slithered and clattered to an awful extent, without making very much progress, and dawn came on before we had reached the desired position. Another quarter of a mile and we should be near the water-path, but it was just too late to get there unseen, so, as the daylight came on, we hid ourselves as best we could, close under the foot of the mountain.

Not far from us we could hear the talking and jabbering of the women and children, altogether unsuspicious of our presence. Parkyn and I then clambered up on to one of the lower *koppies* of the moun-

PARLEYING WITH REBELS

On many occasions we offered the rebels a chance of surrendering before being attacked. To do this, two of us would go near the stronghold, carrying a white flag, and unarmed (at least, as far as outward appearances went, but with revolvers inside our shirts). While talking to them, we kept moving about, because if we stood still, we offered a target to them that was too tempting to be resisted.

197

tain, where we could get a view of what was going on; he took up a good position with his gun to cover my retreat in case of our being nipped there, and I climbed up higher to get a look into this little valley beyond in which all the talking was taking place. I was wearing what remained of my india-rubber-soled shoes, and so was able to get about pretty silently, but just as I was crossing an open space between two rocks, I heard a wild cry of alarm, and all the women calling to each other to run. I thought it was all over with our secrecy, so, clambering down again, Parkyn and I walked boldly out into the open and called to the people not to be frightened—that we had merely come to talk to them.

To my great surprise, it was only then that they discovered us; the previous alarm had merely been given by some women who were lighting up fires which were to blaze up all over their gardens to kill a flight of locusts which had settled there, and they were only calling to each other to run and get out of the way of the flames. However, as we had now shown ourselves, we started a conversation. We told them that we had come to talk peace, and wanted to see Wedza; they informed us that Wedza was not at home, but that anything we liked to say would be reported to him. We soon discovered that it was actually Wedza talking to us; then we proceeded to tell them that a large body of troops were coming to smash them up in their stronghold unless they were wise in the meantime and sent in to make peace. Then Wedza remarked that it was a curious thing for us to come and suggest peace and then immediately to talk war, and especially to talk of smashing him in a stronghold which had withstood many an attack and had never been taken.

At the same time, he would like to continue the conversation with us if we would come a little nearer, as he was rather hard of hearing. We guessed what his intention was, and neither went any nearer—for we were already on the rocks at the foot of the mountain—nor did we cease to walk about the whole time we were talking, because to stand still on these occasions, even though you may be holding a white flag up, often means to get a shot at you so soon as you offer a favourable target. For half an hour we endeavoured to persuade the old boy that he would be wiser to surrender, and we impressed on him that the troops who were coming would be here in a day or two, they would arrive most unexpectedly, and they were the Queen's Own troops, armed with special apparatus for bringing rebellious chiefs out of their caves, means which had never yet failed to effect their purpose. But he only invited us to come and try the experiment with them, and that he would afford the exception that proves the rule.

We then went back to the men, who had all this time been hidden close under the foot of the hill, and moved out into the open to go back to our horses. When the rebels saw this sudden apparition of armed men so close to them, they started yelling and shrieking all over the mountain, and from hilltop to hilltop the cry of warning and alarm was passed on, and very soon afterwards people from outlying *kraals* could be seen running for refuge to the main stronghold in the mountain.

As we recrossed the river to get to the horses, we saw a big crocodile in one of the pools, and the fresh spoor of a hippopotamus along the bank.

We lunched and spent the heat of the very hot day in the open valley in front of Wedza's mountain, watched with curiosity by hundreds of rebels on the hilltops; and then we moved off early in the afternoon to tackle the ridge of hills that lay on the opposite side of the valley. Working our way on to the top of this ridge, we moved along it from end to end, capturing rebels' *kraals*, of which there were about half a dozen dotted along its length. The ridge was grown with thick bush and forest, and though we came across a few natives from time to time, they always managed to elude us in the jungle; we also saw a fine wild boar, which caused quite a flutter in my breast. "If I only had you in

WEDZA'S STRONGHOLD
A mountain consisting of six rocky peaks of about 800 to 1000 ft.: on the summits of these are *kraals* and caves held by the rebels. The position is over two miles long, and one and a half deep.

the open, my friend!" thought I. "If only you had a horse that was fit enough to come anywhere near me!" grinned he. And so we parted.

We took, altogether, four *kraals*, burnt them, and captured half a dozen cattle, and a number of goats and sheep; the natives all bolted into the bush or into caves in the cliffs of the hill. We got down off the ridge just as darkness was coming on, and we bivouacked out in the open plain pretty well tired out; but I have every hope that the advice we gave Wedza, and the surprise we gave him in the unexpected presence of our little force at his doors, and the object-lesson which the burning of the *kraals* and the capture, of cattle on the opposite ridge must have afforded him, will, at least, shake his confidence, and help to simplify our task of capturing his stronghold, for it is a nasty-looking place to tackle, indeed, almost impossible for a small force. Laing had visited it, but considered it far too big a job for a column of 250 men, and it will take every man of Paget's column and mine combined to effect anything. The stronghold itself is a long mountain, consisting of six peaks of about 800 feet high, its total length being about two and a half miles, and its width about a mile and a half.

On the extreme top of five of the peaks are perched strong *kraals*,

FRESH MEAT

For weeks at a time we lived entirely on tinned meat, and it was a great treat to the men when, occasionally, they could get a taste of fresh meat, whether it were buck, goat or horse.

and in addition to these there are three small *kraals* on the side of the mountain; underneath each of the *kraals* are labyrinths of caves. The mountain itself has steep, boulder-strewn, bush-grown sides, generally inaccessible, except where the narrow, difficult paths lead up to the various strongholds, and these paths have been fortified by the rebels with stockades and with stone breast works, and in many places they pass between huge rocks, where only one man could squeeze through at a time. The paths are commanded by loopholes for musketry from the caves.

The *kraals* are collections of circular mud huts with thatched roofs, built on crags near the tops of the hills, and on the most inaccessible rocks among them are perched the corn-bins; these grain stores are little circular pillars exactly like pillar letter-boxes at home, but made of wattle and daub, with a small thatched roof; a little hole is left near the top of the bin, just as the hole for letters in the letter-box, and through this hole the corn is poured into the bin. When full, the hole is sealed up with a flat stone and mortar. When one loots a *kraal*, the first thing to do is to knock out this stone, look in, and if there is corn there of the kind that you require, make a hole in the bottom of the wall and apply the mouth of your sack to it, and the corn will run in.

NATIVE SURGERY
A friendly native wounded in the foot is being doctored by one of his friends.

CHAPTER 15

The Downfall of Wedza
14th October to 21st October.

14th October.—About three miles to the westward of the mountain which we had harried yesterday, lay the solitary mountain peak on which is the *kraal* of Matzetetza, the place which Parkyn and I visited yesterday morning. Owing to alarm-fires having been shown on this hill, we determined now to finally clear it out, so I moved the column soon after daybreak in that direction, sending a message to our camp for the guns to join us near the stronghold. We lay up for the heat of the day within a mile of it, and were joined by the guns in the afternoon.

Although there was a good deal of spoor about, and several rebels visible on the mountain, we could see none in the *kraal*; nevertheless, we put the 7-pounder in position and shelled the stockaded entrance and one or two of the caves; this was done partly to make sure of clearing out any defenders who might be lurking there, but more for the purpose of giving our new gun's crew a little real practice, and also, especially, with a view to letting Wedza know that we were in earnest about shelling strongholds. For we were not five miles from him, and he would hear the gun and see the conflagration when the *kraal* was burnt. We then sent a strong party up into the *kraal*, with covering parties posted to protect their advance in the event of any surprise on the part of the enemy. But the enemy had evidently seen our approach and had hastily cleared to the northward that day in large numbers; they had left behind them a large store of grain and a number of goats and poultry, to which we freely helped ourselves. It was after dark before we had finished our work, and we camped near water within a mile of the place.

At length, runners arrived with a letter from Paget to say that, after all, he would be unable to join us, as had been arranged, for the attack on Wedza.

15th October.—After Paget's message I determined to do as best I could without him; therefore, at a very early hour this morning, we started to tackle Wedza's. It seemed a large order for so small a force—we were only 120 all told; Wedza's mountain, as I have already said, was nearly three miles by two in extent, and had eight large *kraals* on it. His people, therefore, must have numbered something like 1600, of whom 600 or 700 would be fighting men, but worth double that number by reason of their almost impregnable position. I naturally felt somewhat anxious about it. I had prepared a plan of attack for Paget's information, on the supposition that our two combined forces would be available for the purpose, but now that my small party was to do it alone, that plan would not work. To make a direct attack would merely involve certain heavy loss to gain nothing. The only thing we could do was to try and bluff the enemy out of the place.

Wedza's mountain is a kind of promontory standing out from a range of smaller mountains, so I ordered the mounted infantry (York and Lancaster Regiment), under Lieutenant Thurnall, to leave their horses in the open valley at the foot of the mountain, and to gain the neck which joined the mountain to the range of mountains northward. From this position the mounted infantry would command a large part of the stronghold with their fire, and would cut off the enemy's line of retreat to the mountains.

This party were ordered to take up with them their great-coats, water, and two days' rations, for they would have to stay there the whole day and night, and possibly part of the following day; there were only about twenty-five of them, but they were ordered to act as if they were 250, and right well they played their part. My idea was, that, so soon as this party should have established themselves in their position on the neck, I would bombard the central part of the position systematically with artillery and machine-gun fire, and, at the same time, threaten the left (southern) flank, and the rear of the position with parties of 7th Hussars.

I intended to keep up this demonstration during the day and to-night, hoping that such action, combined with the moral effect already afforded by the object-lesson at Matzetetza's yesterday, would so work on the feelings of the defenders, that they would take my previous advice and surrender; or if they did not do that, that, at least, they would be so demoralised that an assault could be carried out with some chance of success on the morrow. For these natives will stand your coming at their position so long as you do so from the expected direction, but if you come at them some other way, or look as if you were likely to cut off their line of retreat, they are very liable to become frightened, and therefore, in dealing with them, it sometimes becomes necessary to disregard the teachings of books on tactics, and, instead of concentrating your force, to spread it about in a way that would invite disaster were you acting against civilized troops. In order to gain our positions to carry out this plan, I took the mounted infantry by one route, and sent the Hussars and guns by another more southerly path—under Major Ridley—to take up their places as ordered.

It was yet early in the morning when, with the mounted infantry, I arrived at the foot of the northern end of Wedza's mountain; here the men left their horses under charge of seven of their number, and started off to gain their position on a dome-shaped mountain overlooking the stronghold. It took them nearly an hour to get up to within reasonable distance of this spot, and before they reached it, their presence was discovered by the enemy, and fire was opened on them as they neared the top. A small but determined party of the enemy, foreseeing their object, established themselves among the rocks of this mountain, and stubbornly opposed their advance; but the mounted infantry, working steadily forward in admirable order, very soon drove these men from their position; and presently signalled down that they were occupying the position assigned to them.

But meantime the sound of the firing had roused the whole of the mountain; from hilltop to hilltop the rebels were shouting to each other, and through my telescope I could see from where I was, with the led horses, that the enemy were rapidly collecting from all the *kraals* fully armed, and were all making towards the position of our little party of mounted infantry. It looked to me that if this movement was allowed to develop, it might prove not only dangerous, but fatal to our handful of men up there. I therefore sent a message to the spot where the guns should be, requesting them to open fire without delay, and thus create a diversion, and retain the defenders of that portion of the stronghold at their proper post. But the guns were not there! It afterwards transpired that Ridley's party had been detained to an unexpected extent by waggons bringing away grain from Matzetetza's.

Something had to be done, and that quickly, so, leaving the led horses to take care of themselves,—no enemy would venture down to attack them, even if they could see no guards with them, as they would

PRINCE ALEXANDER OF TECK
To the fore in the attack on Wedza's stronghold.

be sure to look upon them as a lure,—I took the seven horse-holders, mounted, at the best pace we could command, to the southern end of the mountain, and, crossing with some difficulty the Chingweze River, we worked our way through the bush round to the left rear of the stronghold.

Here there was a large village part of the way up the side of the mountain, and spreading ourselves out in the bush, we opened fire at it as hard as we could go, using magazine-fire, and continually moving about from bush to bush, in order to give the appearance of a large force of men. In this particular village the natives were considerably startled, and ran out in large numbers into the caves among the rocks close by. But we cared not so much for them as for the defenders on the upper part of the mountain; and immediately after our first volley, we could hear the startled cries of alarm from their look-out men on the uppermost peaks, and very soon they began to collect in large numbers on the sky-line overlooking our position. On the great look-out rock, in particular, a mass of them were collected, so, directing the attention of my little band to them, we sighted for 1200 yards, and gave them a volley; the look-out man on the topmost pinnacle of rock fell among the crowd, which lost no time in seeking better shelter! Leaving my small army still in their position, with orders to make a show every now and then with heavy firing,

7TH HUSSARS AT WEDZAS

Our small party of scouts in getting engaged with a stronger party of the enemy stood some chance of being cut off by them. But just as we were thinking of effecting our retreat, a party of 7th Hussars, under Prince Teck, came opportunely on the scene.

I made my way back to the front of the position, and found that the ruse had been perfectly successful; the mass of the enemy, who had been collecting to attack Thurnall, had been surprised by this new attack in their rear, and were now still evenly distributed in the different defensive posts of the mountain. By-and-by the hussars and artillery began to arrive, and it was perhaps better in the end that they did come late upon the scene, because it gave a fresh and increased feeling of alarm to the natives, who, as soon as they appeared in sight, began once more to shout further warnings to other parts of the stronghold.

I thought now that possibly the enemy might think it advisable to come and surrender. The heat of the day was well on, and so soon as the troops had arrived in position, we called a rest; and the doctor, Surgeon-Captain Ferguson, called a rest for *me*, as apparently the flying about this morning round the stronghold had made me look a bit tired, so I lay in the ambulance in comfort, and sucked down some of his excellent Bovril, while the hussars, after feeding and resting their horses, proceeded to take up the positions allotted to them. But no

WEDZA'S KRAAL

A village and granaries on the top of a mountain peak. The only path stockaded and defended by loop-holes from caves, with which the mountain is undermined.

message came down from the enemy, and so, after a time, I thought it desirable to recommence stirring them up, and getting the 7-pounder in position, we opened fire with shells on the more important points in turn.

Before many rounds had been fired, the enemy got on the move within the stronghold, and in doing so, kept giving chances to Thurnall's men up on their mountain, of which they were not slow to avail themselves. By-and-by came a signal from Thurnall, saying, that his men were suffering from the want of water, and we endeavoured to send some up to him, but the party going up were attacked and driven back by the fire of the enemy, and in the end Thurnall's men did not get their water until they had sent down a party after dark to assist the others coming up.

Then another signal came from Thurnall towards evening, to say that numbers of the enemy were making their way out to the rear of the position by a path that was out of his range; so, leaving word with Prince Teck to bring on some of the 7th to that point, I got a fresh horse, and, accompanied by Jackson, the Native commissioner, once more made my way round to the back of the mountain. In passing by the little party that I had left there in the morning, we took three of them on with us, and, riding along the well-worn tracks of the natives, we got into a labyrinth of small valleys at the back of Wedza's mountain.

Then, leaving our horses concealed, we clambered up on to the ridge, looking into the heart of the stronghold from the rear. *Kaffirs* were all about near us, but not in any large number,—single men here and there on the look-out, women and children gathering up their goods, evidently preparatory to making a move; but we could see no large parties of them going away as yet, nothing that we could attack if we brought a force round there; however, we saw the position of their main paths toward the mountains to the north and eastward, and just about sunset we came down again, and made our way back.

Owing to the broken nature of the country at this point, we were forced to carry out what I always consider a most dangerous practice, and that is, to return by the same path which you used in coming, and the danger of it was practically demonstrated on this occasion. Riding quietly along in the dusk, we had just got out of the bad part, thinking all danger was over, when there was suddenly a flash and a crash of musketry from a ridge of rocks close to us, dust spurted up all round, and a swish of bullets whizzed past our heads. My hat was violently struck from my head as if with a stick, and in an instant we were galloping across the thirty yards of open which separated us from a similar parallel ridge; dismounting here, we were very soon busy replying to the firing of the enemy, whose forms we could now and again see silhouetted against the evening sky.

We had had a marvellous escape; Jackson himself had been grazed on the shoulder, his horse had a bullet-hole in its temple, the bullet had lodged in its head, and beyond possibly a slight headache, the gallant little horse appeared to be none the worse. Our position here was not too good a one: the enemy were evidently a fairly strong party, and would merely have to work among the rocks, a little to the right, to cut us off from rejoining our main body. Moreover, they had practically possession, or, at least, command of fire over my hat, which I badly wanted. But it looked as though we ought at once to be making good our retreat, if we meant to go away at all. We were just mounting to carry this out, when out of the gathering darkness behind, there trotted up a strong party of hussars, under Prince Teck, who, hearing the firing, had at once hurried to the spot; his coming was most opportune, and reversed the aspect of affairs. After a few minutes of sharp firing, the rocks in front of us were cleared and occupied by our men, and my hat came back to me.

Teck then posted piquets for the night, extending all round the left flank and rear of the enemy's position. These piquets built fires

"LITTLE MISS TUCKET, SAT BY A BUCKET"
A small girl and her puppy, captured at Wedza's stronghold (on the mountain in the background). She was content to sit for hours by a bucket, and play with empty meat-tins.

at intervals, which were kept alight throughout the night by patrols moving from one to the other. Thurnall had similar instructions to light fires on heights round the northern end of the stronghold; while the men in camp did the same on the plain in front of the central portion of the position. This was done with a view to making the enemy believe that our force was a very large one, encamped on every side of them, and they evidently quite took this view of the case, for during the night they made frequent sallies against one fire after another, never venturing to attack it, but, as a rule, pouring in a sudden volley from a short distance, and then retiring, probably boasting that they had killed untold numbers of the white devils sleeping round their fires.

As a matter of fact, the white devils were specially ordered not to sleep or to remain in the neighbourhood of the fires for that very reason. But our men had a hard night of it, for they had orders not to let the enemy rest, and they carried out their orders well; patrols were constantly on the move opening fire now and then from unexpected points. Sometimes they could see the lights of the enemy moving about among their *kraals*, and these they fired on as a matter of course, but often they fired without any actual object to aim at, merely with a view to keeping up the enemy's state of alarm. It was moonlight up till four in the morning, so that any moves on the party of the enemy in force could easily be seen by our scouts, bands of them were reported getting away by the paths leading towards the mountains.

16th October.—As soon as there was light enough, we began to hammer away with the 7-pounder, the Maxims, and Nordenfeldt, taking each *koppie* and its *kraal* in turn. Through the glass I could see the natives move from the *kraals* into the caves, and when we shelled these, we could see them stealing away through the rocks and bush, evidently anxious to make their escape. Then I sent up the party of volunteers who had joined us from Belingwe to assist Thurnall. He then advanced along the ridge, attacking the *koppies* in turn after they had been shelled, and very soon the flames shot up, and a cloud of smoke rolled out, showing far and near that the first of the villages was taken.

This was Wedza's own particular *kraal*, and in it were found large numbers of Matabele arms, which showed that Wedza's people, although of the Makalaka race, were assisted by a number of Matabele warriors. In this *kraal* was also found a large store of stolen dynamite,

TIRED OUT: PRINCE ALEXANDER OF TECK

and Thurnall was not slow to make use of it; for presently, with a splendid boom, the *koppie* on which the *kraal* stood was blown to smithereens.

While the mounted infantry were thus taking the *kraals* in succession, the hussars were recalled from their outlying positions around the stronghold; and, though pretty well fagged out with the almost incessant work of the last twenty-four hours, they eagerly volunteered to clamber up the mountain and take part with the mounted infantry in completing the destruction of the stronghold; and Major Ridley, with his usual energy, led them up there. All through the heat of the day they were at work, over most awful ground and clambering on to inaccessible peaks, to effect the complete destruction of the enemy's villages and the clearing of their grain stores. It was not till after dark that they were all safely down again, with their work well accomplished, and the blazing evidences of it gleaming out their message to all the rebels for miles round.

21st October.—Excuse bad writing; but the light is waning; it is sunset, the yellow-red sky is cut by the black sky-line of the next ridge and its wooded crest in strong silhouette. Looking from my lair, through the frame of great black tree-stems, our bivouac fires in the gully just below look like ragged bits of the orange-coloured sky dropped into the dark abyss of the bush, and their blue misty wreaths of smoke rise slowly on the breathless air like a circle of ghostly sentries. The men are busy at their evening meal, the murmur of their voices and the crunching of the horses, with their muzzles deep in looted corn, are only sounds that go to emphasize the stillness of the forest.

Overhead, in the darkening sky, "*Celangobi*" (C stands for a Matabele click, with a sound of Kts), the matron evening star, beams calmly on our rest; but, over her shoulder, little, laughing stars are already twinkling at the humour of the thing, for they can see her peaceful gleam glinting sharply from the rifles and sword-scabbards on the ground below; the peace of the scene is but the peace of the hour—tomorrow there will be war again.—What nonsense it is to write all this! but when one is tired, it is as when one is ill: one likes to review such trifles in a dreamy way. I am tired,—we all are tired,—nature herself seems tired tonight. And we've some reason for it.

On the evening of the 19th, we (a party of forty mounted men, hussars and mounted infantry) moved out from camp without encumbrances, but taking two days' rations in our wallets, to follow up Wedza's people in their flight through his country, and to harry them into submission. An evening march, off-saddle in the woods, and on again at 3 a.m. No pipes nor talking as we pass along the foot of the rocky ridge on which the rebels have their *kraals*. Then clamber up on foot, lugging our horses after us, along the steep and rocky cattle track. No cattle now are here—the spoor is old. We break up into small patrols, to each of which is assigned a bit of mountain and its *kraals*.

With my patrol we have a weary trudge—for only twenty *per cent*, of the men have boots still fit for walking—(and I am one of the remaining eighty *per cent.;* my feet are partly through the soles and on the ground; I go, like Agag, "treading delicately"). We see no *kraal;* but the fresh spoor of men, women, and children lies before to guide us. It turns and leads into the boulders on the mountain-side. There, just round the corner of a rock, one spies the eaves of a thatched hut, and, close beside a cave, a few dead branches show there is a cattle *kraal*. We press through thorny bush, and clamber up the slippery granite path, some men working up the right and others up the left.

Behind some rocks we come upon a few huts, all empty but for some calabashes of water and some fetish rags. Then a nasty slit between the rocks has to be approached with care, or others stepped across in haste—these are the caves in which Mashonas love to lie when danger visits their *kraal*. The caves are labyrinths of little passages between the rocks below the ground: and a few men with guns, well posted, can hope with ease to stop a host of enemies.

The path leads up a kind of stair of rocks to a gap between two heavy boulders, and in the gap is fixed a strong stockade of roughly-trimmed saplings. To either hand, interstices between the rocks have been blocked up with stones, and made into loopholes. These defences are without defenders—and we are soon among the better huts of the *kraal* proper, and among the corn-stores.

Each man carries an empty nose-bag, and as soon as these are filled, and some errant chickens killed with sticks, and curios taken from the

A SMELTING FURNACE
Used by the Makalakas for iron-smelting for the manufacture of assegais, etc.
This form of furnace is said to be of ancient origin.

ANCIENT RUINS

huts, we burn the *kraal*, commencing on the windward side. There is a roar, as the pillar of flame shoots up its twenty feet into the sky, the pots and calabashes crack up from heat with the report of pistols, and in a few minutes the village is a heap of smoking ruins—a warning far and near to watching rebels.

After burning two such *kraals*, we make our way back to the horses, the whole patrol reassembles and continues its march, having destroyed five *kraals* among us. Through woods and stony hills into the Sabi Valley. Offsaddle by a convenient water-hole, for breakfast and midday rest. On again in the afternoon, to a bold, upstanding, solitary peak, a regular acropolis, on the top of which are clustered the huts of Monti's stronghold. Keeping under cover of the woods, we divide into two parties, and rapidly surround it. Dismount; and half an hour's arduous climb brings us past caves and barricades up to the summit. Nobody there! Splendid view, fine *kraal*, good huts; fill our nosebags and baskets, clear out, light up, and gingerly, among the sharp stones, down we go again, to the music of the crackling huts behind us.

Then through the forest—up over stony mountains—alternately walking and riding to ease our worn-out nags. Over the Fisu range; then down into an ideal cattle-robber's valley, full of *kloofs* and glades, with a grassy, marshy bottom. Cliffs tower up on either hand, and from their tops we can hear the rebel look-outs shouting their warning of our approach, confound them! They soon know miles ahead that we are there—and the path is far too bad for night marching!

At sundown we off-saddle and bivouac for the night where the gorge opens out a little. High above us towers the rocky Mount Ingona, on the top of which we see the *kraal* of chief Masunda. At dusk voices can be heard in all the rocks around us. It looks as though we were in for an attack—but the niggers vanish like smoke when a patrol goes out to investigate. Lights are seen flitting about Masunda's *kraal*, so we shout to them not to disturb themselves, that if they like to come and talk, we will not fight them. No reply.

Consequently, after coffee at 3 a.m. this morning, we started on foot to clamber up the mountain. The path was steep and the boulders slippery, but we are getting fit at mountain-climbing— still it took us nearly an hour to reach the top. An ordinary *kraal*, with stone and stockade defences, all abandoned. And such a glorious view of the wooded mountains of this Belingwe district, with the many blue ribbons of streams between, so different from the usual South African scenery.

We helped ourselves to all the corn that we could carry, as well as to some little bits of loot, such as a *kaffir* piano and some tambourines—the piano being a small flat board on which is fixed a row of iron tongues, and these when struck give each a different note of soft, metallic sound. We also found some small hard-wood tablets, which are the "cards" by which witchdoctors tell one's fortune.

Then we set the village in a blaze, and made our way down from the breezy height to our tiny laager by the stream below. Got our horses, saddled-up, and after clambering and lugging them over a rocky ridge, we got into the lower valley of the Sabi—a wooded plain, in the centre of which there stood a fine acropolis with another *kraal* on top. Surrounded it. As usual, no one there, but lots of fresh spoor—people evidently gone to earth in the caves below. So we sat down to bathe, breakfast, and sleep (for which the heat, flies, and ants were too much), while the horses grazed.

We had already done a pretty good day's work, but at 2 p.m. we paraded for the *koppies*, in three parties to take the different villages, and in half an hour three fine bonfires were raging, and with more corn in our nose-bags and a few chickens at our "saddle-bows," we rode away to the part of the valley that belongs to our old friend Wedza. Here he had his counting-house—*i.e.* his residential and farming *kraals*. The former was a fine, well-built *kraal*, very neat and clean, but so well concealed among the rocks that it took our patrol some time to find it. In this *kraal*, as in many others we had visited, there was a forge for making nominally hoes, but really *assegais*. The sharpening-stones lying about proved the latter.

The furnace, which is of clay, is in every instance built on this model, which is a very ancient one. Doesn't Bent say Phoenician?

The same march we passed by one of the many ancient (Phoenician) ruins. A small circular fort on a smooth rock; walls, and except where pulled down intentionally, in wonderfully good preservation. Dressed stones without mortar, and the well-known form of ornamentation; a course of herring-bone, tile-like stones, and a dice-board course.

A theory about these forts is, that since they extend in a chain round the gold districts, in which are remains of ancient workings, they were probably built with the object of simplifying the labour question, and keeping the workers in and the agitators out. Couldn't something of the sort be devised for the benefit of England?

Our rations were now at an end; all this clambering of *koppies* had not only pretty well tired us out, but had taken many hours to accomplish; so that evening found us still a long way from the camp near Wedza's stronghold, and we bivouacked, as I began by saying, under the eye of *Celangopi* on the forest hillside, as tired as dogs. We reckoned that a twelve-mile ride next morning would bring us to breakfast at camp. But it didn't.

22nd October.—After making a very early start, on such tea and scraps of bread as we had been able to save, we arrived by eight o'clock, very tired and empty, at the foot of Wedza's mountain. From this (eastern) side it looked not unlike Gibraltar in shape and size; and we really felt a bit pleased with ourselves at ever having had the presumption to go for this place, not to mention at having succeeded in taking it. As we passed round the foot of it, we rather pressed on the pace, in the hopes of breakfast, and in doing so we let three native boys, belonging to Jackson, the Native commissioner, drop rather behind us. Some lurking rebels were quick to see this, and had a few shots at them (one boy afterwards said that a bullet passed between the top of his ear and his head !), and compelled the boys to drop their bundles, which included Jackson's mess-kit, blankets, and, worst of all, a few rounds of ammunition. We were too far ahead to render assistance till too late.

At last we reached our camp-ground. There were the camp-fires cold and white, meat-tins, &c., in profusion, but no camp. A letter from Ridley hanging from a post informed us that in our absence a message had come from Colonel Paget, saying he wanted us to co-operate with him against Monogula near Gwelo, and that, therefore, he (Ridley), as next senior, had moved camp in that direction. We were just about played-out. But we hoped to find him at the next water, six miles on, and so we struggled on.

No; here was another note, saying he had moved a few miles farther on! We off-saddled and sat down, some only to think, others to express their thoughts in words. Then I found a little tea, and Jackson some Boer meal (coarse flour). Of the latter we made a really very good porridge, and had a few spoonsful round and a sip of tea, and on we went through good-looking rebel country, *kraals* and *koppies*, that I had always meant to reserve as our *bonne bouche*—and now they had already been warned by the sight of the waggons, and we were unable to go and tackle them through physical inability. Twelve more miles, many of them on foot, driving our horses over hot, shimmering plains—and at last, in the afternoon, we reached our waggons and

A DANGEROUS PRACTICE

our food.

That night, Ferguson (A.D.C.) rode into camp with a note from the general, telling me to co-operate with Paget (which we were already on our way to do), and also bringing a note from some natives he had passed on the way, which was to the effect that they were messengers from Wedza and Matzetetza, who, after the destruction of their strongholds, had now changed their tone, and were both anxious to surrender, together with their people. So all our toil had not been without effect, and the sixty-mile patrol was rewarded.

CHAPTER 16

Clearing the Mashona Frontier
25th October to 16th November.

For the next four days we have continued our march—practically across country, as there were a few cart-tracks, some leading right and some wrong, but I had got the right landmarks from one of Jackson's boys before he left us (which he did at the end of our patrol). We now left his—the Belingwe—district and got into the Gwelo country.

25th October.—Although it's Sunday, which we generally make a day for divine service and for rest, we have had to put in a lot of marching in order to get to Paget in fair time. One cannot reckon on doing so many miles a day in this country; you can only say it will be so many hours. For instance, it took us five hours to do two miles two different days in this march, *i.e.* in making *drifts* over bad rivers like the Singweza and the Lundi.

We are a wonderfully dirty and ragged-looking crew now—especially me, because I left Buluwayo six weeks ago to join this column only with such things as I could carry on a led pony (including bedding and food) My breeches and shirts are in tatters, my socks have nearly disappeared in shreds. Umtini, my Matabele boy, has made sandals for me to wear over—or at least outside—my soleless shoes. And everywhere the *veldt* has been burnt by grass-fires—every breeze carries about the fine black dust, and five minutes after washing, your hands and arms and face are as grimy and black as ever—as if you were in London again. Bathing "the altogether" too often is apt to result in fever. Too much washing of hands is apt to help *veldt* sores to originate—so we don't trouble to keep clean.

Veldt sores bother nearly every one of us. Every scratch you get (and you get a good number from thorns, &c.) at once becomes a

ROADSIDE INN IN MATABELELAND
Passing, in the Selukwe district, an inn which had been looted but not burnt by the rebels, the comic man of the M.I. acted the part of landlord with the aid of a board and a couple of empty bottles.

A CAVE STRONGHOLD
Elevation and section of the same *koppie*, showing the caves shaded.

small sore, gradually grows, and lasts sometimes for weeks. It is partly the effect of hot sun and dry air too rapidly drying up the wound, and also probably the blood is not in too good a state from living on unchanging diet of tinned half salt beef and tinned vegetables. We have very little variety, except when we loot some sheep or kill a buck. No vegetables, and we are out of sugar, tea, cocoa, and rice. Matches are at a premium, pipes are manufactured out of mealie corncobs and small reeds. Tobacco is very scarce—tea-leaves were in use till tea came to an end.

26th October.—We struck the Gwelo-Victoria road, and it seems quite strange to be once more in civilized (!) country, and not to have to find our own way over every river, and not to be on the look-out for lions at night, &c. Even the spoor of natives fails to excite us much, as most of them about here appear to be giving in. But we hope we may not be too late to help Paget have a final slap at Monogula—one of those *koppie*-holding gentry who has not yet experienced a bombardment by artillery.

It is delightful marching among the hills of this Selukwe district; they are well wooded, and run up here and there into mountains. A lot of the trees are still in their autumn tints, while the others are just budding out (for it is spring here), the young grass is greenifying the low-lying land, and even the black burnt *veldt* is now brightened up with a great variety of wild flowers—these are what I call bluebells, cowslips, dandelions, snowdrops, sweet peas, sweet williams, convolvulus, and poppies, and many more. Not that they are these flowers actually, but as they have some faint resemblance, I like to be reminded by them of the English flowers.

And the woods are cheery with the chirp and whistle of the birds, and though there are no songsters among them, there is a fellow whose note is like a robin, another like a chaffinch, and, best of all, one who distantly resembles a thrush. And overhead the trilling pipe of a big brown hawk brings back at once the glaring heat of India. And then the peeps, between the trees, of wooded peaks beyond show one such colours as can't be found in paint-boxes. Where would you get that pearly lilac of the lit-up face of the rock or the pure deep blue of the shadows? All about among the hills are gold reefs pegged out with notice-boards, and near them the wattle and daub houses of miners—all deserted and looted, but not burnt.

27th October.—The roads are awful for our wretched mules, so hilly, stony, and dusty, but we have struggled on, and at last, on the 27th, we have joined Colonel Paget's column. This column consists just now of merely a squadron of 7th Hussars, the West Riding Mounted Infantry being away on patrol. Such a breakfast they gave us on arrival, with milk (tinned), fish, jam, &c., &c. Beautiful camp under the trees. English mails and newspapers, the first for a month. News of Nansen's return, and of my brother George bringing Nansen home in his yacht *Otaria*, just what I had hoped Admiral Markham was going to do, taking me with him; we talked of it two years ago. In the course of the day two messengers from N'dema (one of the two great rebels of this district) came in to say that he had heard of Wedza's being knocked out of his stronghold, and so had come to surrender, and soon after N'dema himself, and five of his chiefs arrived. They were soon sent off to Gwelo under escort. In the afternoon I went with Paget, Carew, and others, to have a look at Monogula's stronghold from a distance. It did not look a very desperate place.

28th October.—I started off with Carew, 7th Hussars, and a party of ten men, and my orderly, Parkyn, to call on Monogula. We went by moonlight, so that he should not be alarmed at our numbers. On arriving near the stronghold soon after daylight the escort hid in the bush, and, leaving our rifles with them, Parkyn and I rode out into the open in front of the *kraal*, and, waving a towel as a flag of truce, we told the rebels we were men of peace come to talk with them—that the men of war were not far behind us, and would be there before another sun rose, unless they (the rebels) came to talk over the situation.

The great White Queen was getting a little vexed with Monogula; all the other chiefs of note had surrendered or been licked except him: if he did not now take this chance of surrendering, he would be knocked out and his lands given to another, &c., &c. Most eloquent we were! but all in vain. Our shouts only roused up birds from their feeds of spilt grain in the *kraal*. There was no reply, nor was there any fresh spoor on the many paths. We went closer and closer up on the rocks,—nobody fired at us—they were not there! We had a good look round, and then returned to report to Colonel Paget, who had meanwhile moved up the *laager* to within three miles of the place.

When blazing midday was over, the men and the 7-pounder were moved out to the stronghold. The gun fired half a dozen shells into the place, and the 7th Hussars then advanced along the ridge into the *kraal*, while I came up from below with the Mounted Infantry. Suddenly there was an outburst of firing in the *kraal* above us as we scaled the height —I knew it was the 7th Hussars firing into it as a precautionary measure before entering, but the Mounted Infantry supposed that the enemy had been found, and it was a treat to see them dash forward, each man taking his own line, and eager to be first up the rocky face of the *koppie*, and they were very disgusted to find nobody to fight when they got to the top.

A few weeks ago there had been a different tale to tell. A patrol of 7th Hussars under Captain Carew had then got up to the wall that defended the main *kraal*. One man was shot dead close to the wall, when his companion, without a second's pause, mounted the wall and pistolled the firer of the shot. The body of the white man was taken by his comrades to their camp, eight miles away, and buried there with honours. But when our column passed that way two days ago, the cross was there, but the grave yawned wide and empty. The enemy had been there since, and, as they often do, had taken out the corpse to make up fetish "medicines" for themselves.

The caves under this *koppie* were typical of the usual thing met with now. You creep in through a narrow little hole, down crevices between rocks—every here and there a crevice leading to the open air gives you light, and a chance of shooting anybody passing by or looking in from outside. Then you come to a roomy cave, from which other tunnels lead out downwards to more caves—the tunnel being occasionally a perpendicular shaft of twenty or thirty feet, which is negotiated by means of a tree-trunk roughly made into a ladder. The caves and their passages worm about inside the *koppie*, with frequent peeps and bolt-holes to open air, and so are grand refuges for a few desperate rebels. In Monogula's we placed thirty-four cases of dynamite, and at one grand burst blew up the whole *koppie*, so that where there had been hill there remained but a crater. The natives, when they return, will scarcely recognise the site of their once famous stronghold, and they will acknowledge that the white man's God is stronger than their own *M'limo*.

Previous to demolishing the caves, we had of course removed, for our own use, the stores of grain which had been stowed away for the rebel garrison. In searching for this grain, the men had lighted on a place in which the bodies had been thrust of those rebels who had fallen when our last patrol had visited the *kraal*, and, to our satisfaction, we now found that nine were killed, and among them two Cape Boys, one of whom, Hendricks by name, was noted as a rifle-shot. He had two bullets through his head; so the shooting of the hussars must have been pretty straight for the few minutes they were at it! Indeed, the shooting of the Imperial troops in this campaign has been particularly good, and has won the admiration of the Dutchmen fighting with us.

29th October.—My patrol being now over, the mounted infantry started today for their march down country to take ship for India, and I was right sorry to part from so good a lot of soldiers. I only wished that they could have had reward for all their keenness and hard work—in the shape of a really good fight with the Matabele.

I, myself, now took my way to Gwelo, to be examined by a Court of Inquiry as to why I had sanctioned the execution of Uwini. My only defence is, that it was the only right thing under the circumstances.

In connection with what I had done in the case of Uwini, I was rather struck by reading today, about the siege of Delhi, the following remark by John Nicholson to an officer who had said to him, "It is hard, sir, when one has fagged horses and men to death, to be told that one has exceeded orders."

"If you served under me," were Nicholson's words, "that would be impossible; my instructions are, always to do everything that can be done."

Gwelo is on a bare, open flat, with a sea-like horizon of *veldt*. Half a dozen small houses dotted about at two hundred yards apart. A crowded collection of corrugated iron rooms within a rampart of logs and earth forms the fort—kept very clean and neat, which is a change from Buluwayo. But, otherwise, there is not much to commend Gwelo to the artist, traveller, or temperance man. Major Thorold in command has done wonders in bringing order into "the place, and his officers (local forces) ably support him, and—have a very well-done mess.

But the command of Gwelo is no sinecure. There are "lawyers" in the camp. The following are among their ebullitions:—Copy of cablegram to Secretary of State, which would have gone, but that the would-be sender was four pence short of the £24 required for its transmission.

> Man named Thorold questioned my sobriety this morning, and called doctor to decide. Doctor drunk himself, could not decide. I said, willing to put in resignation, as a man is not a machine. . . . Who is this Thorold?

Another man telegraphed to headquarters, to ask:

OUR HORSES

The grey is the sole survivor of my five horses. Prince Teck is looking after him.

When will Gwelo force be disbanded? Without competent officers it is only a farce. Have applied to be discharged; application simply ignored!

The general had telegraphed to me to await him here, as he would shortly be *en route* for Salisbury, calling at Gwelo on the way.

All war is now over in Matabeleland—and Wedza's may be said to have been the final blow. Plumer's corps near the Matopos, and Robertson's Cape Boys have been disbanded, and the 7th Hussars are ordered into rainy-season quarters at Buluwayo. But in Mashonaland the rebels still hold out, and now and then a wire arrives to tell of further fights.

And one I heard of on arriving here was of saddest interest about Major Evans of Alderson's Mounted Infantry, who came out from England with me. I knew him well on board, and two days before we sailed he had married. . . . In his first action he fell, shot through the heart.

Of the officers of this Mounted Infantry who came out with me, several others have been hit in action, *viz*. Captain Sir Horace MacMahon, Lieutenants French and Eustace.

3rd November.—Gwelo is said to have a great future before it, but hasn't much of a present—a little of it goes a long way. Combined with this, a lion has killed two donkeys on the road five miles S.E., and seven lions had been seen five miles N.W., this morning, so I determined to spend my next few days of waiting for the general in an outing for shooting lions. At 2 p.m. I was to start, horses, &c., all ready packed with food and blankets.

At 1 p.m. arrived a telegram from the general, saying that some rebels were reported in the Insimba Hills, near Enkeldoorn, seventy miles N.E. from Gwelo on the Salisbury road, and directing that either

THE YOUNG IDEA LEARNING TO SHOOT

The little Dutch boys practice shooting at a mark (generally an empty meat-tin) with the crossbow. With this weapon the aim and the use of the trigger are very much the same as with the rifle, and in this way they become good shots.

Paget or I should take a column of two hundred there without delay. Nothing would have suited us better. Being all ready to start, Paget sent me off to divert the 7th Hussars, who were expected this afternoon from the Selukwe, on to the Salisbury road, while he (Paget) followed on that road direct with extra supplies. So that night found one again in camp on the warpath.

The next few days was spent marching through green bush country and open grass *vleis*, uninhabited except by game.

Being now a sort of *"serrefile"* or hanger-on to the column, as Paget had come in command, I had lots of time to amuse myself, riding at a distance from the column with my gun ready. We saw wildebeeste, hartebeeste, ostriches, sable and roan antelopes, &c. Carew and I got two beauties of the latter on the 5th, and these supplied the whole camp with fresh meat. I got also a very fine tiger-cat (almost like a small leopard).

The longest march seems short when one is hunting game. Your whole attention is fixed at the same time on "distant views," and on the spoor beneath your nose. Your gun is ready, and every sense is on the alert to see the game. Lion or leopard, boar or buck, nigger or nothing, you never know what is going to turn up. And what an appetite one has at the end of a twelve-mile march, when the folding mess-table is set up, and the Indian cook of the 7th has produced his excellent repast!

My only trouble is that I have lost two of my three horses; they broke loose from camp in the night, and strayed, poor starving brutes, in search of grass, and could not be found. And my remaining horse is very thin and weak. However, I got a pair of *veldt shoen* (Dutch shoes) at Gwelo, and so can do much of the march on foot now. Another blow to me is the loss of Diamond, my Zulu boy, who wants to go home. I offered to take him to Beira, and to pay his passage home from there—but no, he must go back *via* Buluwayo. Why? Because he has a lot of money there,—his savings,—which he has hidden, and no one else can find them. I didn't know till today how to fry liver and bacon—the liver, after being cut in thin strips, should be dipped into a plate of mixed salt, pepper, and dry mustard, before going into the frying-pan. A small matter, but it makes a difference. We journey on by Iron-Mine Hill, Orton's Drift to Enkeldoorn, seventy miles from Gwelo, and forty from Charter.

Meantime, my clothes are in tatters. I remember a lady at a fancy dress ball at Simla figuring as a "beggar maid." She was dressed in a black frock with bits of flesh-coloured silk stitched on to it here and there to look like *holes!* Many people said it was rather *chic* (some using the soft *ch,* others the hard). I am in the same state, only there is no need to stitch on flesh-coloured silk, and I don't know that I look very *chic*; but it's curious to find oneself getting sunburnt in an entirely new place: when bathing, I found that my right knee and thigh have their beautiful alabasterlike surface marred by eight irregular blotches of ruddy sunburn!

Rain has been threatening occasionally. Two or three days have been most oppressively hot, and clouds have gathered at nightfall, with mutterings of thunder, and distant lightning. We have put our waterproof sheets ready on going to bed, and sometimes have spread the wagon-sails over the waggons, and have gone to sleep dreaming of the fate in store for us campaigning in wet weather, with the roads impassable for mud, and the *drifts* unfordable for days together. But we have waked at dawn to find a bright clear sky overhead, and the promise of another sunny, breezy day. But the rains are evidently not far off.

9th November.—Reached Enkeldoorn, just three huts forming a coach change-station, on open, rolling downs. The *laager* made by the Dutch farmers of the surrounding district is three miles distant.

At Enkeldoorn I have been lucky enough to find a covered waggon standing abandoned (one wheel smashed), and have taken possession of it as my house, since the weather is very boisterous and promises rain tonight.

(*P.S.*—The promise was fulfilled—it rained hard, and I was happy. I liked the tilt of my waggon so well, that when we marched next day I took it with me; a frame of poles made it into a very comfortable tent in camp.)

10th November.—We moved to near the Dutch *laager*, and interviewed the Native commissioner and others. The *laager* a most impregnable jam of waggons, strengthened with palisades, sandbags, &c., and surrounded by an entanglement of reims and barbed wire. It was full of women and children and Boers (two hundred of them), from all the farms within a circle of twenty miles round. These farmers brought over two thousand oxen (one man told me seven thousand) to the *laager* when the rebellion broke out, and there were but seventy left—such is Rinderpest.

The people in the *laager* lived on fresh meat very largely, the men going out daily to shoot game. A pile of skulls and horns of sable and roan antelope, wildebeeste, &c., showed how successful they had been.

The boys of the *laager* seemed to be fitted out with hats of such a size that they would have to be grown into, and would then do for them in their grown-up years. The young idea was also learning to shoot by crossbows, and it was interesting to see what good positions they got into for firing in the quickest manner, using aim and trigger just as with a gun. A crossbow should be an excellent instrument for teaching the elements of rifle-shooting.

The Boer pig-sty is a simple one. A round hole in the ground, eight feet across, four feet deep; the pig, once in, can't get out. A dry ox-hide, laid over one side of the hole, serves as a shelter from sun or rain.

Leaving our waggons (except two with rations, &c.) at Enkeldoorn that evening, we marched a few miles in the direction of Taba Insimba, and bivouacked at nightfall. Taba Insimba (Mountain of Iron) is a long wall-like range, with a slice cut through it at one point, looking much like the canal through the Isthmus of Corinth. In this cutting or pass, or, as the Dutch call it, "*poort*," the rebels are said to be living in caves in the cliffs, strongly barricaded with stone walls—about eight hundred of them—very defiant. Soon after our reaching Enkeldoorn they had signalled our arrival with smoke-fires. The place is twenty-five miles from Enkeldoorn, but our horses and mules are not up to dashing to the place, so we have come as light as possible, carrying two days' rations on our saddles, and leaving our waggons to follow. Twenty Boers from the Enkeldoorn *laager* are with us, and also about a hundred friendly natives with Taylor, the N.C.

11th November.—Marched all morning, rested all the day, and marched on again after dark, across the wide, perfectly-open flats, till by 10 p.m., we were within a mile of the place, and then we off-saddled and bivouacked—no talking nor smoking allowed. At 2.30 we were roused up, and formed into our places for the attack. I like the weird, subdued impatience of all the preliminaries for a night surprise.

Colonel Paget was to take the Mounted Infantry and small portable Maxim on to the top of one cliff overlooking the gorge, so as to fire into the caves in the opposite cliff; another party were to be below at the foot of the gorge, to attack these caves under cover of the fire from above. I was ordered to go with Carew's squadron of 7th Hussars, taking our horses (the remainder of the troop were dismounted), over

A CHILDREN'S HOSPITAL

Some women and children had hidden themselves in the long grass between the enemy and ourselves, and four of them were consequently struck by stray bullets. They were brought in, and we bandaged them up and brought them into camp. The 7th Hussars made excellent amateur nurses.

the ridge, and round to the back of the gorge, to cut off the enemy's line of retreat.

We reached the ridge just when it was getting sufficiently light,—as the Dutchman would say, "to see the horns of an ox"—clambered up the steep, stony hill through the bush, then down the other side, where there lay before us, in the early light, a panorama of bush and tree-tops.

Our guide was one Bester, a Boer, whose farm was here. At the outbreak of the rebellion his father had been wounded, his mother killed, and he and his brother only escaped after killing a number of the rebels, and being nearly killed themselves. We passed through the ashes of their home on our way. His uncle I remembered well as field cornet on the Transvaal border, in our operations against Dinizulu, in Zululand, in 1888.

The Magneze Poort, in which the rebels were (for we soon knew that they *were* there by the barking of dogs, the talking of men, and calling of women, &c.), was a huge cleft, with rocky sides, and a bubbling torrent roaring through. On arriving in rear of the place, we found ourselves in a valley between numerous bush-covered hills. The line of retreat open to the defenders of the stronghold in the gorge was across an open glade of long white grass, along the foot of the steep mountain-side.

It was broad daylight by the time we had got to our position, and we had not long been waiting there before we heard excited shouting from the natives on top of the opposite cliffs, answered by those in the gorge below; then *pop—bom—pop—pop*, as the firing began; rifles cracking, and blunder-bores roaring back their muffled reply from caves; soon the *"isiqwakwa"* (Maxim) joined in with its sharp *"rat-tat-tat-tat-tat,"* from the top of the ridge. Ere long, a party of the enemy were seen hastily making their way across the open grass in front of us; a moment later, and a troop of the hussars had burst from their hidden station in the bush, and were galloping, swords drawn and gleaming, straight for the astonished rebels.

But the charge was not to be; the rocky stream, with boggy banks, was the *slip that lay between the cup and the lip,* and baulked the *sabreurs* of their wish; but they did not wait to lament. In a trice they were off their horses, carbine in hand, and soon were popping merrily at the foes they could not get at hand-to-hand. While thus engaged, Carew sent round another troop to cut off any rebels who might succeed in running the gauntlet of fire.

Finding themselves stopped, some ran back among the rocks, and contented themselves with wasting ammunition in long shots at us, while others lay among the tall white grass—to wait until the clouds rolled by. But these latter were soon moved by the clouds, in the shape of Lieutenant Holford and a few dismounted men, moving on them through the grass, and thus compelling their retreat at point-blank range, or their surrender. This party counted fifteen dead bodies, and found a few women and children, whom they brought back. Among these were, unfortunately, four wounded—three children and one woman, hit by stray bullets as they were lying hid in the grass.

Three times in this campaign have I taken out to the field with me a few bandages and dressings in my holster, and on each occasion I have found full use for them. I don't know whether it is coincidence or not—but here was another occasion. Our one doctor was with the main body on the other side of the mountain, so I got to work on the poor little devils. Curiously enough the women and two of the children were hit in the same place, *i.e.* through the lower part of the thigh, clear of bone and of artery; simple wounds, and easily patched up; while the fourth, a small boy, with a very bad temper, had half his calf torn away by a splinter of rock or a ricochet bullet. None of them seemed to feel much pain except him, and he kept kicking and grovelling his poor little leg in the dust when the girl who had charge of him tried to do anything to it. So it was in a bad mess by the time I got an opportunity to get to work on it.

It did one good to see one or two of the hussars, fresh from nigger-fighting, giving their help in binding up the youngsters, and tenderly dabbing the wounded limbs with bits of their own shirts wetted. I invented a perfect form of field-syringe for this occasion, which I think I'll patent when I get home. You make and use it thus—at least I did: Take an ordinary native girl, tell her to go and get some lukewarm water, and don't give her anything to get it in. She will go to the stream, kneel and fill her mouth, and so bring the water; by the time she is back, the water is lukewarm. You then tell her to squirt it as you direct into the wound, while you prise around with a feather (I had lost what I otherwise invariably carry with me—a soft paint-brush). It works very well.

Well, we went on with the squadron among the hills, at the back of the position, and burned a *kraal*. Vaughan, one of Carew's subalterns, has developed a talent as great, or greater, than that of any colonial, for finding native corn or cattle, be they hidden never so wisely. He brought in from the bush a bunch of lively, healthy cattle. Then, firing having ceased everywhere, and smoke of burning *kraals* being seen curling up in columns from the stronghold, we ceased from war, and sat us down in a shady glade by the running stream, and soon had breakfast under way.

Later on we got back to our *laager*, and found that the main body had completely surprised the rebels before they could take to the caves (they had been sleeping outside in huts), and, altogether, twenty-six were killed; the rest had fled in different directions. Our people, well hidden in the rocks and bush, had not had a single casualty.

So ended my most happy roaming on patrol.

The general was expected at Enkeldoorn next morning; so, in the afternoon, I started off, riding one horse and leading another, to do the twenty-five miles between us. At nightfall a heavy thunderstorm rolled up, but I was lucky in being near a deserted farmhouse, where I took shelter, with my horses, in the verandah. A wheelbarrow made me a comfortable lounge in which to eat my frugal but rather in-digestible meal of cold pig, dough and tea. I did not live inside the house, as lurking Matabele fugitives might have watched me in, and could have nicely caught me; but in the open verandah I should be quite a match for them. I was glad next day I had acted so, for Lord Grey's party, camping near the house, found in the rafters of the room a fine, great, green mamba snake.

Well, when the rain was over, I rode on in the night; the spoor I had been following was now washed out, but I steered by moon and time until I thought I was near Enkeldoorn, and, not seeing the camp, then prepared to bivouac till daylight, when a sudden small flash, as of a man striking a match, sparkled on a hill close by; and on I went, and found myself at the *laager*, against the bayonet of a Boer sentry, whose pipe-light had been my guide. Delighted to hear about the fight, he gave me back the news that the general had already arrived. Not long after, I had wedged myself in between Vyvyan and Ferguson in their tent, and was sleeping like a log.

At home it may seem strange to talk of a sentry's pipe, but, in this country, smoking is not a very grave offence. A colonial volunteer officer, hearing of our army orders on the subject, thought to smarten up his men a bit; so, finding one of his night sentries smoking, he ordered him to consider himself a prisoner. The following was then overheard by someone sleeping near:—

Sentry. "What, not smoke on sentry! Then where—— the am I

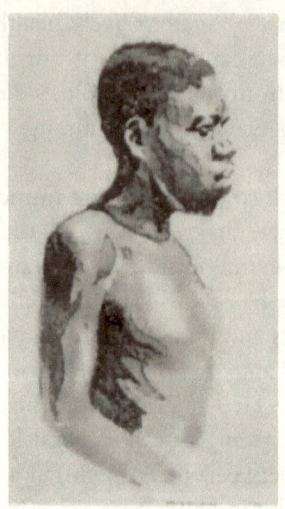

"Diamond"
My Zulu servant. Well-named "Diamond,"
for he was a jewel of a servant.

to smoke?"

Captain Brown. "*Of course* it's not allowed; and I shall make you a prisoner."

Sentry (taking his pipe from his mouth, and tapping Brown—who, in time of peace, was his butcher—on the arm with the stem of it). "Now, look here. Brown, don't go and make a —— fool of yourself. If you do, I'll go elsewhere for my meat!"

And Brown didn't.

CHAPTER 17

Through Mashonaland
13th November to 2nd December.

13th November.—Up early. Paid off and sorrowfully said "Goodbye" to Diamond and Umtini, my two nigger servants.

And in the afternoon the general moved on from Enkeldoorn towards Salisbury. The party consisted of Sir Frederick, Vyvyan, Ferguson, Gormley (our principal medical officer). Leech (who manages our transport), three waggons, a Cape cart, and lots of riding-horses, servants, office-clerks, &c.

This night we camped at Adlum's Farm (the green *mamba* house, where I had "dined" the night before), and found Lord Grey and party also camped here on their way to Salisbury.

I had walked the march on foot, hoping to find buck, and called, coatless and dirty, just as I was, at Lord Grey's camp in passing to our own. Lady Grey insisted on my sitting down to dinner then and there

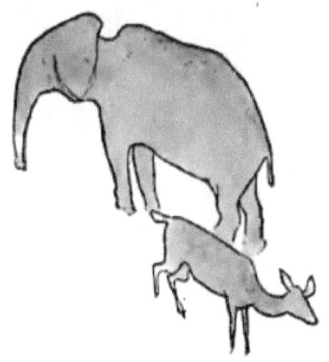

SPECIMEN OF OLD ROCK-PAINTINGS
BY NATIVES IN MASHONALAND.

General Sir F. Carrington Captain Vyvyan, Brigade-Major
Lieut. Ferguson, A.D.C.

HEADQUARTERS' MESS

with them—and a very jolly dinner it was. It made rather a good picture when Lister held the saucepan of rice, while I helped it out to Lady Victoria, who was "asking for more." Lady Victoria has developed the talent for spooring, which will therefore probably become the fashionable pastime among the young ladies of this country; if not, on introduction in England, instead of the usual "Do you bike" you will ask, "Do you spoor?"

That night I had a real good sleep, for out of the previous eighty-seven hours only sixteen had been slept, and many of the others had been expended in pretty good bodily exertion. Sir Frederick had brought me English letters.

15th November. Charter. One has heard of it so much, and seen it writ large in the map so often, that it comes as a surprise to find it is only a tiny *laager* of half a dozen waggons, round which huts are being built, ready for the rainy season. An unhealthy-looking place on low ground, beside a stagnant, muddy stream. Here Sir Frederick, as usual, met an old friend in the first trooper he saw. "Good day, my lad. Not much of a place to be quartered in, this."

"No, sir."

"I have seen you before, somewhere."

"Yes, sir, my name is ———. I was in your Police Regiment two years. I lunched with you at Kimberley Club five years ago. Since then I have been running a 'penny steamer' on the Zambesi. Unhealthy? Yes; always down with fever, but I had luck, and was able to get up again. Came down here to recover, and took on as a trooper for the war."

It is the story of many another cadet of good family moving in these parts. Our ninety-eight miles from Enkeldoorn to Salisbury lay, as per usual, through bush-grown *veldt*, and was a heavy sandy track, and which meant hard pulling for the mules. We generally rolled out of our blankets at dawn—cocoa—and, mounting our horses, rode into the bush with gun or rifle, each taking his own line to the next outspan.

Lord Grey's party shot to northward of the road, and the south side was our preserve; but neither side yielded much game. By seven or eight o'clock the waggons, having done their eight or ten miles, outspanned. A buck-sail stretched over the tilts of two gave a shady room between, in which we sheltered from the midday heat. Then, in the afternoon, we trekked again till sundown. Dinner, and to bed by nine.

A most peaceful, delightful, but terribly fattening life! luckily, some of us had some leeway to make up in that line.

19th November.—On a rock, in a small *koppie* close to our outspan of last night, were a lot of Bushman paintings of animals—some badly, but some very well drawn—in red monochrome. One elephant and a buck were particularly good. We were met by Colonel Alderson and other officers from Salisbury, as we rode in the last six miles of our journey.

Salisbury—two widely-spread townships in a basin among wooded rising grounds, with little of the regularity of building plots as seen in Buluwayo, but altogether a prettier-looking spot. Houses mostly of bright red brick with white tin roofs— all single-storied and verandahed, of course; many of them with nice gardens. One wooded hill overlooks the town, and on this stands the original Fort Salisbury, built by the "pioneers" who first opened up Mashonaland in 1891. At the foot of this hill runs the only regular street of the place—where all the stores, &c., are situated. The rest of the two townships was described to me thus:

> There's the post office, there are the government buildings, there is the hospital, and there is the club—the remainder are mostly drink-shops.

This is maligning the town rather—but it has its allowance of "drink-shops" all the same. We were put up in the Commercial Hotel, and had nice offices provided near the Government Offices. And we settled down in a few minutes most comfortably. It is curious to come off the veldt, where we have not seen a sign of natives for days, almost weeks past, although hunting about—all of us—off the road in the bush, and yet to be told on arrival here that they don't consider the road safe yet—that the rebels are still about everywhere!

Then comes an alarming telegram from Buluwayo to say:

> A white man murdered close to the town; general rising of the natives expected; town-guard of volunteers without pay being formed. &c.

Again one of those unmeaning panics, which seems to strike people who have been living on tenterhooks for a short time—sort of spasms that revisit them now and again till their nerves are restored. But it is very annoying, and often involves moving troops about for fear that *this* time it should be a true report. We have already caught

BLACK AND WHITE

The work of nursing our sick and wounded was undertaken by Sisters of Mercy, who slaved their lives out at the duty, having only one or two native boys to help them in their menial work.

two or three lunatics who had spread such rumours, and sent them out of the country, but there is apparently at least one left. A nervous man is forty thousand times worse than a frightened woman, especially when, as is the case here, he has any number of drink-fuddled "funk-sticks" ready to echo his alarm.

I remember being in a theatre when an inexplicable movement took place among the people in the pit. Almost immediately a "funk-stick" in the dress circle, seeing the commotion, but not seeing the cause for it, shouted out his own fear—"*Fire!*" In a moment others like him echoed his cry, and there was for some few minutes a very pretty exhibition of panic. Manly heroes handing out the women? Not a bit of it; jumping over them to get first to the door! Salisbury is just now full of interesting celebrities—Major Forbes, fresh from the country beyond the Zambesi, where he was administering the company's affairs, and pushing on the telegraph to Khartoum. He had been reported killed in the rebellion, but had got down all right, although his companion was murdered.

Captain Younghusband, sent by the *Times* to report on the South African situation generally, having just done three months' visit to the Transvaal among my old friends Paul Kruger, Joubert, &c., &c., at Pretoria.

H. Cust, M.P., filling himself up with local information and experience, and with lots of good to say of George (of all people!). Lord and Lady Grey and Lady Victoria, Cecil Rhodes, Sir Charles Metcalfe, &c.

21st November.—The general visited the hospital to see the sick and wounded. There were three officers still in. Sir Horace MacMahon and Eustace (both shipmates of mine on the *Tantallon*), both severely wounded in the foot, but going on well.

Montgomery shot in the head, and consequently partially paralysed; trepanned, and doing well. About a dozen men. One poor chap was shot in both arms; one had been amputated, the other was all smashed above the elbow, but the doctors hope to save it. He also had two or three slight wounds about the body, but was as cheery as possible and getting on well.

One curious case we saw there was a young fellow who had been lost on the *veldt*. His party had searched for him several days, but never found him, and supposed that he was killed. Six weeks afterwards, a party of Dutchmen were hunting that *veldt*, and they found a path close to their camp leading down to water with fresh spoor of a man on it. During the few days they were there, they noticed the spoor came fresh each day. They watched, and saw this man come down to drink, but when they tried to approach, he fled, and got down an antbear hole, where he evidently lived. They could not persuade him to come out, and so finally had to dig him out. They found he was quite off his head—unable to talk—living only on roots and berries.

They took him to Salisbury, and when we saw him, he was all right, except he had lost nearly all his teeth, and could not remember much of the time when he was lost. The hospital nursing staff consists of eight nuns, who do excellent work. Like the sisters in Buluwayo, they are most self-sacrificing and constant in their attention to the sick and wounded of the force. The general and I went and saw them in their own house, and had a long talk with them. The superior (a very cheerful, sweet-faced young woman) was an old friend of his, having been a nurse at one of his hospitals for the Bechuanaland Police.

The general and his staff have been supplied with bikes by the Chartered Company (they have a number of them for the police), and they are invaluable for getting about the widespread town. The general takes us for gallops now and then, which really do one a lot of good after a load of office work. The roads are fair and the country open and pretty, and the air most delightful, except when, as it was today, it was dense with locusts.

The outskirts of the township boast a number of nice houses with good gardens and—what is best—deep creeper-grown verandahs.

The house, for instance, where Lord Grey is living (Mr. Pauling's) is a most delightful one—with English furniture; its billiard-room and everything as though in the midst of civilization, instead of being two hundred miles away from a railway. At our hotel I've slept at last in a room—the first time for over two months. I tried it the night of our arrival here, but it would not work, and very soon I had my blankets outside in the street! But this night the clouds rolled up, and the first taste of the rainy season came down in sheets at night.

22nd November.—Among other items of the day, we (the general, Ferguson, and I) rode up on our bikes and called on Rhodes. We found him living in a very pleasant house belonging to Judge Vintcent, who had been commandant of Salisbury all through the rebellion, and being a true old Carthusian, he had his walls covered with photos, &c., of Charterhouse groups, &c. I was very sorry to find that he had gone off to the Cape on leave, on account of his wife's health and his own.

Meantime, Rhodes occupied his house and, when I saw him, his armchair. For Rhodes had been out before daybreak, and was now making up some sleep lost thereby, but in *such* an uncomfortable position.

This was rather characteristic of him: where other people would have been sleepless from discomfort of body and wear of mind, he was sleeping sweetly; but then he is always thinking or doing what you don't expect. In talking over ways and means or plans of campaign, he almost invariably throws quite a new light on the subject, and has a totally different plan, and one which is often the best of the lot, especially from the Chartered Company's point of view, as far as ultimate results go, not present expenditure—that is the point that often makes us pause, but he never seems to think of it, for he looks to the better economy in the end. And while he talks he doesn't sit still, but he'll be sprawling all over the sofa one minute, the next he'll have his legs crossed under him, *à la Turc*—full of restlessness and energy.

23rd November.—Meet of the hounds at Rhodes' house. The pack has been kept in the *laager* during the dangerous time—fed on Boer meal. Is hunted by Graham, the postmaster. We were a field of twenty-seven,—which is not bad, considering how few horses are now fit for work,—all in shirt sleeves. One lady (Lady Victoria Grey). We got on to a buck within half a mile of the house, and had a gallop. I was riding near Rhodes, who was thoroughly enjoying the working of the hounds, till suddenly something better attracted his notice, and we passed under the telegraph line from Cape Town to, or rather towards. Cairo—and he at once went into particulars of that, and showed how the iron posts were made, according to his design, in two parts, so that they would not be too heavy for niggers to carry in the bush and fly country—wooden poles useless, on account of the inroads of white ants; and then we continued our gallop.

Talking of inroads,—we hear that the jigger, an insect the size of a pin's head, is invading South Africa. He came from the West Coast, and is now down as far as Beira. I know the beast: he got me coming back from Kumassi, and planted his eggs under my toe-nail, and I had ten minutes' genuine fun while the doctor cut them out.

Curious how the little pest should be able to cross Africa, and make himself a scourge in a new bit of country,—just as the rinderpest has

THE COUNTESS RESCUES HER SEWING-MACHINE

done,—taking three years to get here from Somaliland.

26th November.—I dined with Wilson Fox, old Carthusian, Public Prosecutor, Director of Commissariat and Transport, and a good singer—so pretty useful all round. This morning I took a toss off my bike and damaged my knees, so that I stand over like an old cab-horse.

27th November.—For the past four days the telegraph line between this and Cape Town has been down, and we have been unable to get sanction to our proposed move out of the country. The rains are beginning (thunderstorms nearly every afternoon), a man per day dying for the last six days, which is a large order in so small a force.

Dined at Lord Grey's tonight, and there also dined the Count and Countess de la P———e. No more interesting couple could be found in the country. I listened open-mouthed to their adventures. He was formerly captain in the French navy and A.D.C. to MacMahon, and has four war medals and ten orders. She was "slavey" in a London boarding-house. They came up here before women were allowed in the country—she dressed as a boy, and so got admitted. They started with £40 and one cow; in three years they owned a large farm and 160 cows, and were clearing £250 a month dairy-farming and butchering. Rinderpest and rebellion suddenly stopped this, and swept away all they had. He took his waggon and span of donkeys to Chimoio, and spent the whole of their money in getting a load of food and luxuries to sell in Salisbury. She remained at the farm, with one nigger boy to protect her.

The count brought his waggon up the road in company with two other traders' waggons—six white men and one American young lady. Thirty miles from Salisbury they found on the road the bodies of a white family—father, mother, and children,—lying, just murdered. They began to bury them, when a volley was fired on them at short range, killing a number of donkeys. They embarked in the lightest waggon, the count losing his waggon and stores. They trekked on, pursued by rebels, who kept firing, without daring to attack, or even to show themselves out of the bush. This went on for two days and one night, till they reached Salisbury. The girl, meanwhile, had been very plucky—merely asked to be supplied with a revolver, with which to shoot herself if the worst came to the worst; and she got one of the men to promise to do it for her if her courage failed.

But they got in all right. Meanwhile, the countess, living out at the farm, five miles from Salisbury, received warning by messenger to come in to *laager*; and when she delayed about it, they sent four friendlies as a guard for her. Her account of it, told in a very matter-of-fact cockney way, was most refreshing,—

> You see, they had murdered our neighbours that day, and I couldn't help thinking about it. So I didn't go to bed that night, but just put on a blouse and skirt, and lay down on the bed, after barricading the door. Well, in the night I was startled first by a waggon going past at full speed; drivers yelling at the mules and cracking their whips,—this was the waggon going to Mazoe to rescue the women there, I could not sleep. By-and-by I heard a noise, and, looking through a hole in the door, I saw niggers—plenty of them—close to the house and on three sides of it. I got the rifle, slipped on my *bandolier*, seized up my revolver-belt, and jumped out of the back window and ran.
>
> As I got over the wall of the garden, I upset an iron bucket with an awful clang. At the same time, my boy, running out of the kitchen, knocked against two frying-pans that were hanging up there, and made worse din. But he got away, and joined me in the bush above the house. There we hid for the rest of the night behind a gravestone. They did not burn the house; and next morning, after waiting some time, to see if any of them were about, I got so impatient about it, that I sent the boy down,—

Younghusband Baden-Powell Sir F. Carrington Lady V. Grey Sir C. Metcalfe Graham (M.F.H.)
Alderson Lord Grey Cecil Rhodes

THE OPENING MEET OF THE SALISBURY HOUNDS (AFTER THE WAR)

to see if my sewing-machine was all right,—and he soon came back with it. He had found it close to the well: a nigger had got it, and was clearing with it, when he was *assegaied* by one of the Zambesi boys.

Luckily they killed him a few yards from the well; another step, and my sewing-machine would have been down the well. But the Zambesi boys were all killed—lying about round the front door. Well, then we made our way into Salisbury; and I had no sooner got there than I found that, like the stupid I was, I had brought the revolver case, empty—in the confusion I had left the revolver behind. So, says I, I must go back and get that revolver.

There was a patrol, just then going out, so I got them to let me go with them and back to my house. I made my way through the murdered Zambesi boys, but I didn't stop to look at them, I was that anxious to get my revolver; and I got it all right, and glad I was to come away with it; not but what it's getting worn-out now, I think, as it wouldn't act the other night when I wanted it to; but it's the one I've shot a lion with, so I like it. Oh, he was only a very old lion; but, ye see, he used to come pretty near every night to our camp, and snap up one or other of the dogs. One night he even got into our dining-hut, where there was a ham hanging from the roof; he got on to the table to reach it down; but the table was a rickety concern and came down with him, and I had stupidly left the cloth on overnight, and a nice lot of holes he made in it with his claws.

Well, one evening I heard the old brute moving in the *sluit*, close to the camp; so I called to the boy to get the gun, and come up with me into the waggon, and I took the revolver. Soon we heard the lion coming along the path, kicking oranges—them hard-rinded things—with his feet. I says to the boy, 'There he is, shoot!' But the boy couldn't see him; and so I says, 'Oh, if you're going to take all night to shoot him, here goes!' and with that I up with my revolver, and lets off a shot at him. The lion sprang forward to the waggon, and I give him another, that sent him back where he came from, and he rolled about a bit in the *sluit*, and died there. I had hit him right in the neck.

What about the other night? Oh, I hate to think of it—my luck was dead out that night! Three nights ago it was, I heard a curious noise at the back of the house, here in Salisbury; so I put on my india-rubber shoes, and takes my pistol, and I slips round to see what it is; and there I find a man—a white man, mind you—trying to break into the house. So I, catches him by the neck with one hand (the countess is a small, slim person), and put the revolver in his face with the other, and tells 'im to keep quiet; but he wriggles, and gets loose. Well, I catches hold of his shirt, and that tears; then I catches his trousers, they tears; and with that he bolts away. Well, I up with my pistol and fired, and fired. But whether it was the cartridges was bad, or there was something wrong with the pistol—go off it wouldn't; and so that man got away.

But if the countess was amusing and original, so was the count in his way. He had been a great elephant hunter in Central Africa. Used to hunt, like Selous, in only a shirt, belt, and hat; no shoes. Killed 103 elephants in one season. Ever charged by an elephant? No, but an elephant was charged by him. Following up a wounded elephant, it took down a steep hillside in thick bush. He tore after it,—an elephant goes very slowly down a steep place,—so he rushed right on to it before he saw it. However, he put up his heavy rifle and fired up into his head and killed it, but the angle of the gun was so great as to knock him down, the stock in its recoil cutting his cheek all open, and leaving him senseless. His boys went back and told his friends in camp that both he and the elephant were killed, the elephant having put his tusk through his cheek. "Srough my cheek! The elephant had a tusk so long as my body, and so thick as my leg, how can he put it through my cheek? I should have no face left."

The count, upon coming into *laager* at Salisbury after the loss of his donkey-waggon, was made a trooper. He an ex-captain of the navy, with four war medals, while his commanding officer was a barman at one of the public-houses! The excuse for this apparent anomaly was that he had known what it was to be an officer, and he might now let the others have a chance of trying. The troop consisted of 120, but of these only fifty were available for duty, the rest were nearly all officers. In spite of having lost everything, the count and countess seemed very cheery and hopeful, and are longing to get to work again on their farm. They deserve to prosper,

29th November.—Part of the Mounted Infantry and the invalids were at last to start down towards Beira for embarkation. The general was to inspect the corps before they started. We went over to the camp (I, being an invalid, owing to my broken knees, was kindly taken by Lady Grey in her Cape cart). Just as we got there, a black wall of cloud arrived from the opposite direction. A roar of thunder warned us off, a sharp volley of rain followed. The general dismissed the parade, and we all scampered for home as hard as we could go, pursued by a drenching downpour. All the afternoon and all the night it came down in sheets; the rains had begun. Now comes the anxiety of learning whether we shall be able to get out of the country at all for the next four months.

The rivers rise, the ground becomes a bog, and mules can't work if their coats are wet, as the harness rubs them raw. It rather shows the danger of working to order at the end of a long telegraph line. Every thunderstorm (and they have been plentiful of late) breaks down the telegraph line somewhere, so that messages take many days to come and go, and we have already wasted a week here merely waiting for replies.

1st December.—For two days it has been fine, as far as actual rain goes, but dead still and hot—boiling hot, banking up for more rain. Very little work and very little play, for Salisbury is, to say the least of it, a little *triste* just now. No news from the outside world at all. The club has a pile of old newspapers (none newer than September 12th) lying on the table, and we go and read these over again like dogs at a bone, hoping yet to find a scrap of interesting matter somewhere in them, even though it be among the advertisements.

We had hoped to start tomorrow, but now as I go to bed another thunderstorm is on us—the roar of the rain is deafening as it falls in a heavy mass on the roof (glad I am to be under a roof, too!). One hardly hears the thunder through, but the lightning is incessant and beautiful; but I wish we were well over the road that lies between us and the sea!

CHAPTER 18

The Situation in Rhodesia

1st December.—The situation in Mashonaland is now as follows:—

In the south-east, Makoni has been attacked by Major Watts, defeated, and captured. Owing to a risk of an attempt being made to rescue him, Watts had him tried by court-martial, and he was condemned to be shot. For this execution Watts was subsequently placed in arrest by the High Commissioner at Cape Town, but was eventually acquitted.

During the early part of October, Major Jenner, D.S.O., had taken a column of 180 men against Umtigeza, south of Salisbury, had captured the chief and destroyed his stronghold, losing three men killed and three wounded in the action. Captain Tennent, Mashonaland Field Force, with 160 men, had made a successful raid on Simbansotas, capturing the stronghold and numerous *kraals*, with a loss of two killed and three wounded.

Captain Sir Horace MacMahon, with 200 men, finally cleared the country north of Salisbury in the Mazoe district, and destroyed the cave strongholds there, losing one killed and three wounded.

Lieutenant-Colonel Alderson conducted an expedition, 500 strong, into the country west and south-west of Salisbury, the Lomagundi district; he captured and destroyed Mashingombi's, Chena's, and Zimban's *kraals*, and blew up the strongholds. He lost four killed and thirteen wounded.

Major Evans, with eighty-eight men, attacked and took Gatzi's stronghold, near the Salisbury-Umtali road. He was most unfortunately himself shot dead during the attack. The effect of these expeditions has been that the rebels have been visited in every part of Mashonaland and smashed, and in consequence are now giving in on every

THE SPECIAL SERVICE
MOUNTED INFANTRY

side. De Moleyns, who was appointed to organise the armed police, is getting together his corps to the number of 580. These are destined to garrison three towns and twelve forts, which latter have now been established in the most important centres of the country.

The men are being recruited in Natal and the Cape Colony; and, pending their arrival up here, we are engaging volunteers to take over their duty in the interim. In this way we shall be able to relieve the Imperial troops, and to get them out of the country before the rains set in fully, and block the roads, and bring the fever.

In Matabeleland the situation is as follows:—

Six hundred police have been posted in the four towns and sixteen forts about the country, while 200 of the 7th Hussars are stationed at Buluwayo.

Plumer's Matabeleland Relief Force and the Cape Boys have been withdrawn from the country, and the local forces disbanded.

Natives are giving up their arms in good numbers, and are settling down to cultivate the lands assigned to them by the Native commissioners. They have been told by Lord Grey that if they still have any lingering ideas of ultimately driving out the whites, they might at

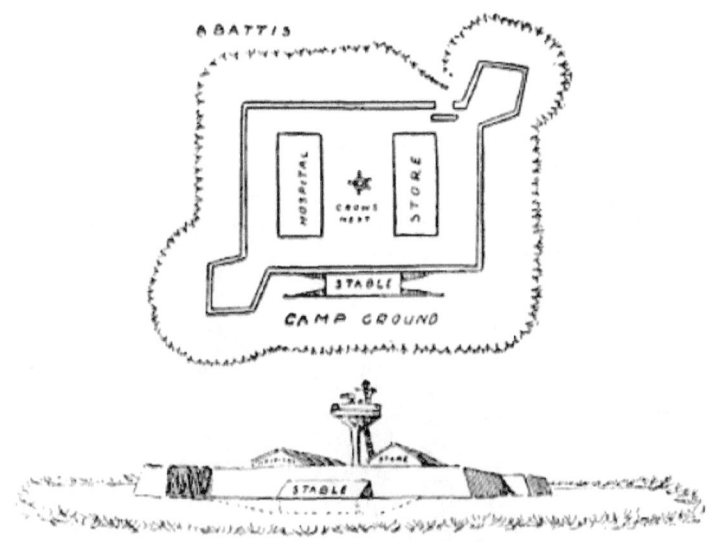

A Fort

The above was the usual type of fort erected for keeping command of a district after its subjugation. Outside the abattis or hedge of thorn-bush a wide belt of grass was left standing, as the dark bodies of native assailants would show up well against its whiteness at night; and beyond the belt it was burnt away to prevent grass-fires coming up to the fort.

once dismiss such thoughts for ever; that the railway will shortly be up to Buluwayo, ready to import thousands of troops, if necessary; that certain chiefs will be reinstated as their immediate rulers; that grievances will be inquired into, and set right wherever it is possible; and that the chief Native commissioner (Taylor) will be the head to whom they will have to refer. This plan has been grasped by them, and agreed to after nearly two months' havering. Rhodes, who had arranged the peace with them, they have nicknamed "*Umlanulang Mkngi*"—the bull who separates the fighting-bulls; and Colenbrander, his *fidus Achates* in the matter, they have called the "tick-bird"—a bird which in this country always accompanies a bull, to relieve him of superfluous ticks.

So that throughout Rhodesia war is over, and there is no prospect of any further outbreak on the part of the people. They have had a heavy lesson which will be further accentuated by the scarcity of food which must result for the next few months, owing to their not having sown their crops. The Chartered Company, having this in view, are

A WAR-DANCE

making every effort to get up supplies of seed-corn and food, with which they will be able to stave off actual famine from the natives.

All that remains to be done in the immediate future is police work: in getting hold of those among the late rebels who are guilty of murders, and in getting hold of the arms that remain still undelivered. This is a matter of time, and may in some cases necessitate small armed expeditions; but there is no likelihood of any further general rising. So far, about four hundred rifles and four thousand assegais have been handed in.

The ultimate arrangements for their government are practically those explained by Lord Grey to the chiefs in the Matopos: The country will be divided into numerous districts, each under its own *induna*, who will be paid by the government, and will be held responsible for the conduct of his district; each *induna* will have about twelve thousand people under him. Native commissioners will be assigned to the districts, acting under the orders of the chief Native commissioners (one in Matabeleland and the other in Mashonaland), and the success of the scheme very much depends upon the efficiency of these officers. The greatest care will have to be taken in their selection and appointment—a point which has in some cases been overlooked in the past, with the recent direful results.

That the white settlers were not entirely overwhelmed in the first mad, blood-thirsting rush of relentless savagery is a matter for marvel; and that they contrived to hold their own for so long, until assistance came, is, as the *Times* has lately said, due not merely to the superior armament of the British, but to their dogged pluck and determination.

For your Englishman (and by him I mean his colonial brother as well) is endowed by nature with the spirit of practical discipline, which is deeper than the surface veneer discipline of Continental armies. Whether it has been instilled into him by his public-school training, by his football and his "fagging," or whether it is inbred from previous generations of stern though kindly parents, one cannot say; but, at any rate, the goodly precepts of the game remain as best of guides: "Keep in your place," and "Play, not for yourself, but for your side."

It is thus that our leaders find themselves backed by their officers playing up to them; not because they are "—— well ordered to" (as I heard Tommy express it), nor because it may bring them crosses and rewards, but simply—*because it is the game.*

Had it not been that this spirit permeated the forces, the campaign might have dragged out interminably, and very probably part at least of the country would have had to be evacuated for a time.

As it was, the operations have lasted for eight months; but in that time the small forces available—amounting to less than five thousand at their very strongest state—have reconquered a country equal in size to Italy, France, and Spain put together, and held by nearly thirty thousand warriors.

The whole of our combined forces amounted to a little over 6000 men (3000 in Matabeleland, 2200 in Mashonaland). This included 1200 Imperial troops, composed of detachments of the 7th Hussars, the Special Service Mounted Infantry, the infantry and mounted infantry detachments of the West Riding and York and Lancaster Regiments, some Royal Engineers and Artillery, Medical Staff, &c.

The local forces included 4200 men—English, Dutch, and Cape Boys; organised in local field forces for each town; also Plumer's Matabeleland Relief Force, the Natal Troop, and the Cape Boys Corps.

In addition to these, we had nearly four thousand eight hundred friendly natives; but, as a rule, they were practically useless to us.

But these, together with the transport *employés*, &c., brought up the number of mouths in the forces to be fed to nearly twelve thousand.

The casualties among the troops (not including the native levies) were as follows ;—

	Matabeleland.	Mashonaland.		Total
Deaths, 134				
Killed, or died of wounds.	51	19	=	70
Died, other causes	48	9	=	57
Killed accidentally[1]	7	0	=	7
Total	106	28		134
Wounded, 173				
Wounded in action	90	68	=	168
Accidentally wounded[1]	13	2	=	15
Total	103	70	=	173

Of the above casualties, 14 officers and 39 men belonged to the Imperial troops. In addition to the above, the number of persons murdered or missing were—in Matabeleland, 140; in Mashonaland, 118; total, 258.

---

1. Chiefly mishandling loaded rifles, and also from a dynamite explosion at Buluwayo.

One of the interesting experiences of the campaign, to a soldier, has been the test of the Lee-Metford rifle in action; and, though a great admirer of the Martini-Henry myself, I have to admit that the new weapon has come through the ordeal right well. It is an excellent gun, more especially in the carbine form. Its accuracy is great, and its liability to jam practically non-existent. The only fault that appears, is the non-"stopping" power of the bullet, which, if it strikes a non-vital spot, does not do much damage to the enemy at the moment. The new bullet will, however, remedy this, its one possible defect. With this rifle the Imperial troops certainly won the admiration of their colonial brothers-in-arms, Dutchmen as well as English, for their accurate shooting as much as for their fire-discipline.

The recent troubles may, after all, bring good in their train, not only to Rhodesia, but to South Africa generally.

They have shown up in a very strong light, firstly, how utterly higgledy-piggledy were the measures and arrangements for military safeguarding some of the most valuable portions of the country, owing to the fact that a false sense of civilization had lulled everybody into a feeling of security. Then, in the second place, the eyes of all have been opened to the immense distances that now divide the portions of civilized Central South Africa, and which demand a more than usually efficient protective organisation, instead of the scattered, disconnected measures that have been deemed sufficient up till now.

Until some guarantee of a better security for all classes and industries be given,—especially with the recent troubles fresh in their experience,—it will be difficult to re-develop enterprise on the part of capitalists and others up north.

But once that guarantee is provided, another link will have been forged in the chain of events which are building the fast-growing Dominion of South Africa.

Within the last twenty years we have had the reduction of the Zulu power by force of arms, in 1876, which gave security to the Transvaal, and opened it to civilization. In 1881 the Boers practically won their independence at Majuba Hill, and were in a position to make use of this security we had obtained for them.

Their filibustering raids in Stellaland and Goschen resulted in the annexation to Great Britain of the slice of territory along their western frontier,—Bechuanaland,—and its protectorate in Khama's country, which brought our borders up to Matabeleland.

Three years later, Zululand again broke out, and was finally gathered into our system, thereby extending our border up to Swaziland, upon the southeast of the South African Republic. Mr. Moffat then checkmated an attempt on the part of the Boers to get Lobengula's country.

In 1889 Colonel Pennefather's "trek" of "pioneers" took up Mashonaland for the Chartered Company, along the northern face of the Transvaal.

Thus penned on every side, the Boers made a despairing effort out towards the east, and Swaziland was given over to their hand, but not the coast they coveted. Tongaland, the last remaining land between them and the sea, became a new protectorate of England.

And to the north, under Mr. Rhodes' direction, the Company extended far and wide its sway. In 1890 it crossed the Zambesi, and, adding Barotseland within its sphere, moved up its borders to Nyassaland.

In 1893 the inevitable conflict between the rival powers north of the Limpopo came to a head, with the inevitable result—the power of Lobengula, King of the Matabele, went down before the white pioneers of civilization.

And while the white power of South Africa was thus spreading its far-reaching arms to enfold these enormous possessions, its heart was gaining strength and power in Kimberley and Johannesburg. Enterprise, backed by gold, is a life-current in the veins of a developing country whose value cannot be denied. But when the child is overgrowing itself, it is a dangerous experiment to endeavour to increase the functions of the heart by tinkering at its valves. Nature, if left to herself, will bring it right in the end.

The aim of the higher policy of South Africa is the amity and co-operation, if not the absolute confederation, of her various white states for their mutual good. The effect of the raid will merely be to put back the consummation for some years longer.

That higher policy is a matter which, apart from its present money aspect, should be of deepest interest to the people of England. Our Colonial expansion, especially in South Africa, is not undertaken with any idea of show-off, but for the actual use of our overflow population now, and, more especially, in the near future. Rhodesia comprises all that is worth having in the unoccupied parts of South Africa, and its ultimate development is perfectly assured, without the addition of the riches even of Johannesburg. Ten years back Kimberley was the heart and centre of South African wealth, as Johannesburg is today;

(as at time of first publication), and there is no reason why, within the next decade, an entirely new centre should not have sprung up in the virgin territories of Rhodesia. The chances are, in fact, largely in its favour. Even without a special boom, that part—and, indeed, the whole of civilized South Africa—will press steadily and rapidly forward; and it is even possible that out of the late evil good may come, and the lessons learned in the past few months may be of greatest value in guiding the steersmen in the future.

No doubt the two foremost obstacles to development in this part of the world are: firstly, insecurity; secondly, want of labour. And these are evils that seem to be capable of remedy.

In the matter of labour, the situation in South Africa is briefly this—in the mining and agricultural centres of the west and north, native labour is scarce; whereas in the south and east, where there is little demand for it, native material is lying idle in masses. The problem before the local statesmen is, how to effect a redistribution that would remedy this, and readjust the balance of supply and demand. The system which at present obtains in the east is to herd the natives together in "reserves," where, assured of a certain amount of land and perfect security, they settle themselves down to what is their ideal of life—namely, to bask on a sunny blanket, while their women raise the food. There is not the slightest incentive offered them to work or to improve themselves. They merely increase their numbers and hatch grievances, and thus become a danger in the land.

In Natal they number nearly three millions, against the six hundred thousand whites. Various plans have been considered for the amelioration of this state of affairs. It has been proposed so heavily to tax them, as to force them to work in order to raise the necessary cash; or to grant them freeholds for farming; or to transplant bodily whole reserves to mining centres; and so on. Whether one plan or many should be tried is a moot point; but it is very certain that some move in this direction is necessary for the development of the almost boundless resources of the country. White labour, if it were content to labour, and not to strive at once for fortunes, would, in that climate, thrive and do well; but it is a dream which, at present, does not work in practice. Were this otherwise. South Africa would prove a richer agricultural garden than Canada.

The sense of insecurity, which is the other stumbling-block to African development, arises from various causes, all of which seem open to remedy. The chief of these is the mutual jealousy and bad feeling between races and countries which are here crowded together. In addition to the native danger from Zulus, Swazis, *kaffirs*, Basutos, Matabele, and others, there are conflicting white interests. From the mining centres the Boers find themselves elbowed out by the capitalists; these, in their turn, are stirring against each other in the struggle for wealth,—German Jews competing with British prospectors, American experts against French financiers, and so on.

And, outside, colonies are mutually working against each other—Cape Colony against Natal, Chartered Company against the Transvaal,—all against all. Result general war of rates, freights, and customs, to the great detriment of the trade of each and the whole. Could the local statesmen rise above their present petty jealousies, and take a broad survey of the whole question of South African progress and prosperity, what a vast stride it might bring about in their mutual well-being, and in abolishing the present situation, where some parts of the country are intoxicated with wealth, while others are parched for want of it!

Chapter 19
After War—Peace

2nd December.—On the road at last. Although Salisbury has its charms as a dwelling-place, we were getting a bit anxious to be nearer the coast, and this afternoon we started with our three waggons and Cape cart and our riding horses.

Our last and least pleasing item in Salisbury was the hotel bill—for twelve days—five of us—£258. Board and lodging being two guineas a day, exclusive of drink, which is at the rate of 3*s.* for a whisky and soda. Eggs had touched 47*s.* a dozen. Ducks are still at 30*s.* each. Flour £7 10*s.* per 100 lbs. Tinned meat 2*s.* 3*d.* per lb. Fresh mutton 4*s.* 6*d.* per lb.

However, in spite of siege scarcity, I must say our manager, Rosenthal, did us wonderfully well. He contrived to give us eggs and bacon, omelets and fresh vegetables, cooked by a French *chef*, so we could not complain.

When we had outspanned near Ballyhooley (a place almost as pretty as its original in Ireland), and had just finished dinner. Lord Grey arrived there too, ahead of his waggons, with Lady Grey and Lady Victoria, and Howard, and they came and dined with us, pending arrival of their outfit. The ladies are bound for Beira, and for the ship that we hope to go in.

3rd December.—This Mashonaland is far prettier than Matabeleland, in some places beautiful, and very green after the recent rainstorms.

The wayside stores and inns, having been three years longer in existence than those in Matabeleland, are far more complete, well-built, and home-like, with some flower gardens, farmyards, pigsties, dove-cotes, &c., &c.—but all looted and empty, with recent graves and rough crosses near them.

4th December.—The country now is all green, wooded with rocky, bushy ridges and frequent tumbled-up granite *koppies* (some quite fantastic), and water in the streams.

My horse, the sole survivor of four, is picking up flesh rapidly with good grazing and corn, and being well looked after by a soldier servant whom I have got from the Irish company of the mounted infantry. This man, M'Grath, pleased me this morning by describing the horse as a "tedious feeder" (pronounced in the richest brogue)—meaning he was slow in eating his corn.

I gave up the horse this day in favour of the bike, and had a most enjoyable ride. Bikes have been issued to the police to use in place of horses, as the latter are hard to feed, and die in large numbers every year of horse sickness. But I think they ought to have tandem bikes,—not single ones,—because police should always go in pairs on long patrols, On a tandem one man can watch the ground and steer, while the other can look about lot enemies and can use his revolver—which cannot be done by single bikers.

5th December.—We passed the Mounted Infantry and the wounded going down from Salisbury to the coast, and met the men for the new police force jest coming up. A large number of them are Australians—a very fine-looking lot of young fellows.

This would make a grand country for colonizing. Judging from the few families we have seen, the locally-born children are as healthy and well-grown as you could wish. The great want in the town is that of cooks and domestic servants. With a good supply of these would follow much marrying and settling down on the part of many of the young prospectors, police, and farmers, who at present pour all their earnings into the hands of canteen-keepers. It is a pity that some system of importing a good class of women domestic servants is not tried, similar to that employed in Canada.

At Marendellas (fifty-one miles from Salisbury) we passed one of the fortified road posts, where we saw the graves of poor Evans, Barnes, and Morris, and of several men, all killed in action in the neighbourhood. At Headlands (eighty-eight miles) and Fort Haynes (a hundred and five miles), similar forts, were more such graves, including that of Captain Haynes, R.E., and others killed in the attack on Makoni's.

Near Fort Haynes were said to be some ancient ruins—so we rode over to see them. There were the remains of an old *kraal*, strongly fortified with a circular stone wall, a wide ditch, and a triple circle of trees which are now very big. It was certainly an ancient ruin, but not of the class of the Zimbabye ruins near Victoria. The general even said he had seen better stone walls in the Cotswold country. But in a neighbouring *koppie*, which was the burial-place of Makoni's father,—and a very sacred place to the natives,—we found a bit of wall made of square-cut stones neatly fitted together, much more like the Zimbabye style. The rocks within this wall formed some natural circular enclosures; one rock stood up on end, and several of them were pockmarked.

I don't think that Bent mentions whether the stones at Zimbabye are also pock-marked, but Ross, the Native commissioner with us, said they were. Well! the Phoenician temple at Hadjiar-Kim in Malta, and the Giant's Tower in Gozo, both contain pock-marked stones and rocks. These are supposed to be artificially worked to represent the firmament. Perhaps this should be another clue as to who were the builders of Zimbabye and other prehistoric ruins in Mashonaland, since they seem to have treated pockmarked stones as sacred.

Taberer, chief Native commissioner, who was with us, attributes the fortified *kraals* to the Vorosi people, who inhabited the country before the Mashonas, and have now disappeared northwards. They are a far cleverer race than most South African natives. The rock drawings in Mashonaland generally attributed to Bushmen, he says, are by them, and are superior to the usual Bushmen drawings.

7th December.—We got into broken, mountainous, and bushy country, and descended the Devil's Pass, a hundred and seventeen miles from Salisbury, a long descent among granite *koppies* and shady woods. A lion had been seen on the road the previous day here, but we saw nothing, though we used all our eyes. I hiked the afternoon trek, and got thoroughly drenched by a downpour in doing so. Next day I went to look for lions in most liony-looking country, but only saw one solitary steinbuck—which I shot.

9th December.—Umtali at last! A small town in a green basin among the mountains. A pretty, but dull place. "*A fair field and no favour*" is the reception with which Sir Wilfred Lawson would meet were he to come here. The surrounding greenery and its backing of wooded hills remind one of beautiful Sierra Leone, and, if the fever fiend be absent, still the drink fiend is there in its place.

Although we found rooms engaged for us at one of the hotels, we prepared to camp just outside the town. And we are certainly most

Maori B———e

comfortable in camp. The general lives in my little Cabul tent, and we other four fill a bell-tent. Our dining-room is a space between two waggons, roofed in with a roomy "buck-sail." Our table is a door laid on a trestle bedstead from a looted farm. And when we dine, we might imagine ourselves in a room, did not the lanterns light up in strong relief the massive wheels and under-carriages of the waggons on either side of us. Our conversation, too, is nearly drowned by the crunching of the mules feeding at their manger, which is hung along the *disselboom* (pole), and he who sits at the head of the table stands a good chance of being landed by a kick which he is well within reach of.

Tonight we had to dinner "Maori" B., who was with me with the Native Levy in Zululand in 1888. Celebrated over Africa for his yarns of fighting and adventure. Originally of a fine old Irish family—arrested, while a schoolboy from Cheltenham on his way to shoot at Wimbledon, on suspicion, of being a Fenian; enlisted as a gunner; blew up his father with a squib cigar; shot his man in a duel in Germany; hiked into the Lake of Geneva; went to New Zealand, where for twelve years he fought the Maoris; ate a child when starving; and afterwards hunted the bushrangers in Australia; took a schooner in search of a copper island, or anything else of value; next, a Papal Zouave; under Colonel Dodge, in America, he fought the Sioux.

When with Pullen's corps in South Africa, his men shot at him while bathing; he beat them with an ox-yoke; they stole an ostrich and hid it; a row among themselves followed, begun by a Kentish navvy, who complained he did not get his fair share of the "duck." B. denies that in the Maori war the Maoris displayed a flag of truce for more ammunition, but to ask the troops to stop firing shells into town, so as to let them have water—"else how can you expect us to fight?" they said. Then he became gold digger; later, fought in the Galeka war, then the Zulu, Dinizulu, first Matabele campaigns, and lastly the present operations, in which he is a major in the Umtali forces.

10th December.—The general and our party went out to the Pennalonga Mine, seven miles through pretty wooded hills, every one of which showed signs of having been prospected. At the mine, Jeffreys, the manager, and his bright bride did us right hospitably, and after lunch we went over part of the mine. Their working is simple; having found the reef in a watercourse in the mountain-side, they have followed it with "drives "both ways, and have met it with other drives from the opposite side of the hill. The ore (of "*gallina*") containing something much over 20 oz. of silver and 11 dwt. of gold, a lot of it very pretty with the garnet-like crystals of chromate of lead. We walked into one *adit* about four hundred feet, and saw the working; cross-cuts showed the reef eighteen feet across. The air was not very good, and we could with great difficulty keep our candles alight.

They have just put up a 5-stamp battery to be worked with a turbine, the water being led from the top of the mountain above the mill

A ROADSIDE HOTEL IN MASHONALAND
The nearest hut is the "Coffee-Room". The farther one is the "Bedroom."
The "Smoking-Room" is in the open air.

by pipes which are now being laid, so that in a short time the mine should be in full work. The only obstruction at present is the famine price of food, which prevents the company employing sufficient black labour (which they have to feed).

There are several other mines in the valley, but none so forward as this, though one has a splendid waterfall to supply its power in the future.

We saw some gold-washing done as the prospectors do it. With a pestle and mortar the quartz is crushed to powder, and then washed in water in a shallow pan (which has a tip in it for the use of unskilful washers, for washing is a knack).

The liquid mud is then swirled around and shaken, so that the heavier ingredients work to the bottom of the sediment, and the waste is poured off. As this in its turn gets washed out with fresh water, a little "tailing" of yellow dust is seen at the edges of the sediment, which is then washed out till nothing is left in the pan but the thin little streak of gold dust. If 8 dwts. of this can be extracted from a ton of ore, it will be sufficient to repay expenses of mining.

16th December.—Packed up our kits and started on our last trek, from Umtali to the coast. Umtali itself is very pretty, but when five miles from there we came to the top of Christmas Pass, and began to descend, we had splendid view of grand, rolling mountains, with wide, rich valleys, and wooded hills.

We crossed the site of New Umtali, whither Umtali is to be moved to be on the railway line. (While we were at Umtali, the inhabitants came to claim compensation from Rhodes. Of course he had some new way of meeting the difficulty. It was reported that he took each man in turn, got at his price, and by the afternoon had bought Umtali as it stood for £40,000.)

At New Umtali I spotted *such* a site for a house!—with a view in front of it that will make me yearn that way for a good long time to come.

Our road went down and down (splendid run had one been on a bike; the whole distance, Umtali to Chimoio, has been done in nine hours on a bike), diving down into deep, dark valleys between thickly-wooded hills, then through forest plains, with peeps between the trees of great blue mountains looming high on either side.

Frequent along the road are inns—clean and neat, all kept by Englishmen—in thatched wattle and daub huts.

At Massi Kessi (*alias* Macequece) we got into Portuguese territory. Massi Kessi was the place where the Chartered Company's forces (consisting of thirty-three men) were attacked by the Portuguese to the number of seven hundred (five hundred of them native troops). A few volleys and rounds of case-shot from the British sufficed to drive back the enemy; and their officers, unable to rally the men, stood on one side and surrendered. The British force then went on to the fort—a very strong place from which the Portuguese had sallied—and took it with all its contents. These included the flag (which had been left flying in the hurried departure of the garrison), some guns, machine guns, and mess furniture, which are still in use with the Chartered Company's forces. That Massi Kessi has since been replaced by the present township, eight miles from it.

This is a township of one square of about fifteen houses altogether, of which one is the Government House, and twelve are drinking bars. In Rhodesia liquor is not allowed to be sold to coloured men, but in Portuguese territory there is no restriction; consequently all our drivers (seven) and those of Mr. Rhodes' and Lord Grey's waggon, which were with us, all got more or less drunk—most of them more. They had saved up their pay in anticipation of this occasion. I was not sorry to hear that two of them, having got hopelessly incapable, were robbed of £30 by the liquor-seller. We had to adopt strong measures with our own hands the next two nights to keep their fighting and noise within tolerable bounds in camp.

17th December.—At the Revuwe River and hut hotel we were overtaken by Cecil Rhodes, Sir Charles Metcalfe, and others, also travelling to the coast.

Rhodes had asked us to stay at his beautiful old place near Cape Town, Groot Schur, but when he met us this morning, he said, "I am sorry to find that I shall not be able to give you accommodation at my house. It has been burnt to the ground. It is a great pity, because there were some old things there that could not be replaced. I liked my house. Providence has not been kind to me this year, what with Jameson's raid, rinderpest, rebellion, famine, and now my house burnt, I feel rather like Job, but, thank God, I haven't had sores yet. Still, there remains some of the year, and there is yet a chance for me to develop some totally new kind of boil. That would be the height of evils, to have a boil called after one. Fancy being inventor of the Rhodes boil!" And then he sent a telegram: "Having heard indirectly that my house has been burnt, please put up tents in the garden, as I don't want to live at an hotel."

Our last trek, eight miles today, brought us to the railway. It was a delight to come on an embankment with its rails and telegraph in the midst of wildest-looking bush—and then to hear the shriek of the engine as an empty train came rumbling up to fetch us to the coast. All that night and up to four o'clock next day we rattled along through the bush, at first among small hills, latterly over the flats—all the time in deep, soggy heat. How one longed for a breeze—and when it came, how disappointing it was—like hot eiderdown pressing against one. At times in the thicker bush one could well imagine oneself on the new railway in Ashanti.

18th December.—Early in the morning, about four, a hurried whistling of the engine and much jabbering of our nigger servants in the baggage truck apprised us that three lions were calmly walking along the line in front of us, thinking the road had been made especially for them. They deigned to make way for the beast that breathed flame and smoke, and they skipped off into the jungle. A month ago a prospector named Brown was killed by lions, while walking along the line here.

Now and again we pass camps of railway men, a white overseers' tent, with a few straw huts of native labourers; and once or twice small stations where up and down trains pass each other, and travellers can get food; but we had no need to avail ourselves of them, for our train was full (too full for comfort) of railway officials and others, each of whom had brought a box of food, chiefly champagne, beer, and sandwiches; and at odd hours of night as well as day one thirsty soul or another would get at his box, break bulk, and wake up everybody to have a snack. They meant well, but eternal champagne and beef, especially at 5 a.m., when one would have given worlds for a cup of tea or coffee and some bread and butter—it was *cloying*, to say the least.

Fever was evident everywhere. At one station the telegraph clerk handed us in some perfectly illegible and nonsensical telegrams. He was half-unconscious with fever, and we never discovered who were the senders or what the purport of these messages. We had to change engines, as our driver had an attack of fever. At a new bridge five out of eleven white men were down.

At Fontes Villa, a little town built on piles, at present the railway headquarters, we *déjeunered* with the manager of the line in a beautifully green verandah. Such fruit I mangoes, bananas, *grenadillas*, limes, and pineapples. Thermometer 115° in the shade.

Smart, gentlemanly young fellows acting in all the lower as well as upper railway capacities, but with lots of life and lots of death, for Fontes Villa possesses two cemeteries—one, the "old" one (three years old), being full, the new one had been made nearer to the station, to be more "handy," and this one also looks like being full very soon.

About twenty miles farther on, somebody spied the masts of a ship above the bush, and soon we ran into the station at Beira.

Beira is a long town of about 1500 inhabitants, the houses built along a spit of sand for two miles between the sea and a mangrove creek. With good wharf, storehouses, a tile-roofed hospital, and a curiosity in a great square red and white lighthouse, substantial-looking, but on close inspection showing itself to be of corrugated iron, painted.

We did not wait to look at these, but got ourselves and baggage transferred without delay to the s.s. *Pongola*, lying off the shore in the mouth of the Pungwe River. The Pungwe here opens from its flat mangrove banks into an estuary some ten miles across.

After dinner (which happily was laid on deck, after the manner of the Florio-Rubbatino ships in the Mediterranean), the general, Rhodes, Sir Charles Metcalfe, and I went ashore to call on Colonel Machado, the Portuguese commandant. We found him a handsome, clever-looking man of forty-five, speaking English well, and full of knowledge of the country, and very friendly; but his house was mighty hot, and we were glad to get back into our homeward car in the open air.

The roads in Beira are of deep soft sand by nature, but their imperfections had been got over by art. A little tram line runs along the main street, with offshoots to all the by-roads. Public and private tramcars, holding four persons each, run along the rail, propelled by shoving niggers.

19th December.—After a general farewell visit of friends from the shore, we got under way at 10 a.m.

How good it is to feel the first few heaves of the screw as the ship is being turned in the yellow tide to set her head for home!

We steamed out through the seventeen miles of sandbanks that form the mouth of the Pungwe and Busi Rivers. We stuck for half an hour on one shoal, but floated off with the rising tide, and soon dropped the low flat shore of Beira out of sight.

22nd December.—Passed along the coast of Zululand in the morning, seeing familiar spots like Etschowe (Signal Hill), the Tugela, and finally reached Durban—steaming boldly into the harbour and alongside the wharf, where ships were moored two deep. At Durban we landed the troops, and spent four hours.

How the place has grown since I was here seven years ago! The long road from the Point to the town is lined with villas and gardens in place of sandhills and shanties. The streets are full of bustling people—English ladies, carriages, tramcars, and 'rickshaws. The latter in swarms, with Zulu runners dressed up in war headdresses and with rattles on their legs, "playing at horses" as they run, great children that they are—tossing their plumes and stepping up to their noses.

Saw old Reuben Beningfield, and had happy reminders of old shooting days with him; Little, 9th Lancers, and Sir Walter Hely Hutchinson, the governor, and Jameson, who does not alter one jot, and many other friends. At six we sailed again for Port Elizabeth.

After this brief flash of life in civilization we are once more getting along, butting against obstructive wave power, and pressing into the darkling haze.

23rd December.—Cloud-wrack and wind, and pale, deceitful sea. Heaving along, we churn our way, till out of the dark swish of the driving rain on a rushing, riotous sea, we suddenly emerge into sunshine and calm in Port Elizabeth roadstead.

Amid the blaze of bunting, and a babel of steamers' whistles and cheering masses, we follow Cecil Rhodes ashore into the Liverpool of South Africa—and Liverpool at Christmas time (for today is Christmas Eve). A banquet lunch of five hundred in the Feather Market, and a dinner at the club at night. Torchlight procession, bands, and "waits." The whole town—with deputations, too, from all the other "Eastern Province" towns—was keen to do him and Sir Frederick honour; and we, the staff, came in for the full benefit of reflected hospitality. They did us royally! But the genuineness of the feeling towards Rhodes was unmistakable and impressive. It was not a gust of got-up welcome, but a spontaneous burst of enthusiasm, in a place that formerly was distinctly hostile to him. He made five separate speeches in the course of the day—all characteristic.

Christmas Day.—From the rush and whirl of yesterday, one woke to absolute peace in a bright, English-looking bedroom, looking on an English garden with a something more than English wealth of flowers. One could not stay in bed on such a cheerful, sunny morning. After a grand freshwater tub, Vyvyan and I sallied out to stretch our legs. We started at half-past eight, and only returned ravenous to the club three hours later, after walking out and round the whole of Port Elizabeth. Our walk showed us the miles of busy railway and shipping-wharves, and the stores along the sea-front. Then, by mutual consent, we got out on to the *veldt* outside the town, both impelled by the same object, *viz*. to get our coats off. The feeling of sleeves on our arms, when we had been going bare-armed for months, was too irritating to be borne; so we offed coats, rolled up our sleeves, and were happy on the open, breezy racecourse downs, with views of inland veldt and mountains.

Then the Park and Botanical Gardens; and the upper town, with avenues of pretty suburban houses, deep sunk in their shady verandahs, with their trim and flowery gardens. In every other one, jolly English children were playing about, and raising their cheery shouts. I only thought how good an object lesson it would be to ship a load of "Little Englanders" out even to this spot alone, just to open their eyes to what a busy, homely colony it is (and yet it is only one of many), and to see what an enormous future generation of strapping colonists is growing up in the glorious sunlight here, for the service of their mother-country.

After breakfast to church. Everything exactly ordered as if at home: the Christmas Day choral service, with a good choir and a fine organ.

And as the anthem of peace and goodwill rolled forth, it brought home to one the fact that a year of strife in savage wilds had now been weathered to a peaceful close.

DOLCE FAR NIENTE

General Sir F. Carrington and Mr. Cecil Rhodes on the homeward journey.
N.B.—A lady critic has written to say that although not an admirer of my sketches generally, in this instance she is pleased with "Rhodes' feet"!

L'envoi

There is little more to add.

That night we were on the ocean steamer *Moor*. Two days later found us at the Cape.

2nd January.—Table Mountain grows grander and more living every time I see him. His personality grows on one, like that of the Taj Mahal at Agra. I can quite understand certain races worshipping a mountain as their idea of Divinity. Always steadfast and stupendous. You may turn your back on Him and wander away for a while; but whenever you choose to look back, He is there, the same as ever. You have only to go back into His shadow, to find a haven from the chilling wind or withering sun. And you may climb up to Him, to where He sits above the clouds,—which is feasible in proportion to the state of training you are in,—and when you have reached the summit, you can lay you down in peace upon His breast, and contemplate the world below which you have left behind,

6th January.—Cape Town is very busy now, with crowded streets, big shops, electric lighting everywhere, electric trams cavorting through the streets and out to Claremont: such a change from the sleepy, old-world place it used to be. It is much *en fête* for Rhodes.

Today we embarked on the *Dunvegan Castle* (Captain Robinson); splendid new boat. Also on board Cecil Rhodes, Miss Rhodes, and Colonel Frank Rhodes; Lady Grey and Lady Victoria Grey; Sir C. Metcalfe; Olive Schreiner and her husband; Lord C. Bentinck; Hon. J. Ward, M.P.; Rochfort Maguire and his wife; Wilson Tod and Critchley, 4th Hussars; "Bob" Coryndon (also styled Selous the Second), Ronny Moncreiffe, Sir Horace MacMahon, and Eustace, Blewitt, &c., &c., and hardly any Jews! A most interesting shipload.

And we left the Cape and its old mountain bathed in the glow of its summer sun—sorry, and yet glad, to go.

A good deck cabin, and the many comforts of Sir Donald Currie's finest ship, coupled with the varied cheery company on board, made the time fly by. We slipped past Cape de Verd on the 13th, and Madeira at night on the 18th.

27th January.—It is a day to be remembered, is that of a return from foreign parts.

As we head into the green heights around Plymouth, there is one excited old Colonist, button-holing everyone in turn, shouting with eager irony, "Saw you ever *veldt* like yon green hills?" And as a fog of driving sleet bursts like a blizzard on us, a mad heart-choking cheer goes up of joy to see real snow again.

A little red-bearded Scottish missionary is dancing wildly about the deck, with his coat-tails flying, yelling, "Man! I haena seen the snaw for twenty years!"

Why does not someone laugh at him? We can't.

We are back once more in the yellow fog and the grimy slush of thawing snow in dear old, same old England.

Then, from the rushing hum of the special train, through the roar of the sloppy, lamp-lit streets, to the comfort and warmth—of Home.

The Downfall of Prempeh, a Diary of Life
With the Native Levy in Ashanti, 1895-6

Contents

The Author's Apology to the Reader	279
Reasons for the Ashanti Expedition of 1895-96	281
Preliminaries to the Expedition	295
Local Preparations	300
At Cape Coast Castle	305
The Levy Starts	306
In the Bush	308
Pioneer Work	315
The Scouts	323
The Bekwai Column	326
Forward Movements	335
In Kumassi	338
Preparing the "Coup"	344
The Downfall	346
After Events	352
The Coastward March	356
Homeward Bound	364
The Formation of a Native Levy	369
Policy and Wealth in Ashanti, 1895	379

The Author's Apology to the Reader

One lives but to learn.

Whatever may have been the political result of the late expedition on the Gold Coast, its military aim was altogether defeated by the passive submission of the Ashantis.

I am not too proud to take a cue from our late foes. Therefore, in offering these notes to the public, I would at once disarm any intending critics by giving in to everything they may urge against me.

The book does not purport to be a full and detailed history of the operations,—my position with the native levy, at a usual distance of several days' march from the central direction of affairs, precludes the accuracy and personal knowledge necessary for such a task, and I should hope that there will be many historians far better qualified, who will produce the necessary history.

My sketch—for it shall be nothing more—will merely be a rough diary of the campaign from my point of view. I have one object, and one only, in writing. That object is, to escape the further importunity of my friends.

On every side I am badgered—and I suppose that most of the other members of the expedition have been similarly badgered—with the remark:

"Oh, you have come back? Now I *do* hope you are writing a book about it. You are wasting your opportunities if you don't."

These importunities have reached a climax. I will take the plunge. I will shut myself up for four days, and will overhaul my diary.

I only beg of the reader not to judge me harshly, but to picture me entering on the fray with a faltering pen, dragged on by overzealous friends, and bolstered up with the kind assistance of the *Journal of the Royal United Service Institute*, the *Daily Graphic*, the *Daily Chronicle*, and the *Graphic*, whose editors have generously allowed me to draw upon them for material.

That my tale should not be entirely futile, I shall endeavour to make it point a moral, and to save the reader the trouble of wading through its tedious pages. I will here at once say that the moral may be summed up thus:

A smile and a stick will carry you through any difficulty in the world, more especially if you act upon the old West Coast Motto, "*Softly, softly, catchee monkey.*"

This axiom would not have been offered did it not hold good equally in the lesser as in the larger developments of the campaign. The expedition itself, well-disposed, yet determined, was at once a smile and a stick. By quietly taking possession of Ashanti, it has practically acquired the vast Hinterland beyond—it has softly caught the monkey. And the principle is being carried out in all quarters of the world. In Siam, in Venezuela, and up the Nile, England goes softly, softly, catching her monkey.

And what is a sound principle for an empire is a safe one for an individual.

R. S. S. B-P.

Chapter 1
Reasons for the Ashanti Expedition of 1895-96

In the African bush one may see a lion making his meal on the beast which he unaided has hunted, and is slain by his mighty power; and round him, shrieking and snarling, snatching and tearing, there skips a craven pack of jackals.

One need not go so far as Africa to seek a similar scene. Within a hundred miles of Westminster it may be found.

When a travelling Briton has returned from roaming among the broad lands of our empire beyond the seas, he finds that his ideas have become enlarged, his "bosom swells with pride" at his being a heritor of this vast prize of generations of British lions, and he realises for the first time what it is "to be an Englishman," and how there is not much temptation "to belong to any other nation "so long as our navy rules the seas.

But should he feel a little too "uppish" in this elation and pride of birth, he can readily find an antidote. Let him obtain a ticket for the Strangers' Gallery in the House of Commons, and let him go and see for himself the working of what the nation is pleased to call its brain. There he will find—on both sides of the House (for I have no party predilections)—a few lions and a great many jackals behind them. The petty jabber and snarl of these as they snatch and worry at the subject under discussion well-nigh drowns the occasional, meaning "sough" of their betters.

A growl is enough to scatter them all like chaff, but only for a moment, and *anon* they are back again, blathering as before.

The scene fills one with a sense of humiliation, and yet, on the other hand, it shows the lions in even a better light than before: they have to carry out their hunting not merely unaided, but handicapped by the incessant yapping at their heels of a pack utterly incapable of hunting for itself.

To one just back from Ashanti not many days ago, it was particularly pleasing to hear the Secretary of State for the Colonies replying, with reference to that country, to a chorus of yaps. In a brief but very complete manner, he stated the reasons which had led to the despatch of the expedition under Sir Francis Scott.

The main contentions which he had to meet were, firstly, that the claim on the King of Ashanti which produced the expedition was absolutely unjustifiable; and, secondly, that even if it were justifiable, it could have been secured by a means much less costly than an expedition to Kumassi. As a preliminary to dealing with these questions, Mr. Chamberlain disclaimed any ulterior motive in the expedition as having respect to the doings of the French in West Africa—the expedition was undertaken solely in the interests of the Gold Coast Colony, and at the request, often repeated, of the inhabitants of that colony. Both they and the government considered that steps must be taken to suppress what was neither more nor less than an intolerable and injurious nuisance. The government of the King of Ashanti had, ever since 1874, stood in the way of civilization, of trade, and of the interests of the people themselves, and should, on these general grounds alone, be put a stop to. He put it thus:

> From the date of the war in 1873 and 1874 this district of Africa, which is, I believe, extremely rich—certainly rich in natural resources, probably rich in mineral resources—has been devastated, destroyed, and ruined by inter-tribal disputes, and especially by the evil government of the authorities of Ashanti. No sooner was the present ruler installed as king of the country than he began to make war upon every tribe in the neighbourhood, and the consequent loss of life was very great. I often think it is so extraordinary for gentlemen like the hon. member for Caithness to talk of the loss of life involved in the expedition.
>
> It cannot be placed in the same category as the loss of life which has been going on year after year, month after month, simply because we had not the courage and the resolution to make the expedition. (Cheers.) I think the duty of this country in regard to all these savage countries over which we are called

upon to exercise some sort of dominion is to establish, at the earliest possible date. *Pax Britannia*, and force these people to keep the peace amongst themselves (cheers), and by so doing, whatever may be the destruction of life in an expedition which brings about this result, it will be nothing if weighed in the balance against the annual loss of life which goes on so long as we keep away.

What is the state of things in Ashanti and in many other of these West African and African possessions? The people are not a bad people. The natives are, on the whole, perfectly willing to work, and if they fight, they fight because they cannot help themselves. They would always rather settle down to commercial or agricultural pursuits if they were allowed to do so, but in such cases as that we are considering, the government is so atrociously bad that they were not allowed to do so. No man is safe in the enjoyment of his own property, and as long as that is the case, no one has any inducement to work.

But in addition to these general grounds for action being taken against the Ashanti regime, there exist more particular reasons for it in the refusal of the king to carry out the provisions of the treaty of 1874.

The danger of allowing treaty contracts to be evaded is fairly well understood among European nations, but the results of slackness or leniency in their enforcement are none the less dangerous when the treaty has been made with an uncivilized potentate, since his neighbours are quick to note any sign of weakness or loss of prestige on the part of the white contracting party, and they in their turn gain courage to make a stand against the white ruler and his claims over them.

In Ashanti the abuse had been allowed to go on far too long. Natives near our border—ay, within it too—had seen year after year go by, and the Ashanti liberty taking the form of license more and more pronounced, with little or no restraint beyond mild and useless remonstrance on our part. Naturally this raised the Ashantis once more in their estimation, while it lowered our prestige in a corresponding degree; and although the people were sufficiently knowing to see that under our government they were their own masters and were able to carry out any ideas of commerce that they might entertain, still they also saw that, as far as local indications went, the Ashantis were equal in power to the white men, and, as a natural consequence, they were

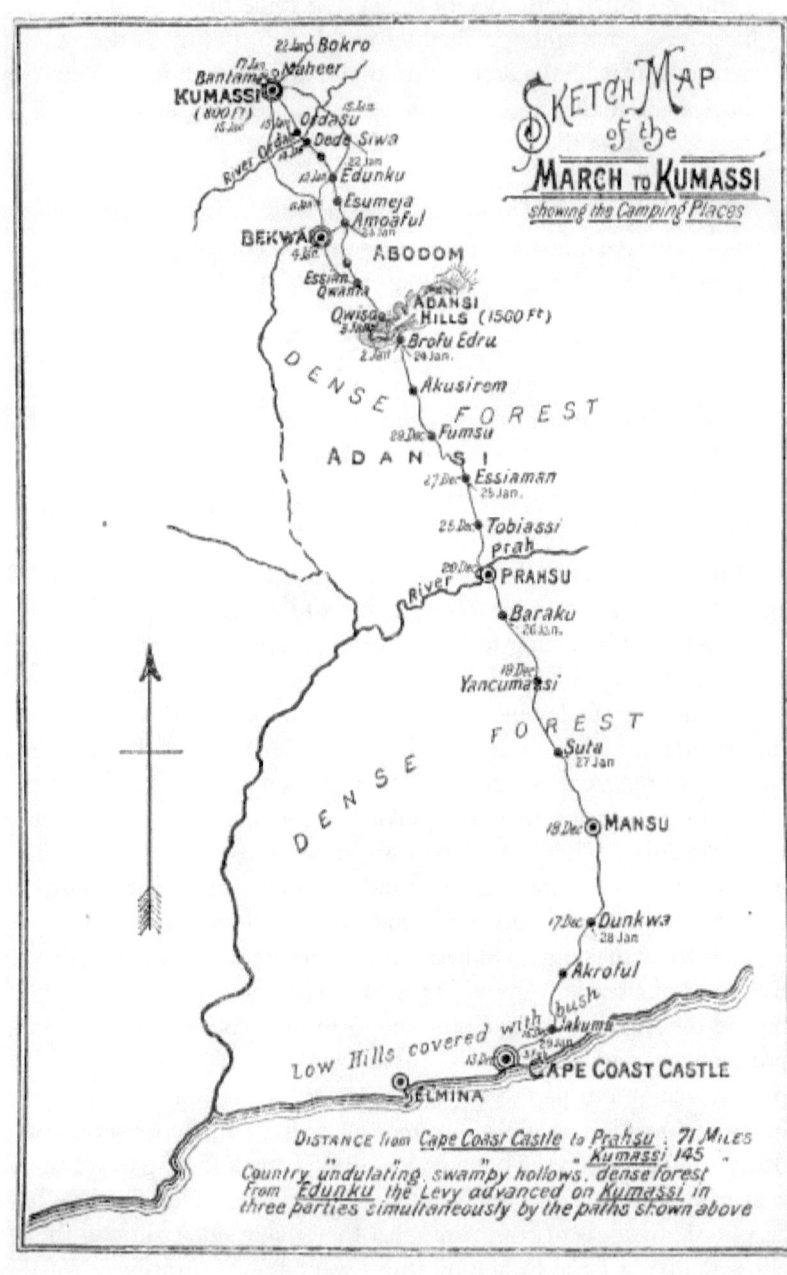

much inclined at least to waver in their allegiance to us.

"*Britons never will be slaves*," and Britons are so peculiarly imbued with a notion of fair-play that they will not see anybody else in a state of slavery either, if they can prevent it.

Slaves in some parts of the world form the currency of the country; in others they are the beasts of burden and the machinery; often their lot is mercilessly hard, though not always.

Wherever there is a good market for them, it is to the interest of the owner to keep them well fed and in good condition. In those parts where domestic slavery prevails, there is often little or no hardship. An occasional lick from a whip is, to an unintelligent savage but a small matter where in the opposite scale he has the very substantial compensation of protection, food, and home—advantages which are not always shared by his white brother when fate has frowned and has turned him into the cold to work out his living among the unemployed.

The worst part of slavery is, as a rule, the hardships entailed in the slave-caravan marches, which have to be conducted at a forced pace over desert and devious routes, in order to avoid the good intentions of the European antislavery forces.

But in no part of the world does slavery appear to be more detestable than in Ashanti. Slaves, other than those obtained by raids into neighbours' territory, have here to be smuggled through the various "spheres," French, German, and English, which are beginning to hem the country in on every side. The climate they are brought to is a sickly one for men bred up-country.

They are not required for currency, since gold-dust is the medium here.

Nor are they required to any considerable extent as labourers, since the Ashanti lives merely on vegetables, which in this country want little or no cultivation.

And yet there is a strong demand for slaves. They are wanted for human sacrifice. Stop human sacrifice, and you deal a fatal blow to the slave trade, while you render raiding an unprofitable game.

Up till the time of the expedition raiding had been carried on systematically in direct contravention of treaty.

> The expedition was necessary also for the protection of other tribes. Every tribe in the neighbourhood of Ashanti lived in terror of its life from the king, who had on several occasions

destroyed, one after another, tribes which had sought our protection. There were at least half a dozen separate tribes under separate kings or chieftains who had been driven out of their country and to a large extent destroyed, the whole trade and commerce being utterly ruined in consequence of the continued raids, made against the representations of the British authorities, by the King of Ashanti. In order to prevent that, from time to time the British Government took some of the tribes under its protection. In my opinion a great mistake was made in refusing sooner to take under our protection tribes that asked that protection merely in order that they might engage in peaceful commerce, always with the result that the tribe was immediately afterwards eaten up by the tribes of Ashanti.

On one occasion the tribes of Ashanti marched into another kingdom which had been taken under the protection of the British Government. We had to send, at considerable expense, an armed force in order to protect these territories. It is true that in the presence of that force the tribes of the King of Ashanti were withdrawn. But it was only under threat of our intervention that they were withdrawn. The finances of the colony have suffered for years by keeping up larger forces in order to protect tribes under our protection. I think I have said enough to show that we should have been wanting in our duty if we had not insisted that this state of things should be stopped.

In England we scarcely realise the extent to which human sacrifice had been carried on in Ashanti previous to the late expedition, but evidences were not wanting to show it.

In the first place, the name *Kumassi* means "the death-place."

The town possessed no less than three places of execution; one, for private executions, was at the palace; a second, for public decapitations, was on the parade-ground; a third, for fetish sacrifices, was in the sacred village of Bantama.

Close to the parade-ground was the grove into which the remains of the victims were flung, and which very aptly was known as "Golgotha" to the members of the force. The ground here was found covered with skulls and bones of hundreds of victims. At Bantama was the celebrated execution bowl, which was fully described by Bowdich in his account of Kumassi in 1817. It is a large brass basin some five feet in diameter. It is ornamented with four small lions, and a number of round knobs all round its rim, except at one part, where there is a space for the victim's neck to rest on the edge. The blood of the victims was allowed to putrefy in the bowl, and leaves of certain herbs being added, it was considered a very valuable fetish medicine. The bowl has now been brought to England. Then in Kumassi are two blocks of houses occupied entirely by the executioners—one being assigned to the sacrificial, the other to the criminal executioners. Among the loot taken in the houses of Prempeh and of his chiefs were several "blood stools," or stools which had been used as blocks for executions, and which bore very visible signs of having been so used. In these notes, be it remembered, we are only dealing with Kumassi, but every king—and there were some half a dozen of them in the Ashanti empire—had powers of life and death over his subjects, and carried out his human sacrifices on a minor scale in his own capital.

In fact, the ex-king of Bekwai was deposed on account of his overindulgence in that form of amusement.

Any great public function was seized on as an excuse for human sacrifices. There was the annual "yam custom," or harvest festival, at which large numbers of victims were often offered to the gods. Then the king went every quarter to pay his devotions to the shades of his ancestors at Bantama, and this demanded the deaths of twenty men over the great bowl on each occasion. On the death of any great personage, two of the household slaves were at once killed on the threshold of the door, in order to attend their master immediately in his new life, and his grave was afterwards lined with the bodies of more slaves who were to form his retinue in the spirit world. It was thought all the better if, during the burial, one of the attendant mourners could be stunned by a club, and dropped, still breathing, into the grave before it was filled in. In the case of a great lady dying, slave-girls were the victims. This custom of sacrifice at funerals was called "washing the grave."

On the death of a king the custom of washing the grave involved enormous sacrifices. Then sacrifices were also made to propitiate the gods when war was about to be entered upon or other trouble was impending. Victims were also killed to deter an enemy from approaching the capital; sometimes they were impaled and set up on the path, with their hand pointing to the enemy and bidding him to retire. At other times the victim was beheaded and the head replaced looking in the wrong direction; or he was buried alive in the pathway, standing upright, with only his head above ground, to remain thus until starvation or—what was infinitely worse—the ants made an end of him. Then there was a death penalty for the infraction of various laws. For instance, anybody who found a nugget of gold and who did not send it at once to the king was liable to decapitation; so also was anybody who picked up anything of value lying on the parade-ground, or who sat down in the shade of the fetish tree at Bantama.

Indeed, if the king desired an execution at any time, he did not look far for an excuse. It is even said that on one occasion he preferred a richer colour in the red *stucco* on the walls of the palace, and that for this purpose the blood of four hundred virgins was used. I have purposely refrained elsewhere from giving numbers, because, although our informants supplied them. West African natives are notoriously inexact in this respect. The victims of sacrifices were almost always slaves or prisoners of war. Slaves were often sent in to the king in lieu of tribute from his kinglets and chiefs, or as a fine for minor delinquencies. Travelling traders of other tribes, too, were frequently called upon to pay customs dues with a slave or two, and sometimes their own lives were forfeited.

When once a man had been selected and seized for execution, there were only two ways by which he could evade it. One was to repeat the "king's oath"—a certain formula of words—before they could gag him; the other was to break loose from his captors and run as far as the Bantama-Kumassi cross road; if he could reach this point before being overtaken, he was allowed to go free. In order to ensure against their prisoners getting off by either of these methods, the executioners used to spring on the intended victim from behind, and while one bound his hands behind his back, another drove a knife through both his cheeks, which effectually prevented him from opening his mouth to speak, and in this horrible condition he had to await his turn for execution. When the time came, the executioners, mad with blood, would make a rush for him and force him on to the bowl or stool, whichever served as the block. Then one of them, using a large kind of butcher's knife, would cut into the spine, and so carve the head off.

As a rule, the victims were killed without extra torture, but if the order was given for an addition of this kind, the executioners vied with each other in devising original and fiendish forms of suffering. At great executions torture was apparently resorted to in order to please the spectators. It certainly seems that the people had by frequent indulgence become imbued with a kind of blood-lust, and that

Human sacrifice at Bantama

to them an execution was as attractive an entertainment as is a bull-fight to a Spaniard or a footballmatch to an Englishman.

This custom is one which a clause in the treaty of 1874 stipulated was to cease, but the contract was never carried out by the king. In spite of his promises, sacrifices went on up till the time of the expedition. It was even said that an execution came off at the palace the day after our arrival at Kumassi.

Another clause of the treaty which King Prempeh had failed to carry into effect was that which promised the maintenance of an open high-road from Kumassi to Cape Coast Castle. The idea of this road was not only to render communication with Kumassi comparatively easy, but also to open a way through the two hundred miles of impassable forest which shut off the rich plains of the Hinterland from access to the coast. It was argued, with reason, that if such road were kept open for pack caravans, a big trade would at once be opened up with the interior; but the king neglected to carry out his part of the treaty.

The road was allowed to become overgrown again with the rank, thick jungle of the bush, and the slight foot-track to which it dwindled was used by a few small bands of rubber-dealers, but these traded at great risk and for small returns, owing to the heavy dues and peremptory punishments imposed by the Ashantis on traders passing through their country. Remonstrance had no effect. Without an expedition it looked as though the mass of trade awaiting an outlet from the Hinterland would either die off or would be diverted into neighbouring countries belonging to France and Germany.

Another item in the bill against the king was the payment of the war indemnity for the last expedition. Of this the first two instalments had been paid, but since then not a *stiver*.

Briefly, then, we may look on the following as the main reasons and objects for the expedition:—

To put an end to human sacrifice.

To put a stop to slave-trading and raiding.

To ensure peace and security for the neighbouring tribes.

To settle the country and protect the development of trade.

To get paid up the balance of the war indemnity.

Experience had shown that it was of no avail to trust to the king carrying out the terms of a treaty, and therefore it was considered necessary to appoint a resident at Kumassi who would see that the king carried out his engagements.

The king was asked whether he approved of this plan. At first he

PORTRAIT OF KING PREMPEH

altogether refused to accept a resident. Then he sent insulting replies. Another time he sent no reply. And, finally he declined to deal with the governor of the colony, but sent envoys to England. The story of this part of the case was thus stated by the Secretary of State for the Colonies:—

> The king said he had sent his messengers to see the Queen of England and make known his wishes. Lord Ripon sent word to the Governor of the Gold Coast to tell the messengers if they came to England that they would not be received by the queen or her representatives. He actually forbade their coming to England, although he did not feel justified in preventing them by force. On what grounds did Lord Ripon take this course? He had many grounds. In the first place, that their character was bad; in the second place, that they were representatives of a king who indulged in human sacrifice, and that the representatives of such a potentate were not to be received by the Queen of England (cries of 'Oh, oh!'); and, in the third place, that in dealing with these subject tribes under the circumstances which I have detailed, it would be absolutely ruinous to the governor on the spot if, at any moment you chose, you could pass him by and claim to be received directly in London.
>
> We place a great responsibility upon the heads of the governors whom we send out to those distant places, and who have to act very often on the spur of the moment; and if we ourselves reduce their authority in the eyes of these subjects, there would be simply no end to the representations with which we should have to deal in this country, and to the tricks by which these savage rulers would escape from their responsibility. When I came to office the matter came before me, having been already decided by my predecessor. I do not want, on that account, in the slightest degree to lessen my responsibility. If I had occupied office at the time Lord Ripon did, I should have taken exactly the same course.
>
> These persons came to England, and I refused to receive them. Representations were made to me on their behalf by a member of this House; and I said I would be most happy to receive him, but I refused to recognise him as their representative. He did not desire to be recognised as their representative, but wished on his own account to place before me some statements which

he had heard from them. Their statement was to the effect that they had credentials from the King of Ashanti; that they had plenipotentiary authority from him to deal with me as the representative of the government; and, finally, that they were prepared to accept the terms which I informed the gentleman who saw me it was our intention to demand.

Well, I told them I accepted their assurances for what they were worth (laughter); but that Her Majesty's Government would not on that account countermand the expedition. It is very easy, of course, to say we should have stopped the expedition; that we would have saved the expenditure and attained the same result. That is a hypothetical statement. I confess I have not the remotest belief that we should have attained the same result, or anything like it. And I think I have some reason for saying that when I had to make my decision, of course, I did not know all the facts, but what I did know was that if the expedition was held back, and if, thereafter, these so-called envoys were repudiated by the King of Ashanti, not only would great expenditure have been incurred for no purpose, but we should have to repeat the expedition at a time when, owing to the difficulties of season and climate, the loss of life would have been very much greater.

I thought the risk too great. What justification has come to hand of the action which we took in this matter? In the first place, these so-called envoys had absolutely no authority whatever to make the terms to which they gave their signature; their credentials were forged credentials, the seal of the King of Ashanti was manufactured in London after they came here (laughter); they had no power whatever to accept the conditions imposed upon them by Her Majesty's Government; and the only authority they had was authority which they themselves had sought to obtain redress from Her Majesty's Government for the grievances of the Ashanti people. And it is perfectly clear that what I feared would have taken place, and that if they had gone back without an expedition they would have been repudiated, and properly repudiated, by the Ashanti king. Then it is said, 'Why this display of force?' In order to avoid bloodshed. (Cheers.)

It is also said that all this might have been done by a small force, and I believe that is true, but it would not have been done without bloodshed. If we had gone there with a small force we should have tempted the Ashantis to war. Do not let it be supposed that the Ashanti king had no idea of resistance. You will find that he sent an embassy to Samory, who is a powerful chief, inviting him to join in resisting the British attack; and nothing but the sense of his own impotence prevented a collision which must have resulted in a very considerable amount of bloodshed.

Indeed, as it was, the men had all been called out for war, and had the expedition been a little slower in coming upon the scene it would, without doubt, have met with a determined resistance. The king would not bring his army into the field until he had had the report of his envoys from England. When they arrived at Kumassi the expedition was close upon their heels. The Ashantis take time to mobilize and to get all the preliminary fetish-eating and oath-swearing completed, and thus, before they were ready, the British troops were already in Kumassi.

The force then present was sufficiently large and powerful to overawe the natives, who were assembled, be it remembered, under arms, in the villages round about Kumassi; and it was able to effect the arrest of Prempeh, together with the whole of his leading chiefs, at one swoop.

Had a smaller force, or one composed entirely of Houssas and West Indians, attempted a similar *coup*, there is not the slightest doubt that bloodshed, and very probably disaster, would have resulted. In a word, there could not, by any possibility, have been a clearer vindication of the policy of sending a compact force of white troops on this expedition.

CHAPTER 2

Preliminaries to the Expedition

14th November, 1895.

The pink " flimsy" bearing the magic words, "You are selected to proceed on active service," gives to the recipient a gush of elation such as a flimsy of another kind and of a more tangible value would fail to evoke. From that moment he is a different being. He treads on air, the envy of his non-selected fellow-aspirants. He is like to the happy man who has received a favourable answer to his suit, not only from "her," but, what is more to the point, from her stern parent. He becomes an object of interest to all, and especially to himself. His arrangements for the campaign do not take long. He looks into the sundry packs and parcels that contain his field kit, always ready, and notes deficiencies that have to be made good.

No sooner has his name appeared in the list, as published by the press, than circulars flow in upon him from outfitters, moneylenders, insurance agents, and others, anxious to utilise such a chance of sucking money as the occasion may afford. And his daily post is further swelled by letters of congratulation from his friends both far and near. Envious comrades congratulate him, while they beg his help to get them taken too, and ill-spelt appeals come from his men for him to get them to the front. At the War Office he finds that bustle without fussiness prevails, but the number of officers seeking their orders there is far outnumbered by those who have come to beg for any vacancy that may occur.

And then he has to face a medical examination by a board of doctors, who test his soundness in wind and limb and eyes; the dentist sets him up for faring on "hard tack," and the surgeon vaccinates him, as the Gold Coast now teems with smallpox. At stores and shops he spends much time in choosing what he wants from endless stocks of what he is pressed to take. The dealer's estimate of what is necessary differs in a wonderful degree from that which is the outcome of experience. Kind friends press on him presents of varied utility, from hip-baths to teacoseys. On every hand he is asked—as though the fact of his being appointed to the expedition made him *ipso facto* a full-blown authority on it—what is to be the actual good of the campaign, apart from the active employment it may give to eager officers and men. And where does the return come in for the expenditure of thousands of pounds and many lives on a bit of West African swamp that can be of no use to anybody?

So he turns to the handbooks and returns of the United Service Institute, and there he finds that this Gold Coast Colony produces an annual revenue of some 202,000*l.*; its expenses run to something under 180,000*l.*; it has an export and import trade of over 720,000*l.* each, of which some 530,000*l.* goes to the United Kingdom; and that the amounts are steadily increasing year by year. But all this trade is only derived from the eastern and western extremities of the country; the trade of the centre remains stagnated and barred by the opposition of one tribe there located, namely, the Ashantis. Were these people to act in a friendly and peaceful manner towards their neighbours, a large increase in the prosperity of all would result; but now, as of old, they remain an obstacle to progress and development.

In early times the Phoenicians, and in later times the Portuguese, had exploited the riches of the Gold Coast. So long ago as 1366 French traders from Rouen settled there for the purpose of digging gold, and styled their port La Mina (Elmina). These remained there for nigh a hundred years. Danes, Dutch, and English, Portuguese and Swedes soon followed them with trading ventures all along the coast. In 1672 the English Royal African Company established itself at Cape Coast Castle, as well as at several other points, and paid its way till 1821, when, damaged by the abolition of the slave trade, it transferred its property to the Crown.

Meanwhile, the Ashantis had already made themselves unpleasantly known as the bully tribe of that region by their raids on their more feeble neighbours, especially the Fantis of the coast. These latter had come to be considered as the *protégés* of the English. Consequently, after two such raids, in 1807 and 1817, the English established a Resident at Kumassi, but he had to be withdrawn after a short residence, and again the Ashantis came down in 1819. In 1823 they proceeded to invade the Wassaw territory, but the Gold Coast was now a colony of the Crown; the governor, Sir Charles Macarthy, with 500 native troops and twelve European officers, endeavoured to oppose their advance. He had, however, committed the usual British fault of underestimating the strength of his enemy; ammunition ran out (it is even said that through one of those mistakes that do sometimes occur, the kegs which had laboriously been carried to the front as bearing ammunition were found when opened to contain but supplies of vermicelli)—the result—disaster.

The governor's head went to make a drinking goblet for the savage king, and very few survivors lived to tell the tale. The Ashantis' further advance was only stayed by a deadly outbreak of smallpox in their ranks, so that for a season they withdrew. But two years later again they took the field, this time to find us with our allies well prepared and organised. The result was a very decided victory in our favour, which brought about a lengthened spell of peace and prosperity to the colony. In 1831, Governor Maclean concluded an important treaty with the Ashantis, Fantis, and other tribes, in which the Ashantis renounced their pretended suzerainty over all others, while the Fantis on their part agreed to abstain from giving cause of offence and retributory raids, and all consented to refer to British arbitration any disputes that might arise. To this treaty a further clause was added in 1848, in which Governor Winniett obtained the abolition of human sacrifices by the Ashantis.

But the Ashantis were not made for peace or treaties. Blood and loot had for them charms that could not be resisted. In spite of treaties, human sacrifice at the rate of 3000 per annum still went on. Raids were attempted in 1853 and 1863. Then, in 1872, the Fantis provoked attack from their ever-ready neighbours by quarrelling with a tribe of Ashanti allies at Elmina. Fighting took place. The British were dragged into it partly to defend their Protectorate and maintain treaties, and partly because the Ashantis had seized and held as prisoners certain Europeans.

Experience had then shown that the natives never felt bound to any extent by treaties, however solemnly they might have been entered upon, and that any show of hesitation, or even of leniency, on the part of the British was construed by friends and foes alike as a sure sign of weakness. Consequently, the expedition under Sir Garnet Wolseley was organised on a footing such as precluded all chance of failure. His main column of 1400 white troops advanced direct on Kumassi, while columns of native allies made demonstrations to divert the Ashanti forces. The king, recognising our determined front, sent in message after message of submission and promise of amendment in the future, but Sir Garnet took them for what they were worth, and never paused in his onward march; and it was only after the pseudo-submission had been broken down in a series of toughly-contested bush fights that he finally captured and destroyed the capital, and left the king a fugitive.

In the treaty of peace which thereupon resulted, the Ashantis promised to renounce all *suzerain* rights over various neighbouring tribes, to open their country to trade, to stop human sacrifice, to pay a war indemnity of 50,000 ounces of gold, and to keep the road from Kumassi to the Prah open and clear of bush. And how have these promises been observed? The Ashantis have raided their neighbours, have taken over 2000 Koranzas, traders cannot pass through Ashanti, the main road has never been kept clear of bush, the war indemnity still remains to be paid, and human sacrifice continues as before—to wit, some 2000 captured Koranzas are said to have been decapitated in the past two years, as many as 400 being killed at one time on a special occasion.

As for the expedition itself, matters are being now organised on the most practical and economical basis. A picked and compact force is being sent out, consisting of some 2000 regular troops in all. By the time they arrive on the Gold Coast, the staff sent on in advance will have prepared the road before them for the first 70 out of the 120 miles to Coomassie. Five depot camps will have been established between Cape Coast Castle, the base, and the river Prah, which forms the frontier. Bridges will have been built over the numerous rivers and streams, telegraphic communication will have been set up all along the line, and two fortified posts will have been made beyond the Prah to cover the cutting of the road and to protect communications in the enemy's country. Twelve thousand carriers will have been collected for transport of supplies, baggage, and sick. So that our troops will, on arrival, have nothing to do but to march straight forward on to the enemy's capital at the best pace the climate will allow.

Already to the northward officers are organising the Koranzas to threaten the Ashanti rear, while native troops are getting into position on his eastward flank. One of the highest authorities in the land has prophesied that the Ashantis will make a stand, and come into action with us about January 9th, near Edunku. What wonder, then, that he who has his orders for the front presses on his final arrangements with a feverish haste, and will only be happy when, one fine morn, he stands upon the deck, with pyjamas blowing in the land breeze, to receive the snaky welcome of the misty, low-lying shore?

Chapter 3

Local Preparations

8th December, 1895.

M'Lala-Pahnsi, or "the man who lies down to shoot," is the name by which a Zulu describes the man who lays his plans carefully and with full completeness before he embarks on his enterprise. It is the name which such Zulu, were he here, would apply to Sir Francis Scott. Every point that can be foreseen as requiring attention in the present expedition is being provided for. Critics may say that to get everything cut-and-dried beforehand is to dig for oneself a groove that will hold one when a change of circumstances may require a corresponding change of action. But it does not follow that when you have selected your line in the run, you may not change it if the fox alters his course. Moreover, it must by these critics be remembered that in the present enterprise we have not merely one, but two enemies opposed to us. One is King Prempeh, the other, and more formidable, King Fever. It is against this latter, as much as against the former, that the plans are being laid. His tactics are well known and unvarying, and are therefore to be met with equally regular fore-thinking.

On arrival at Grand Canary on the 1st inst.. Sir Francis found little news awaiting him beyond the disappointing fact that his advance party, owing to stress of weather, was now but four days ahead of him instead of at least a week. The threatened extra delay will probably be got over by extra exertion on the part of all concerned; but extra exertion is above all things to be avoided in the Coast climate if sustained working power is to be maintained. The main duties of the advance party and of the officers already on the spot are—

    1. To enrol carriers.
    2. To prepare road stations.

In order duly to appreciate the great importance of these two services, it is necessary to consider the nature of the road from Cape Coast Castle to Kumassi.

In the first place, the so-called road is merely a narrow pathway—the best part of it, from Cape Coast to the Prah, is only sufficiently wide for two men moving abreast; beyond the river it has yet to be cleared. It leads for the greater part of its 150 miles through heavy primeval forest. The thick foliage of the trees, interlaced high overhead, causes a deep, dank gloom, through which the sun seldom penetrates. The path winds among the tree stems and bush, now through mud and morass, now over steep ascent or deep ravine. The heavy dews and mists that come with night are laden with malaria for men, while the tsetse fly and horse-sickness infest the forest, and bar it as a death-trap to all beasts of burden.

To plunge a force of white troops at once into this forest, to set them to march and fight and bivouac in the usual way, would be to lay them low at one stroke with sickness. For the first seventy miles of its course, from Cape Coast Castle to the Prah River, the road lies in our own territory, and it is this portion which is now being fully prepared beforehand for the ultimate rapid and unhindered advance of the British troops when they arrive a fortnight or three weeks later. Since baggage animals cannot be employed owing to the "fly" and absence of forage, and Decauville, or other mechanical means of transport are impossible by reason of the nature of the ground, it is necessary to use the ordinary system of the country, namely, porters.

For mere regimental transport, that is, conveyance of men's kits, regimental ammunition, sick, &c., the number has to be computed at one carrier per head, which will entail close upon 2000 of them. In addition to these, an army of porters will be required for transport of ordnance, commissariat, hospital, engineer, and other stores. Large supplies and reserve stores of ammunition, arms, food, not only for the fighting men, but also for the host of carriers themselves, stretchers for sick, medicines, telegraph and bridge-making equipment, and a hundred other necessary items, have all to be moved up beforehand to the ultimate base, at the Prah, at Prahsu.

For the whole of this work, then, it is estimated that some 10,000 or 12,000 carriers will be required. The work of collecting these men will in itself be no small task; for although there is not the drain on the local manhood that there was in the last campaign, to serve as armed levies, yet their natural laziness, timidity, and general disregard of their engagements, make it extremely difficult to get them even to come to the scratch. In fact, it is only possible by means of bribes and rewards to the various chiefs—awarded in proportion to the number of men supplied. Then, when they have been assembled and registered, there is a great deal to be done in organising them into proper gangs under responsible men, and in assigning the gangs to their various duties under white officers, and in providing for their punctual rationing and payment, and for their discipline and sanitation.

All this has to be done before the stores can be moved from the landing-place at Cape Coast Castle. Then the limit of work of which a carrier is capable is to carry a 50-lb. load for ten miles, with one day's rest in every five. The relay posts will, therefore, be established at every ten miles, and will include standing camps for the reception of the troops as they march up. But these stations have all to be prepared, bush being cleared, huts erected, water supply perfected, fuel collected, and rations and supplies stored before they can be pronounced ready for use; and furthermore, the advanced base at Prahsu has to be completed with all the bulk of supplies necessary for carrying the troops on beyond the Prah up to Kumassi and back.

This means the transport of hundreds of tons over 70 miles of narrow bush path in 50-lb. packages. To help matters, the path has to be "corduroyed" over bogs, 200 bridges built, and telegraph set up. Then the standing camps, to be effective for preserving the health of the men, have to be prepared in a very thorough manner. Huts are built with wattled walls and palm-thatched roofs, 60 ft. long by 20 ft. wide, with a raised platform along each side to serve as a bed. These will accommodate fifty men each. Eight of such huts, together with others for officers, hospital and supply stores, will constitute a station. Of these stations there will be seven between the coast and Prahsu, near the following points:—Jakuma, Akroful, Dunkwa, Mansu, Suta, Assin, Yankummassi, Baracu.

Huts are essential to the health of the troops, as the only protection against the ordinary heavy dews of night and the frequent thunderstorms and tornadoes that sweep over this region. And although thus sheltered overhead, it is of equal importance that the men be protected against the natural poisonous exhalations of the ground; and the best means to this end is the provision of bed-places standing at least two feet above the floor level. Plenty of fuel is to be provided at each station, not only for cooking purposes, but also for drying the air inside the huts. The supply of abundance of good filtered water forms another important item in the preparation of each station. The comfort and well-being of the men, healthy as well as sick, is being catered for in a most thorough manner, even down to the daily supply of fresh oranges and bananas. Camp police have to be organised to ensure the due observance by the large detachments of carriers of the orders regarding sanitation and discipline laid down for them. Thus it will be seen that there is much to be done before troops need, or should be, landed. Lying idle at the coast while waiting for the road to be completed would inevitably lay them low with fever.

Pushing forward before the supplies and camps are ready would equally mean unnecessary hardships and consequent sickness. And with so very small a force every man is wanted for the fray, especially if Samory, with his mounted braves, should try to pass our flank in the open valley of the Volta. The Ashantis will not move away; our target is a fixed one, and in preparing to shoot at it we should be mad to fire before we have got into the best position for doing so. As our chief is acting on this principle, we may hope, with all confidence, that there will in this case be no repetition of the French campaign in Madagascar—an instance of a fine expedition nearly wrecked by want of sufficient forethought and preparation.

SIR FRANCIS SCOTT AND PRINCE CHRISTIAN VICTOR
LANDING IN A SURF-BOAT.

CHAPTER 4

At Cape Coast Castle

13th December.

At last we have arrived at the end of our three weeks' voyage, and Cape Coast Castle has shown itself to our longing eyes much as the books describe it. A large, rambling, whitewashed fort standing on a group of rocks on the surf-washed beach. Behind it lies the dull red native town of earthen flat-roofed houses, interspersed with whitewashed bungalows of merchants, and all around the town there rise a mass of small, steep, wooded hills, two or three of which are topped with buildings.

Great open surf-boats take us to the shore, each propelled by a dozen lusty paddlers, sitting sideways on the gunwale, and timing well the dipping of their three-pronged blades with choruses which at times are quite harmonious. Then, as we near the seething beach, a rush of naked helpers runs the boat well up, and we are landed dry-shod at the castle water-gate. Within the courtyard, with its galleries all round, the bustle and the noise are almost overpowering, as gangs of earners, both male and female, bring the loads of stores just landed from the ship, to be checked and stored for further use. Perhaps nowhere will you find a more well-trodden grave than that of L. E. L., the poetess, who lies beneath the flags of this same courtyard.

Here, too, are crowds of natives being enrolled and told off into gangs as carriers, to form the chain of depots that have to be made in anticipation of the arrival of the troops.

Chapter 5

The Levy Starts

14th December,
Preparations such as those I have described take some doing, as they have to be completed before the white troops can usefully be landed; and they have to be pushed on well into the proximity of the enemy. For this reason they demand the presence of a covering force to protect their progress. A small body of Houssas is already engaged on this duty near Prahsu. (Houssas, I may explain, are disciplined native troops drawn from the fighting Mohammedan tribes of the Gold Coast Hinterland, and commanded by white officers; they do not call themselves either "Hoos-as" or "Hussars," but "Howsers.")

An order has now been given that an additional force, composed of native warriors, shall be organised and pushed up to act as covering force in front of the expedition.

It falls to my lot to get together and organise this corps. Fortunately I have the advantage of the valuable assistance of Captain Graham, D.S.O., 5th Lancers, whose other name is "The Sutler." If this implies that he is as business-like as he is enterprising, the title is not inappropriate. One hundred of the Adansi tribe have already been collected and armed by the civil authorities, and have taken up their position as outposts beyond the Prah, in the country from which they have lately been driven by the aggression of the Ashantis.

In addition to these we are to get the services of men of various tribes living nearer to the coast within the colony. Numbers of them are promised by the various kings and chiefs, who, however, on the slightest pretext go back on their engagements with most annoying promptness. At last, after three days of alternate cajoling and threatening, we get these chiefs to undertake to produce 500 men on December 16th by noon.

16th December, Noon.

The parade-ground outside the castle lies an arid desert in the midday sun, and the sea-breeze wanders where it listeth. Not a man is there. It is a matter then for a hammock-ride through the slums of the slum that forms the town. Kings are forked out of the hovels where they are lodging, at the end of a stick; they in their turn rouse out their captains, and by two o'clock the army is assembled. Then it is a sight for the gods to see "The Sutler" putting each man in his place. The stupid inertness of the puzzled negro is duller than that of an ox; a dog would grasp your meaning in one half the time. Men and brothers! They may be brothers, but they certainly are not men.

If it were not for the depressing heat and the urgency of the work, one could sit down and laugh to tears at the absurdity of the thing, but under the circumstances it is a little "wearing." But our motto is the old West Coast proverb, "*Softly, softly, catchee monkey;*" in other words, "*Don't worry; patience gains the day.*" It was in joke suggested as a maxim for our levy of softly-sneaking scouts, but we came to adopt it as our guiding principle, and I do not believe that a man acting on any other principle could organise a native levy on the West Coast—and live. Gradually out of chaos order comes. Kings and chiefs are installed as officers, and the men are roughly divided into companies under their orders.

Then the uniform is issued. This consists of nothing more than a red *fez* for each man, but it gives as much satisfaction to the naked warrior as does his first tunic to the young hussar.

Arms are to be issued to the corps at Prahsu, and that the intervening seventy miles may not be traversed uselessly each man is now supplied with a commissariat load to carry on his head. At three o'clock the levy is ready for the march.

His Excellency the Governor inspects the ranks, and says a few encouraging words to the leading chiefs and captains. Among the men we muster a few with guns and others who are artists on the horn. The horn in this case consists of a hollowed elephant's tusk, garnished with many human jaw-bones—its notes are never more than two, and those of doleful tone; but at the signal for the march these horns give out a raucous din which, deepened by the rumble of the elephant-hide drums, imparts a martial ardour to the men, and soon the jabbering, laughing mob goes shambling through the streets, bound for the bush beyond.

CHAPTER 6

In the Bush

Prahsu, 21st December.

On the road at last—from Cape Coast to, or at any rate towards, Kumassi. For the first few miles after we have cleared the bazaar of Cape Coast Castle, the road, a hard gravel path, runs through a labyrinth' of small bush-covered hills; but although there is very little sun today, the heat is very great, and one is fain to give up one's first resolution doing all the march on foot in favour of an occasional, if not a frequent, lift in the hammock. The hammock as a conveyance, once you have become accustomed to its motion, and have fitted its hang to suit your taste, is said to be luxurious. Personally I prefer to walk, except where a lift may serve to keep one's feet from wet or head from sun. The hammock itself is a common string one, with a crossbar affixed to each end. The cross-bar rests on the heads of the bearers. Over all a light canvas roof is fixed, which serves to keep off the worst of sun or rain from the occupant. The four bearers shamble along at a good pace, balancing the concern on their heads, and can carry one for long distances by day or night without stumble or false steps. The drawback to this method of travel is that the springiness of the motion forbids all reading or writing that might otherwise usefully occupy many of the hours spent on the march.

But so far as it has gone—some five days between Prahsu and Cape Coast Castle—the journey has in no way palled upon us. About fifteen miles from the coast the bush gradually grew in height and density, until the huge bare shafts of the cotton-trees began to tower here and there among the palms, giant ferns, and smaller trees that formed the general mass of foliage. Then we gradually came into regular forest scenery, from which we shall not again emerge till our campaign is over. This same scenery, we were told, would appal us with its deadly dullness, and the depression of the forest would affect our minds most powerfully.

Possibly our minds are not sufficiently prehensile to catch the morbid sensation that was promised, and in all the wondrous woodland that has charmed our eye at every step, the only inharmonious quality that has struck us is its aroma. Yes, walking down the solemn shady aisles of forest giants, whose upper parts gleam far above the dense undergrowth in white pillars against the grey-blue sky, or passing from a sunlit glade into the deep, dark crypt of massive bamboo clumps—places that have aptly been compared with the scenery of the depths of the ocean—everywhere there hangs the noisome scent that meets you near old cabbage-plots in England.

The rule here seems to be, the prettier the spot, the more deadly is its air. Where you see the brilliant red wax-flowers gleaming beneath the great angle-buttresses of a cotton-tree, whose stem is covered for fifty feet with ferns and orchids, till 150 feet of creeper, hanging in one dense curtain, meets them from the upper branches, you stand a moment to wonder and admire, when, faugh! the loathsome smell assails and drives you forward. In all the forest scarce a bird or living thing is seen. An occasional robin's song is heard, or the tuneful wail of the "finger-glass bird," while at night the whistle of the crickets and the roar of frogs is broken by the dismal childlike shriek of the sloth.

The path is now narrowed down, and being almost all in shade, is far more cool for walking than at the outset of the journey—in width about four yards, but often by overgrowth reduced to one. On either side, the dense mass of fern and bush and tangled creeper set in swampy ground prevents all moving off the path. And thus our pace is checked as we find the road in front blocked with a slow-moving mass of loaded carriers—hundreds upon hundreds of them, all working along in gangs, with loads upon their heads of about 50 lbs. apiece. Each gang works under its own chief, and is distinguished by armlets of a certain colour, each armlet bearing the classifying letter and number of the wearer.

Here we find yellow armlets carrying cases of "bully "beef; then come grey ones with lime-juice; soon after we find white ones carrying tarred rope for the bridge over the Prah; and then a "lady-pack," with blue and white policemen's armlets, carrying biscuit cases, many a one of them with an additional load in the shape of a brown nodding little baby on her back. The whole of this mass of usually blundering natives was working just like clockwork all along the line within three days of its organisation in the hands of Colonel Ward and his never-tiring staff. Not a load gets lost or even delayed, not a man is in arrears of his daily pay.

Every three or four miles one passes through a native village—generally a single street of some twenty or thirty houses. Each house consists, as a rule, of three or four small huts or sheds, facing inwards, and forming a little courtyard. These huts are on built-up platforms, with hard mud walls, and roofs thatched with palm-leaves, and their front steps faced with a smooth red-coloured cement. They are kept fairly clean, so that we generally occupied one for our half-way breakfast, or on occasion to sleep the night. In the centre of each village is a tree with seats round it, formed of untrimmed logs, on which the elders of the village sit and smoke and gravely talk.

As one leaves the village and plunges once more into the bush, one passes the village fetish ground, well marked by rags and stones and broken pots, all offered as propitiation to the presiding demon of the place. Deep in the bush behind the huts one sees the giant leaves of the plantain groves that yield the staple food of the inhabitants. At every village as we pass we interview the headman on the subject of his crop, and warn him that a daily market must be open for the sale of yams and plantains to our host of carriers; and though he looks a knowing and a high-class kind of man when strutting forth in his *toga*-like garment, we find it hard to make him grasp the full meaning of our demand. The brains of these Ashantis are assuredly most non-receptive.

At nearly every ten miles we come upon a rest-camp, in a more or less completed condition, for occupation by the British troops when they come marching up. With no little labour, bush has been cleared away for many hundred yards, and huts have been built up of bamboo frames, with trellis sides and palm-thatched roofs. Within them tables, seats, and bed-places have been made again of split bamboos—accommodation sufficient for some three hundred men, with complement of officers. Store-sheds are being quickly filled with food and ammunition for the force. A.S.C. officers in *déshabillé*, and steaming, are hard at work from dawn till dusk. And then, as far at least as Mansu, half-way to the Prah, the telegraph runs near the path, but taking a more direct line through the bush by a track recently cut out with much and heavy labour. After Mansu the "fetish cord," as the natives call it, no longer hangs on poles, but lies along the ground close to the path. It is the mere field cable of the engineers that now takes

Laying the Field Telegraph in the Bush.

the place of the more permanent line; and as we press forward, we at length overtake Captain Curtis, R.E., working himself, like his men, half-stripped, and laying out his line at the phenomenal rate of two and a half miles an hour. This in itself is a record that would be hard to beat when all the difficulties of country, climate, and circumstances are taken into consideration.

Here and there along the road we come to bridges over streams and causeways over swamps, all in course of construction at the hands of scores of natives, working with an amount of energy that is most surprising when one sees how few and far between are the ever-travelling, hard-worked white superintendents. Here we meet one gaunt and yellow. Surely we have seen that eye and brow before, although the beard and solar *topee* do much to disguise the man. His necktie of faded "Old Carthusian" colours makes suspicion a certainty, and once again old schoolfellows are flung together for an hour to talk in an African swamp of old times on English playing-fields. Again we press on through the never-ending dark green aisles, until at length, one sweltering afternoon, we tramp in a melting state—although in the airiest of costumes—into the village camp of Prahsu. Prahsu is our advanced base on the River Prah.

The big yellow river slowly slides along between its forest-clad banks, and on a low, reed-grown spit the camping-ground is cleared and huts are being built. One double-storied house exists, the headquarters of the post, where Major Gordon reigns supreme. A company of Houssas—the war-loving native armed police—is quartered here; a base hospital and base supply and ordnance stores are being made. There is an accumulation of barrels waiting for the rope with which the pontoon bridge is to be constructed.

As we arrive at Prahsu, rumours there are of encounters between our scouts and those of the enemy, and of blood drawn on both sides. We are told that King Prempeh laughs to scorn the proposal that he shall come down to meet the governor in conference. "*The King of the Ashantis is the lord of heaven and of earth.*" This is an Ashanti proverb up to which the king and his captains are said to be ready to act. To-day, too, (as at time of first publication), we hear that the best Ashanti scouts are now out and about Bekwai to watch our doings, and that the Ashanti plan of campaign is to draw on our force, and then to cut in in rear of it. At any rate, they seem inclined to fight. That they will do so is the great hope of those who toil through the long hot hours in this steaming fetid atmosphere. Nor can one well grudge them the feeling. Of the little band of eight white men now preparing matters in Prahsu, even as I write, three are down with fever. Still they peg away, one day down, the next up and smiling again—but sometimes the smile is a little wan. All that buoys them up is hope—hope that through their "bucking up" their side will win the game.

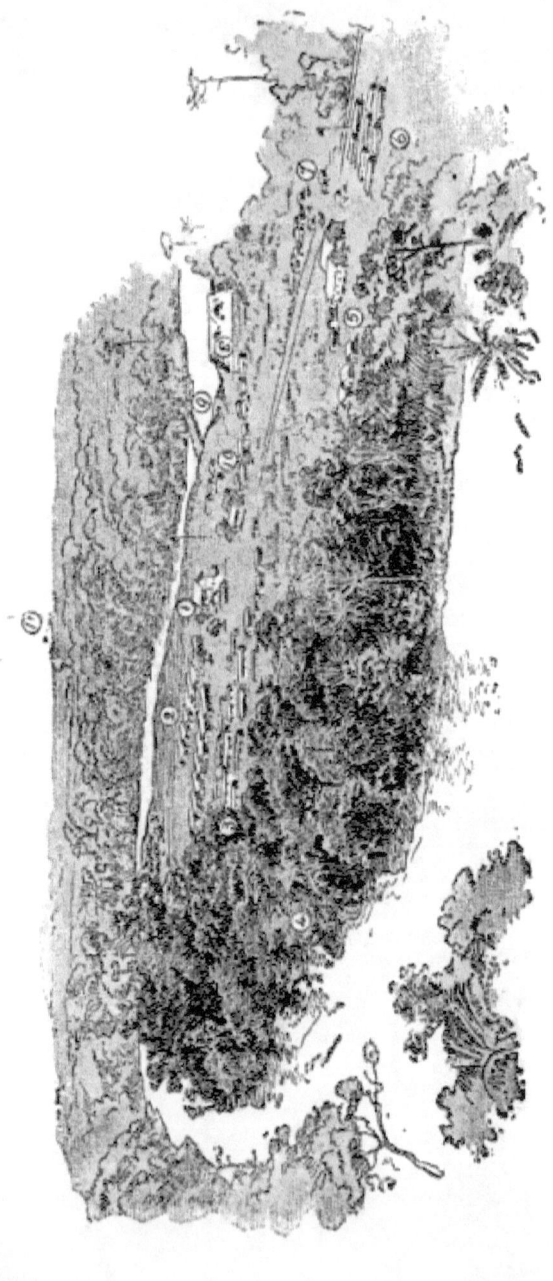

Bird's-eye View of Prahsu.

1. Commandant's House. 2. British Troops' Company Line. 3. Houses and Lines. 4. Cemetery and Magazine. 5. Hospital. 6. Major Baden-Powell's Regiment. 7. The Village. 8. Supply and Ordnance Store. 9. River Prah, and Pontoon Bridge. 10. Officers' Huts and Lines. 11. Ashanti.

CHAPTER 7

Pioneer Work

Prahsu, 22nd December.

When one speaks of the boundary between Ashanti and Cape Coast Colony, one's ideas picture the Prah as the natural mark of the border, whereas the actual boundary lies much farther north, beyond the Adansi Hills. Historically and politically, and for most practical purposes, the Prah remains the boundary all the same. The Adansis, who used to inhabit the British portion beyond it—and so formed a buffer tribe between the Ashantis and the colony—have been removed to more eligible quarters in the south, and the district remains a no man's land, and practically a bush desert. For the purposes of the expedition the camp at Prahsu, on the bank of the Prah, is a half-way house to Kumassi—comparatively safe from attacks of the enemy by reason of its position at the end of a good road from the coast, and in a land of plentiful supplies. It is as much the frontier and advanced base today as it was in 1874, when it was actually on the border of the enemy's country.

An immense depot of supplies has now been formed here, and when the forward move commences, no doubt a further advanced base will be formed at the Adansi Hills, thirty-five miles farther on. The supply of stores will be pushed up there for the maintenance of the troops within striking distance of Kumassi. The long line of road between Prahsu and the Adansi Hills has, however, to be prepared with a chain of defensive camps, where convoys can defend themselves should the Ashantis endeavour to cut in on our lines of communications. This is a very favourite manoeuvre of theirs, and constitutes one of their avowed plans of campaign for the present war. Their system is to secretly cut a path for themselves through the bush away from the line of the main road, but parallel to it.

When their scouts have warned them that they have well passed the main force or depot whose destruction they desire, they cut their way to the road, and then lie in ambush for parties endeavouring to pass up or down, or they make a raid on a convoy in camp; thus with a comparatively small body they are enabled to completely cut off their enemy from his base. It is to guard against such tactics that the native levy has now been ordered into the country across the Prah, together with about 150 of the Houssa police. The advanced outposts are formed by our Adansi company, of 100 men. These are posted on the actual border north of the Adansi Hills, and the scouts are watching every move on the part of the Ashantis; for there are moves of Ashantis going on—small ones, it is true, but they are often the grains of dust that tell which way the wind blows.

The Adansis being bushmen and hunters by nature, and subjects for many years of oppression at the hands of the Ashantis, have entered on the work of reconnoitring *con amore*; and although they are only armed with flint-lock guns, they show an amount of keenness in their work that is very noticeable in a country where energy or enterprise on the part of the natives is usually so conspicuously absent. Our main body consists of some 300 Krobos under their king Matikoli, and 100 Mumfords, under Chief Brew, and a company of Elminas, under the veteran chief Ando. This fine old warrior bears on his breast the medal for the last Ashanti campaign, where he served for some time in Sir Evelyn Wood's Native Levy and afterwards as native adviser on the staff of Lord Wolseley.

23rd December,

At Prashu, after handing over to the commissariat department the loads which we have brought up for them, we have got to work on the more complete organisation and training of the levy. After begging and borrowing (sometimes even stealing) any tools of any kind whatsoever, we have started the levy to work in clearing the bush, in building huts, in road-making, and in other useful pioneering work. And in addition to this we are exercising the men at outpost work, and we have issued arms to some of them. But the arms, being very inferior flint-locks,—many of them wanting even the flints, do not inspire great confidence, and we only hope that ere long a supply of Snider rifles may be issued in their place.

Fumsu, 27th December.

On the 24th December, after four days usefully, but anxiously, spent at Prahsu, the permission arrived for the levy to cross the Prah, and to continue its advance into the enemy's country. The permission reached us at three o'clock, and by five the major portion of the levy had been ferried across in the great ferry-boat (a "dugout" hewn from the trunk of an enormous tree, and capable of carrying thirty people). A slight delay was occasioned by one tribe declining to move, but the argument *pro* and *con* did not last long, and eventually we found ourselves practising night-marching up till about nine o'clock, when we reached our camping-ground,

Beyond the Prah we find a very different state of things to that on the southern side. Our road is no longer the comparatively broad, direct, and well-cleared way, but has become a twisty, zigzagging footpath—now clambering over fallen tree-trunks, now twisting through a bog—so narrow and broken as to forbid the use of a hammock for any distance. Villages are very few and very small, and consequently supplies are very scarce for our men and for the carriers of the expedition who are to follow. Road-makers and bush-cutters cannot now be obtained among the native population. Thus the work that falls upon the levy is exceptionally heavy, especially as our supply of tools is somewhat limited, and the natives' idea of using those they have is even more so. Give a man a felling-axe, and he will think it a good weapon for scraping up weeds, and a spade he will use for cutting down timber.

Yes, life with a levy, where there are only two of you to work six hundred, might, for a few days, be a diverting experience, if the climate were good and if there were no immediate necessity for the work to be carried to a result. But as things are, it is a pretty powerful exercise, both mental and physical, and by the end of the day one wants but little here below but to drink and to lie down and sleep—or die, you don't care which.

Here is our usual day's routine:—

At early dawn, while the hush of the thick white mist yet hangs above the forest, a pyjama-clad figure creeps from its camp-bed in the palm-leaf hut, and kicks up a sleeping drummer to sound "*Reveille*." Then the tall, dark forest wall around the clearing echoes with the boom of the elephant-tusk horns, whose sound is all the more weird since it comes from between the human jaws with which the horns are decorated. The war-drums rumble out a kind of Morse rattle that is quite understandable to its hearers. The men get up readily enough, but it is merely in order to light their fires and to settle down to eat plantains, while the white chiefs take their tubs, quinine, and tea. A further rattling of the drum for parade produces no result.

The king is called for. "Why are your men not on parade?" With a deprecatory smile the king explains that he is suffering from rheumatism in the shoulder, and therefore he, and consequently his tribe, cannot march today. He is given a Cockle's pill, and is warned that if he is not ready to march in five minutes, he will be fined a shilling. (The luxury of fining a real, live king to the extent of one shilling!) In five minutes he returns and says that if the white officer will give his men some salt to eat with their "*chop*" (food), he thinks they will be willing to march.

The white officer grimly says he will get a little salt for them, and proceeds to cut a specimen of a particularly lithe and whippy cane. A hundred pair of eyes are watching him. They read his intention in a moment, and at once there is a stir. A moment later, and *that* portion of the army are off in a long string upon the forward road, with their goods and chattels and chop tied up in bundles on their heads.

But the whole levy is as yet by no means under way. Here a whole company of another tribe is still squatting, eating plantains, and jabbering away, indifferent to every other sound. "Call the chief." Yes, the chief is most willing to do anything; would march straight on to Kumassi if ordered. But his captains are at present engaged in talking over the situation, and he cannot well disturb them. The white chief does not take long about disturbing them, but still the rank and file don't move. The captains have something they would like to communicate to the white chief "Well, out with it."

The head captain has come to the conclusion, from information received, that the Ashantis are a most cowardly race.

" Quite right. Just what I have told you all along; and if you will only hurry up, we can get right up to them in a few days and smash them."

"Ah! the white chief speaks brave words, but he does not know the ways of the bush warriors. No; the plan which the captains in council have agreed upon is to draw the enemy on by retiring straight away back to Cape Coast Castle. The enemy will follow them, and will run on to the bayonets of the white soldiers who are coming up from the coast."

"A very good plan, but not quite identical with that of the white chief. There is only one plan in his mind, and that is to go forward, and this plan must be carried out by all. He has in his hand a repeating rifle which fires fourteen shots. When the regiment begins its retirement, he will go to the head of it and will shoot at each man as he comes by. Fourteen corpses will suffice to block up the path. And now any who like to go back on these conditions can do so; the gun is already loaded. Those who like to go forward to get their chop at the next halting-place can move on. Those who like to sit where they are can do so till it is their turn to be tied to a tree, to get a dozen lashes, commencing with this gentleman."

Loads are taken up, and in a moment the whole force goes laughing and singing on the forward path.

On through the deep, dark aisles, still foggy with the morning mist and wet with the dripping dew. Twisting and turning, now up, now down, clambering over giant tree-roots or splashing through the sucking mud—all in moist and breathless heat, till, tired and dripping, we reach the next site for a camp. Two hours' rest for mid-day chop, and then parade. More delays, more excuses, and at last every man has his tool issued to him, and every company has its work assigned to it. No. 1 to clear the bush. No. 2 to cut stockade posts. No. 3 to cut palm-leaf wattle. No. 4 to dig stockade holes. No. 5 to mount sentries and prevent men hiding in huts; and so on, till every one is at work. We lay out the plan and trace of the fort that is to be built, and of the huts that are to form the camp.

"Hallo! where are the hole-diggers?"

"They have retired to have some *chop*."

"*Chop?* they've only just finished two hours of *chop*."

"Yes—but the white chief works them so hard that they have big appetites."

"They—and you, their chief—will all be fined a day's pay."

"Yes; well, the white man is powerful. Still, we prefer that to not having our *chop*. Many thanks."

"Oh, but you'll have to work as well. See this little instrument? That's a hunting crop. Come, I'll show you how it can be used. I'll begin on you, my friend!"

No need to. They all fly to their work. Then you go round. Every company in turn is found sitting down, or eye-serving.

"Down with that tree, my lad— you with the felling-axe! Not know how to use it?"

For three days I felled trees myself, till I found that I could get the tree felled equally well by merely showing the cracker of the hunting crop. The men had loved to see me work. The crop came to be called

"*Volapük*," because it was understood by every tribe. But, though often shown, it was never used.

The bush-clearing company are sitting down, not a yard of bush cut. "Why?"

"Oh, we are fishermen by occupation, and don't know anything about bush-cutting."

The bush soon comes down nevertheless, and, what is more wonderful, by sunset there is an open space of some seven or eight acres where this morning there was nothing but a sea of bush jungle. Large palm-thatched sheds have sprung up in regular lines, and in the centre stands a nearly finished fort, with its earth rampart bound up by stockade and wattle. Within it are two huts, for hospital and storehouse. Trains of carriers are already arriving with hundreds of boxes of beef and biscuit to be checked, arranged, and stored. At sunset sounds the drum, the treasure box and ledger are opened, and the command comes up for pay.

"First company—how many men present?"

"Sixty-eight, sir."

"But it has only got fifty-nine on its establishment!"

"Next company."

"All here, sir, but some few men away sick—and two he never come"—and so on and so on. At last it is over, except that a despatch-runner comes in with a telegram, forwarded from the last telegraph station, to ask from Cape Coast Castle offices immediate reason why the men's pay-list has been sent in in manuscript, instead of on Army Form O 1729.

27th December.

From the advanced scouts to the main body of the expedition is a long step. The antennae are at Dompoassi, the head and brain are at Prahsu, and the body extends from that place to Cape Coast Castle. The white troops are getting along well now that they are in the bush, but the first march on the coast claimed, alas, two victims to the heat. At Prahsu the headquarters staff are at present concentrated, and occupy a position where they are completely in touch with the whole of the long line of the force, a line a hundred miles in length. The field telegraph is of the greatest value in directing and controlling this immense chain, and has now reached Akuserim under the energetic arrangements of Captain Curtis. Plenty of work for everybody is the talisman which has so far happily kept the staff in an excellent state of health and energy. Sir Francis Scott appears the picture of life and freshness. Prince Henry of Battenberg, as military secretary, is in constant attendance on his chief, and shows no sign of feeling the heat. Having allowed his beard to grow, he is now the counterpart of his brother. Prince Louis. He has imported chargers into the country in the shape of a pair of riding donkeys, which are, so far, standing the climate well; but shortly they will have to face the ordeal of the "fly," for about Esiaman, a short distance north of the Prah, the tsetse fly abounds. This little pest—about the size of a large house-fly—although to men it is no more harmful than a mosquito, is fatal to a horse or domesticated animal. One bite is said to be sufficient; the system gradually becomes poisoned, and the animal loses strength and dies—all the more rapidly if the weather is wet. Wild animals—probably through generations of inoculation—are proof against the poison, and donkeys are said to be less susceptible to it than other tame beasts. Therefore, it is possible that Prince Henry's stud may live to carry him through the campaign. Working hard at his duties as A.D.C., Prince Christian Victor gets through a great amount of work in the day, and, in opposition to Prince Henry, he has shaved even his moustache. Major Belfield, on whose shoulders the main work of the expedition falls, luckily keeps as well and as energetic as ever was his wont. But there is sickness in the camp, and far too much of it. Three of the medical officers are down with it, and several of the non-commissioned officers and men—especially of the Royal Engineers.

All along the road progress continues. The carriers, thoroughly organised in gangs, are working like clockwork. Tons of supplies are being placed ready in the camps all along the route as far as the Adansi Hills. Over these and beyond, the road is still being cut, and camps being laid out and built. News trickles in daily from the outposts. We now know that Prempeh ordered a council of war last week at Kumassi, and that most of his chiefs attended it, but that several did not, and business was adjourned for their attendance. In the meantime, the envoys who had been to England have returned. The council has again been called, and again one or two chiefs have refrained from attending. The most notable among these absentees is the King of Bekwai, who has a force of some 2000 men, and whose country would be the first to receive the British invasion. He has sent messengers to Sir Francis Scott expressing his desire to come under British protection. But it is evident that such protection must take an active form, and promptly, for there is little doubt that should Prempeh discover his subject's treason before the British help arrives, the King of Bekwai will lose his head. It is probable, therefore, that a small flying column will be sent with all speed to occupy Bekwai and afford protection to its people. In doing this, such column would also occupy a very strong strategical point on the enemy's flank, which might possibly affect in an important degree the future plans and moves of the Ashantis. Of these there are now collected in Kumassi some 8000 warriors armed with guns and rifles, but apparently not well supplied with ammunition for sustained fighting. The ceremony of taking fetish for war is gradually being carried out—in the leisurely fashion peculiar to all business, however urgent, in this part of the world. Taking fetish is practically the taking, by all the captains and chiefs, of an oath to fight. When all have completed the ceremony, the king gives his assent and his orders for the war.

The system of the army appears to be to sit quietly awaiting the development of affairs, and they protest that they have no intention of fighting the English. This same protestation they made in 1874, and continued to do so until within a few hours of the Battle of Amoaful, so that no reliability can be placed on their statements; and there seems little doubt, from the fact of their being already assembled in arms, that they intend to resist, at any rate, any attempt to take their capital or their king. But once they have thus satisfied their conscience and established etiquette, they will be only too glad to lay down their arms and to welcome the new order of things.

The whole country seems sick and tired of the continual state of war in which they have lived. Over the border they see the people who used to be their slaves now thriving, fat and happy, under the English flag, and they begin to long for something of the kind for themselves. Custom and superstition still partly hold them to the old order, but with very little pressure they will gladly throw that over and accept the new— much to the benefit of themselves and their neighbours.

CHAPTER 8

The Scouts

Dompoassi, 28th December,
Leaving the main body of the native levy at their work of building forts and making roads and camps ready for the advance of the expedition, we come, by a very rapid transition, into another state of things. The road, narrow as it was and broken, now becomes a mere foot-track, twisting in and out between the trees, impeded with gnarled roots and boggy ruts. Every now and again a huge fallen tree-trunk blocks the way—sometimes the path goes laboriously round the end of it, at other times one clambers over, and when one has clambered over some four or five of these impediments in the course of a hundred yards, one begins to realise what delay they would cause to a long train of troops on the march. Streams and bogs have to be waded through, being so far innocent of bridges and of "corduroy." These are points that will be corrected as the levy moves along.

Meanwhile, there is a certain pleasure in thus pushing through the bush in its more natural everyday condition. Villages now become very few and far between: mere clusters of huts in forest clearings, containing a population of about a dozen each, all told. Tracks of animals and of hunters become more frequent in the tangled bush. These are tracks that are used by Ashanti scouts, and we notice that our carriers now no longer straggle along the path or spend their voices in loud jabbering, as they have done before the Prah was reached.

At last two figures meet us, quite in keeping with the scene. No clothes beyond a few discoloured rags—their bodies girt about with leathern thongs from which hang powder-gourds and knife-sheaths and bullet-bags of deer's hide. On their shoulders they carry immense long flintlock guns, and round their necks are strings of fetish charms. They come gliding on, laughing, bowing, and shaking hands—these are the first we meet of our scouts. They have heard—goodness knows how—of our arrival, and have come out to meet and escort us on the way. Their coming to meet us means a little step of ten miles or so over the mountain, but that is as nothing to these fine wild children of the bush. Now we come on a clearing in the bush, where two or three huts are all that remain to show the one-time thriving village of Brofu Edru. Villages of this name are frequent along the road. It means, literally, "the power of the white man"—indicating that the place was instituted when the white man had brought peace to the land in 1874. From this particular Brofu Edru we get our first view of the Adansi Mountains—merely a high bush-covered ridge rising above the surrounding trees, less than a mile away.

Soon we commence the ascent. Almost direct the path climbs up—perhaps the straightest piece of road we have so far met with. Scarce a vestige remains of the beautiful zigzag way that was made by the Royal Engineers on the last campaign. As we rise, the air seems fresher, and much we want it, for never was the meaning so nearly brought home to us of the term *"bathed in perspiration"* as in our last efforts on the steamy flats. At length we reach the top—breathless and panting, longing for the view. But view there is none. All round us the same impenetrable bush, and where the foliage occasionally grants us a glimpse of the world beyond, we see a rolling expanse of treetops, looking sky-blue in the overhanging haze.

Now we descend down "Richmond Hill," past "Greenwich"—a stream where little fish like whitebait may be taken by using your mosquito curtain as a net. Suddenly a figure is before us, where a moment before was nothing but a curtain of bush—another scout stands glistening like a polished bronze statue in a sunlit spot. Again the cheery smile, bow, and handshake. He is one of the sentries from the neighbouring piquet. Already the horn is sounding, like a deep-toned steamer's whistle, to call the men together, and a few minutes later we are among them—good, cheery-looking bush-warriors, and well up to the work of keeping watch. Then we have a talk.

How they enjoy the *palaver* in which I tell them that "they are the eyes to the body of the snake which is crawling up the bush-path from the coast, and coiling for its spring! The eyes are hungry, but they will soon have meat; and the main body of white men, armed with the best of weapons, will help them win the day, and get their country back again, to enjoy in peace for ever." Then I show them my own little repeating rifle, and firing one shot after another, slowly at first, then faster and faster, till the fourteen rounds roll off in a roar, I quite bring down the house. They crowd round jabbering and yelling, every man bent on shaking hands with the performer.

Later on we visit other piquets and their outposts. The sentries lie about within the bush close to any main paths, at such distance from the piquet as will allow of them being called in by the horn. Patrols of two men each go out along all paths for some eight or ten miles every day. At night the watch is kept by small parties of half a dozen men, who camp out on the paths a mile or two beyond the piquet. Like most natives, they will not work alone at night, but in small parties they do their night work admirably. Indeed, with such outposts in front of them, our expedition is pretty safe from any surprise by the enemy. Nor is their work by any means confined to passive watching, for far and wide, and well into the enemy's country, our scouts and spies have spread themselves—even in Kumassi itself.

In this way not only are the actual moves of the Ashantis known to us, but also their every plan and preparation. At one piquet there stands a little group that interests us all. Two of the naked Adansi scouts have charge of a prisoner who is tied to one of them by a withe of monkey-creeper. It is an Ashanti spy whom they have caught within the outpost line. An hour's interrogation gets little but contradictory statements from him, so he is remanded, under guard, for further inquiry. Other men are caught hiding in the bush, but evidently more fools than knaves, and they are sentenced to help in cutting the track and clearing the path. So, although at present we have not so far come to blows, life at the outpost is not altogether without its charm and interest.

CHAPTER 9

The Bekwai Column

5th January, 1896.

A night march is, as a rule, a slow and tedious business, unless there is some little excitement to enliven it. Last night we had the experience of a night march, in which the spice of adventure relieved the tedium, although it did not, and indeed could not, do much towards making it a rapid one. The King of Bekwai, a tributary of Kumassi, had sent to the governor messengers asking that he might come under the British flag, and that protection might at once be sent to him, as otherwise he would be taken by Prempeh and executed. A small flying column was therefore organised, and ordered to proceed at once from our outposts to the Bekwai capital, some twenty miles distant through the bush. The one road to it was held by an Ashanti piquet.

The column was ordered to take a week's supplies, in order to render it independent of its communications should it become cut off, in the defence of Bekwai, from the main body of the expedition. But this carrying of provisions, together with medical stores, ammunition, &c., involved the addition to its personnel of some 450 carriers, and as the whole force could only move in single file through the narrow jungle track, it may be imagined how great an incubus to its fighting efficiency was this long train of defenceless people. Even were the head of the column to succeed in driving the Ashanti piquet out of its position, the certainty was that the men composing it would scatter into the bush on either side of the track, and there lie ambushed until the non-combatant portion of the force came up before they opened fire.

The effect on unarmed carriers—who by nature are at any rate no braver, if half as brave, as most people—would have been excellent from the enemy's point of view, and would possibly have meant disaster to the little expedition. Moreover, the expedition was not a reconnaisance in force to drive in outposts, but rather a relief party, whose one object was to put itself as quickly as possible in touch with the place it was ordered to succour. It was, therefore, determined to make a secret flank march past the Ashanti outposts by night, and so gain a position where, on the one hand, we should be in touch with Bekwai, and, on the other, be in rear of the outpost, and so able to attack it with full advantage.

From Dompoassi, to reach Bekwai, the flying column would have to follow the Kumassi road as far as Esian Kwanta. At this point the Bekwai road branches off to the left; but it was at this same point that the Ashanti piquet was posted. About a mile away, to the left of Esian Kwanta, deep in the bush, is the village of Obum, connected with the Bekwai road by a path which joins it near Heman. This village, Obum, was not connected with the main Kumassi road until our scouts came and cut a path. And it was by this route, Obum and Heman, that the flank march was to be conducted. The flying column under my command was composed and formed as follows:—

First, a section of the scouts ranging well to the front; then an advanced guard, followed by one company, headquarters, and drums of the Gold Coast Houssas, under command of Captain Mitchell. Then came the long string of carriers, among whom were distributed the Elmina company of my scouts for their better protection. Behind the carriers came a second company of Houssas, with a rearguard; and finally, in rear of all, another section of scouts, the whole comprising 700 men, and extending, when closed up, over a mile of path. No orders had been given to the force as to its march or destination till after dusk. It was then too late for would-be deserters to abscond; they would rather face the enemy with the crowd than venture alone on the ghost-haunted path that led homewards; and for the same reason, Ashanti spies, if there were any, having seen the camp apparently settle down for the night, would have gone back to report all quiet.

We gave orders to parade at moonrise—that was at a quarter to nine—and shortly after that hour the column stood ready to proceed. In the bush-clearing, which is the site of the former town of Dompoassi, the rising moon, gleaming dully through the heavy night mist, gave sufficient light to show the long line of men standing motionless and dead silent—like a wall. The orders were given out and explained as to what was to be done by every man in the event of attack; ammunition was cast loose—with no little pleasure on the part of the

Houssas—and presently the word was given to march—not that any word was heard, but the ghostly wall was seen to be slipping quietly along to where it was lost in the dark tunnel of the bush.

And then began a night of trouble. Dark as pitch, one's only guide to the path was the white rag or package on the next man in front. With stick in hand, one groped one's way through the deep, dense gloom, hoping that as the moon rose things would improve—but they didn't. Buried in this bush, below the over-laced tree-tops, scarcely a ray could penetrate. Now a jerk down as one stepped off a hummock, now a stumble over a root, now caught in a prickly creeper, now ploughing through the holding swamp; and all around the deep silence of the forest, only broken by the rare crack of a trodden stick. One could scarcely believe that several hundred people were with one, moving—slowly, it was true, but still moving—ever forward. The carriers carried, in addition to their loads, their own packages of food and furniture—the furniture consisting of a mat, the food of plantains and dried fish.

It was this dried fish that was my trouble. It was horrid; but one felt comforted to think that two atmospheres, namely, malaria and fish, could not have a place on that path together. Fallen trees were frequent, and tangled bush and streams combined to check and break the column. Each man took his several seconds to negotiate the obstacle, and lost a few yards of distance in doing so, thus every minute saw the column growing longer. This could only be remedied by frequent halts and slow marching at the head. Occasionally the check would come from the head itself. Marching with the advance guard, there would be a sudden bump against the man in front of you, and, like a train of trucks, the whole party bumped to a standstill; then the whisper passed that the scouts had discovered the enemy. Suddenly a flicker and a flare of light in the bush well to our right. Enemy? No, it is the advanced scouts on our road, which twists and serpentines in a marvellous way, who think they have discovered an enemy's ambush. They creep around the particular thicket they suspect, then suddenly lighting brands, they hurl them into the hiding-place to light up the hoped-for target.

This time they draw blank, and we move on again, grateful even for this little excitement. The march does not appear so tedious or so slow when one moves among the scouts. These fellows are on the *qui vive* all the time—now stopping to listen, now diving into the bush, with scarce a rustle, to search the flanks. Nor is their watchfulness too great for the occasion, for twice we come upon the glowing logs of outpost fires that have hastily been quitted; but those are the only signs of men—whether friend or foe—being in the forest besides ourselves. At length the scouts creep forward, spreading out in an open clearing, and we reach the village of Obum. It is occupied by Bekwais, who, as they peer startled from their doors, tell us no Ashanti scouts are there. But we do not pause; clearings are more frequent, and consequently the light is better, and now we are on a well-worn path things seem better; but there is very little improvement in pace—the carriers are tired, and the column keeps ever trailing out.

It is long past two in the morning when our advanced guard reaches the village of Heman, and an hour later before the tail of the column comes in. Only nine miles in six hours, and everybody fagged! But we have gained our point; we have passed the outposts, and are in Bekwai country, within reach of the capital. We learn that the Ashantis have not yet advanced against it, and all is quiet. So after planting our outposts, we spread our beds in the verandahs which form the houses here, and roll off to sleep in no time. But it is not for long. Four hours' rest and a light breakfast set us up for further work. One company of Houssas move off, with all the carriers, for Bekwai, some ten miles distant, while the remaining company, together with the scouts, prepare to turn on Esian Kwanta to clear the Ashantis out of it.

The Houssas turn out with an eager alacrity that reminds one of our little warriors in other climes—the Ghoorkas. But once again, alas! their hopes are disappointed. The native scouts sent on ahead to reconnoitre Esian Kwanta come trotting back to tell us the enemy are not waiting for us to attack, but have bundled themselves out and away towards Kumassi. This renders the main road clear for those coming after us, and leaving a piquet of the scouts to occupy Esian Kwanta, we march away for Bekwai.

4th January,

One emerges from the shady forest on to a red, bare rising ground, on which are two long straggling streets of huts crossed by two others at right angles—open and airy, but unimposing. This is Bekwai.

The Ashanti houses are similar in design to those of the Adansi country, in that a house usually consists of a collection of four small verandahs facing inwards, with walled backs. They thus form a little court, with a small portico all round—not at all unlike the Pompeian houses, the more so as they are *stuccoed* with a smooth red-coloured cement. The houses differ in construction from those of the Adansis in being made of wattle and daub, and in having very high-pitched roofs. So long as the fine weather, with which we have luckily been blessed, continues, they form ideal houses for living in—shady, airy, and fairly clean.

Immediately on arrival of the flying column in Bekwai, I proceeded to the so-called palace, where I was received by the king in council, and after giving the king a letter, assuring him of British protection, I received the evidently earnest thanks of the king for the prompt coming of the protecting force. The following morning (5th January) was devoted to the ceremony of hoisting the British flag, and small as the matter seemed to be at first, it developed into a very impressive function. African monarchs are very hard to hurry, but there was much business to be done, and business on an expedition such as this has to be done quickly. So that, after several messages requesting the king's wishes as to where and when the ceremony of hoisting the flag should take place, I had the staff set up in a spot of my own choosing, paraded my force, and sent to tell the king that all was ready.

This had the desired effect in the end, although the guard of honour of Houssas and of the B.P. Scouts had some time to wait before the din of drums and horns and the roaring of the crowd told that the royal procession was on the move. Presently it came in sight—a vast black crowd surging and yelling round the biers on which the king and chiefs were borne. Above and around them twirled the great state umbrellas. In front were bands of drummers with small drums, then dancing men who leaped and whirled along, fetish men in quaint head-dresses, drummers with kettledrums, trumpeters with their jaw-bedecked ivory horns, and then the great war-drums, carried shoulder-high, and hung with skulls, which were, however, for this occasion covered with a strip of cloth, signifying that it was a peace ceremony. There were the king's court criers with their tiny black and white caps, and running before and behind there rushed the crowd of slave boys carrying their masters' stools upon their heads.

The roar and the drumming became intense as the procession came rushing up the road—for it moved at a fast pace—and the umbrellas whirling and leaping gave a great amount of life and bustle to the scene. At last the throne and chairs were set, and the people marshalled by degrees into some kind of order. I then offered to the king the flag with all its advantages, which the king, with much spirit in his words, eagerly accepted; every phrase he used, besides being formally

Hoisting the flag at Bekwai

applauded by the chorus of court criers, was evidently fully approved of by the concourse.

The king then moved from his seat to the flagstaff. Though it was but a few paces, the move involved no small amount of ceremony. The umbrella had to be kept twirling over him while the bearer moved only on the ball of the foot. Men went before to clear every stick and straw from the royal path. The fetish man, in a handsome Red Indian kind of feather head-dress and a splendid silver belt, appeared to bless the scene. One man supported the king by holding his waist, and was himself similarly supported by two or three others in succession behind. Another mopped the king with a handkerchief, while boys armed with elephants' tails kept off stray flies from the royal presence.

The king was dressed in a kind of patchwork toga with a green silk scarf, on his head a small tortoiseshell cap, and on his wrists, among the pendant fetish charms, he wore some splendid bracelets of rough gold nuggets and human teeth. In all his barbaric splendour the king moved up to the flagstaff. The flag was at the masthead in a ball, and as he pulled the halyard that let it fall out in long gaudy folds, the band of the Houssas struck up "God save the Queen," and the troops presented arms. The king made a gesture as of going to sleep, with his head on his hand, and said that under that flag he should remain till he died. The officers of the Houssa force then came up and were introduced to the king. These were Captains Mitchell, Aplin, and Middlemist, Dr. Murray, &c.

Later in the day the king and chiefs came in procession and called upon the British officers. This consisted in their filing past, bowing to each officer, and holding the hand out as if to bless him—the greater chiefs shaking hands. The king himself shook hands three or four times over with me, calling me his friend and deliverer, and then proceeded to favour the company with a few steps— a proceeding almost unprecedented in the annals of Bekwai, and intended as a very special compliment. This was the end of the ceremonial palaver; but later in the day there came a business palaver, the first of a series which lasted over the next two or three days, whereat the king was asked to make some return for the privilege he now enjoyed of being a British subject, such as supplying men to act as carriers at a shilling a day, men to act as armed levies, assistance of villagers in cutting roads through the bush, and in supplying vegetable markets, &c.

To each and every proposal he found some insuperable objection. A thousand carriers were required in two days' time; he could produce only two hundred in six days. Two thousand armed men were wanted to form a levy; he could only produce one thousand. This was accepted, and the thousand soldiers transferred to be carriers. He had not reckoned on that, so added they could not carry loads, did not know how, and could not be collected in less than ten days. Endless argument, promises of reward, only passed hours of fruitless talk.

"Was this the way he showed his gratitude for being saved from the Ashanti?"

"Yes; he was very sorry, but he could do no more."

"Very well, then, tomorrow the flag would be hauled down, and the troops would march away."

Thereupon, he thought that possibly six hundred carriers might be got in four days, and so on, until at last all was promised as desired, and eventually the promises have been very fairly carried out. But it was a very wearisome business, this long preliminary haggling. The king, too, was generous in his way. A long string of slave boys brought us a pile of good things, such as yams, plantains, *pawpaws*, chickens, eggs, sheep, and even a bullock. And what a brute a man becomes after even a few weeks in the bush! We simply revelled in this fresh food. And yet, up to the present, we had had no cause to complain; modern "canning" science has shorn a campaign of much of its hardship; we are well supplied with Maconochie's rations, and as a great authority has said, "*an army can go anywhere and do anything, so long as it possesses morale and Maconochie.*"

On the 5th January we were joined by a new white officer, Captain Williams, South Staffordshire Regiment, better known as "Litre-billee." He came to us practically for the purpose of replacing "The Sutler," who had at last fallen into the clutches of the fever fiend, and had to be sent into the newly-established hospital at Qwisa. But "Litre-billee" was already ill when he reached us at Bekwai. And soon we heard that yet another officer, Captain Green of the Houssas, who had been sent to command a wing of the levy then on a reconnaissance westward, had also been struck down. The fever, too, was not of a kind that had a set-to with you and then retired, but after giving a shattering blow, he hung around and kicked at you at intervals; so that these officers, after their first seizure, were never up to the mark again, although between the attacks they went to work as energetically as ever.

6th January.

This day was enlivened by an incident which, small as it was in itself, had a large effect on our dealings with the King of Bekwai. My report to the assistant adjutant-general thus briefly describes it all:—

"I received this morning your orders to stop communications between the King of Bekwai and messengers from the people at the coast or at Kumassi.

"I accordingly sent out piquets on the roads; and hearing that two native clerks had just arrived from the south, simultaneously with some envoys from Kumassi, and that all were about to confer with King Bekwai, I marched half a company of Houssas to the king's house, surrounded it, called him out, and ordered him to hand to me the strangers. This he did, and I have them under guard in different houses. Neither the Cape Coast men nor the Ashantis have had any interview with the king. Two of the king's men tried to escape during the arrest, but were captured by the Houssas at the back of the 'palace.'"

This somewhat high-handed procedure evidently startled the king, and showed him that we did not blindly believe in him. The result was that from that hour he exerted himself, and carried out fully one-half of his promises.

While at Bekwai, we have been joined by Prince Christian Victor and Major Piggott, who have come up to see the place, and who evidently mean to make themselves welcome to headquarters when they return with the numbers of fowls and eggs they are purchasing from the natives.

CHAPTER 10

Forward Movements

On 8th January we interviewed a party of envoys sent from Kumassi to ask us to delay, if not to abandon, our advance upon that place. Then, after a run back down to the road to report progress at headquarters (which were now at Qwisa), I pressed on with the levy in continuation of our work of road-making. One good I got out of my hurried trip to headquarters was, that I obtained the valuable services of Major Gordon, 15th Hussars, for the levy, in lieu of Captain Graham and the others who were still sick; but a cloud hung over that day, as I heard of the death, at Prahsu, of poor Victor Ferguson, Royal Horse Guards. "*Beloved by all*" stands true for him. And Prince Henry too was just struck down, and lying sick in camp.

15th January.
We have pushed on from day to day, bush-cutting, camp-building, bridging, and corduroying in the never-changing, never-ending forest. On the further bank of the Ordah River we clear a large amount of bush, to form a field of fire for a rough bridgehead, which we hastily construct of brushwood—for 'tis here we might expect to be opposed, as happened in 1874. Indeed, so hopeful are the troops at this point that the noise of our axes as we were felling trees brought up the Special Service Corps at the double, since it sounded like the dropping fire of rifles. It was here, too, that "The Sutler" reappeared, pale from his bed of sickness, but resolved to be with us for the advance on Kumassi. And how our "red-caps" cheered to see him with them once again!

At Ordasu once more we meet an embassy from Prempeh. To Captain Donald Stewart, our political officer, they offer his submission—complete and unconditional. Alas! this looks like a peaceful end of all our work. Yet at the moment there have been the makings of a row. A panic among the attendants of the envoys induced a rush into the bush, and as they blundered through our active outposts, the latter, naturally thinking something wrong, started in chase, and chairs and stools, state swords and oof-bags were dropped in wild confusion. But confidence was soon restored, losses made good, and the summary punishment of one or two detected looting put all on friendly terms again.

Yet, in spite of all assurances, we cannot trust to what Ashantis say. We know their warriors are not far away, and every care must still be taken as we near Kumassi.

The following is the formation ordered for our final advance into the place:—

The levy, being now 860 strong, is able to find two flanking parties on by-roads to the town, in addition to its main party on the central road.

Baden-Powell's Command.

☐   ☐   ☐

Distance variable.

Advanced Guard. { ☐ } Two Companies Gold Coast Houssas and Maxim.

Distance, quarter mile, communication kept up by men dropped by the Gold Coast Houssas.

Nearly nine miles long.

☐ Special Service Corps.
†† Two guns.
† Maxim.
☐ Headquarters Staff.
☐ Half Bearer Company.
☐ Six Companies 2nd West Yorkshire Regiment.
†† Two guns.
†† Two rockets.
☐ Half Bearer Company.
☐ Ammunition Column.
☐ Baggage Column.
☐ Supply Column.
☐ Field Hospital.

} One Company 2nd West India Regiment distributed by half sections through this portion of the column.

Rear Guard. { ☐ Two Companies 2nd West Yorkshire Regiment.
☐ Lagos Houssas, with Maxim.

CHAPTER 11

In Kumassi

Kumassi, 17th January.
Kumassi at last! And what a disappointment! For a long and toilsome march to end in a scene of such meanness and squalor; for a well-equipped, expensive expedition to have attained its goal with so very little return to show for it—all contribute to depress everybody with a feeling of bitter disappointment rather than with the high elation that had been hoped for. Especially hard has it been on the men in the ranks. For weeks past they have been borne up by the one hope—they have struggled on—more than manfully—against all the evils of the climate and the country. Through the endless, sickly forest they have dragged on mile after mile, literally fighting down leg-weariness and fever; every man meaning to be "in it" when the fight came off; and after that—well, they didn't care whether they lived or died—better perhaps to get bowled over by the fever then, as it would mean riding in a hammock back to the coast. But as things now stand, even without the fight, the expense will be the same in valuable lives and good constitutions lost.

All yesterday my force was working its way by three different paths towards the capital. Here and there we captured armed Ashantis watching in the bush, but no kind of resistance was offered to the advance. One curious incident occurred to waken up those spirits of the main body who had begun to despair of getting a fight. Major Gordon was commanding the right flank party of the advanced force. A crumpled scrap of paper arrived by a native runner from this part of the command, bearing the ominous words,—

Major Gordon
Killed 14th inst.

This, of course, caused much discussion and rumour in the camp, till someone discovered a faint pencil note of receipt initialled by Major Gordon himself, and it then was remembered that a piece of fresh meat had been sent off to him a day or two previously, with this selfsame label attached to it.

A few miles in rear of my crew came the main body, headed by Houssas and the Special Service Corps, and, with its long string of supply, ammunition, and hospital columns, it covered something like nine miles of road.

The duty of the advanced force was to scout and to cut the road for the main body, but there was now. no time for building huts, as had been the practice up till now; accordingly the troops had to make their own bush-shelters or pitch their *tentes d'abri*.

Most unfortunately a tornado paid us a visit last night. A violent thunderstorm and torrents of rain lasting several hours played havoc with the slight, improvised shelters, and turned everybody out in good time for an early start, but as wet and bedraggled as it was possible for men to be. Still, as usual, the wetter and more miserable his surroundings, the more cheery is Tommy Atkins, and today was to be the last of the march. Reports were flying around that the enemy meant to oppose us at the gate of Kumassi, to make one stand there, and if beaten, to blow up the city, and disperse into the bush. "Gates," "city," "king's palace;" all sounded well, but what did we find?

Through dense, high elephant grass, along a little beaten footpath—which was strewn with fetish dolls—we got near to the place. As our scouts warily approached, the drums could be heard rumbling and booming far and near. Presently we passed a cluster of the usual mud huts, then another; several other clusters were in sight, with patches of high jungle grass between. Then a bare open patch of ground 200 yards across, with huts about, and more thatched roofs in the hollow beyond.

This was Kumassi.

With Graham and myself and our scouts came Captain Donald Stewart, the Political Officer, and Major Piggott, with the Union Jack on a silver-mounted hog-spear. Then came the native levies, followed by a company of Houssas with their drums and fifes, under Captain Mitchell. Within a few minutes of our arrival there appeared from the right of the town Major Gordon's flank detachment, and shortly after from the left a similar party of the levy, who had cut their way through the bush where no road lay. So that, had the enemy resisted the entrance of the centre main column, he would have found himself immediately attacked on both flanks simultaneously, and the fight, had there been one, could not have lasted long. The advanced force now formed itself upon the so-called parade-ground, and sent piquets on beyond the town to guard approaches, while the main body was moving up from out the bush.

The drumming in the town was getting louder, and the roar of voices filled the air; but, alas! it was peace drumming. The great coloured umbrellas were soon seen dancing and bobbing above the heads of the surging crowds of natives. Stool-bearers ran before, then came the whirling dancers with their yellow skirts flying round them. Great drums, like beer-barrels, decked with human skulls, were booming out their notes, and bands of elephant-tusk horns were adding to the din. The king and all his chiefs were coming out to see the troops arrive. Presently they arranged themselves in a dense long line. The umbrellas formed a row of booths, beneath which the chiefs sat on their brass-nailed chairs, with all their courtiers round them. This was nine o'clock, and there they sat till five.

Often had they sat like this before upon that same parade-ground; but never had their sitting been without the sight of blood. The object of this open space was not for parading troops, but for use as the theatre of human sacrifice. Orders had been given before our arrival to clean away all signs of this custom, nor were the people to speak of it to the white men; but with very little cross-examination all the facts came out. Indeed, while standing about the parade-ground, "The Sutler" peered into the coppice close by, where the trees supported a flock of healthy-looking vultures, and there at once he found skulls and bones of human dead.

And there sits Prempeh, looking very bored, as three scarlet-clad dwarfs dance before him, amid the dense crowd of sword-bearers, court criers, fly-catchers, and other officials. He looks a regal figure as he sits upon a lofty throne with a huge velvet umbrella standing over him, upon his head a black and gold tiara, and on his neck and arms large golden beads and nuggets. Presently a little party of our force comes hurriedly across the ground, three white soldiers with four natives carrying a reel and winding off the field telegraph; and thus within a few minutes practically of the arrival of the advanced force in Kumassi, the fact would have been known at home had not the previous day's tornado destroyed the line in sundry places. But this feat has not been performed without cost. Of the telegraph section, Captain

KING PREMPEH WATCHING THE ARRIVAL OF TROOPS.

Curtis is in hospital with fever, as are also many of his men; and it is a fact worthy of record how, in spite of this and of the heavy work connected with the laying and the working of the line, its completion has been carried out with such rapidity and efficiency.

The billeting officers sent forward under Colonel Ward, the assistant adjutant-general for B duties, have been busy in allotting different portions of the town to the various units of the force as quarters, so that no time need be lost in housing them on their arrival.

And presently they come. The advanced guard of the Houssas lead the way.

Then come the Special Service Corps. Wet, and white of face, but going strong and well, they march up in their little companies to their places on parade, amid the admiring cheers of those of us who were already there to greet them. Close behind the 7-pounder guns came up, carried on bamboo poles.

And then Sir Francis Scott and staff, all looking hale and well. In rear of these there marches in the West Yorkshire Regiment, all ranks of most soldierly and most workmanlike appearance. A thousand pities that there is so little for them to do!

No time is lost. The billeting officers show the way, and soon the units are filing off to their various quarters about the town, the advanced force continuing its move to a mile beyond the town to Bantama.

Later in the afternoon, Sir Francis Scott, with all his staff, seated in a semicircle on the parade-ground, received a visit from King Prempeh and his chiefs. There had been some conjectures as to what Prempeh might do when asked to come down from his throne to meet the commander of the troops, but he came down without a word; indeed, it looks as though the Ashantis had agreed to give in to their visitors on every point that might be raised—until their backs are turned!

The usual long string of chiefs, each with his little court, came thronging by, saluting with outstretched hand the officers; and finally King Prempeh came himself, supported and even jostled by his swarming courtiers, his flabby yellow face glistening with oil, and his somewhat stupid expression rendered more idiotic by his sucking a large nut like a fat cigar.

Sir Francis told him in plain terms that he would have to make his submission in accordance with native forms and customs to the governor, who would shortly arrive in Kumassi. Beyond that he did not enter on political questions, but merely gave a few necessary orders regarding the provision of markets and the maintenance of order, etc., and the interview came to an end.

The queen-mother followed, and looked a good-natured, smiling little woman; but beneath that smile she is said, like others of her sex, to hide a store of villainy.

Chapter 12

Preparing the "Coup"

20th January,
A very lively day today was preceded by almost as lively a night. It was known that some of the leading chiefs now in Kumassi, and even Prempeh himself, might endeavour to slip away during the night; therefore every road and bush-path leading out of the place was quietly piqueted by our levy. During the day piquets had been posted on all the main paths, more for protecting villagers bringing in supplies to the market than for any defensive purposes. But after dark these piquets were strengthened, and extra ones were added to prevent egress as well as ingress by natives.

It was soon evident, from the prisoners whom the outposts secured, that the palace people were anxiously reconnoitring the various roads only to find them all barred. John Ansah was seen by several of the piquets, and was finally captured by one posted on a by-path leading from the palace to the bush.

In the evening a council had been hastily summoned at the palace, and it sat nearly all the night.

After going round all the piquets, we put out our torches, and went as what is termed a "hanging patrol"—a party of men who "hang about" for a few minutes here and for an hour there, as the commander may deem desirable.

Our hanging about was chiefly near the palace. Twice we visited the sacred fetish grove, in front of it, where some newly-turned earth made one suspicious of hidden treasure that they might think necessary to dig up and remove to safer quarters.

Then we went and squatted in the shadow of some huts, and had hardly settled ourselves when a gleam of light came from the palace doorway, and a procession with torches issued forth? Was it Prempeh making off? The time was now three o'clock, and there was a thick, wet mist. The string of white-robed figures, looking most picturesque in the strong light of the torches, drew silently near, and then we saw, from the big hand-screen carried by the attendants, that the queen-mother was the leading notability in the group. Silently they passed up a by-street within twenty yards of us, and very softly we followed them until we had marked them down into the queen's residence. . Then back to our ambush. In a few minutes more a councillor on his way home, attended by a slave boy carrying his stool, walked into our midst. He was too startled to speak before he had been told that silence would save his life.

Soon a fast-footed pair of men were heard pattering up. Just as they came close upon us, they suspected something. One of them stood within arm's length of me, peering into the darkness in the opposite direction. I stood up, and he did not move. I reached out and got hold of him, and luckily gripped the gun he was carrying. Others of the patrol were on to him in a moment, but he fought like a maniac, wriggling and twisting till he got one hand free and dived it into the back of his skirt; but he was pinned in good time, and a handsome knife in a leopard-skin scabbard was added to our spoil.

His companion had meantime made a dash for liberty, but was tripped up and caught by a couple of quick Adansis. He proved to be a servant carrying his master's spare clothes and bedding. Hardly had these been stowed in the shade, ere an old man was heard coming slowly, slipperty-slop in his sandals, evidently loafing home after the council. We sat silent, and he passed between our ranks without ever dreaming that he was within arm's length of a dozen enemies. One or two more councillors fell into our hands, and then reveille began to sound in one camp after another round the town; strings of water-carriers began to pass our lurking-place; the mist grew lighter overhead, and our night-watch was over.

Prisoners were separately examined and released—the armed man minus his gun, sword, and knife; and soon we were back in camp, breakfasting with the keenest of appetites, and cheered by the knowledge that we had got Prempeh and the queen-mother "marked down" all safe for the morning's doings.

Chapter 13

The Downfall

10th January.

Nor were these long in beginning. Six o'clock had been named as the hour for Prempeh and all his chiefs to be on the palaver-ground. This was done, well knowing that he might then be expected about seven, and it was desirable to make an early start with the ceremony, in order not to keep the white troops exposed to the sun in the middle of the day. Soon after seven o'clock the troops began to form up on the parade-ground, but still no sign of any of the Ashantis coming; nor even was there any of the usual preliminary drumming that invariably goes on to summon all the retainers who usually form the procession.

Nearly two hours' grace had been given him; it looked as though Prempeh did not mean coming. The order was accordingly given for the Special Service Corps, assisted by the native levy, to surround the palace and the queen-mother's house, and to bring Prempeh and the queen to the governor. Captain D. Stewart went in to "draw" them.

The native levy, in view of such course becoming necessary, had during the previous day cut away the bush adjoining the palace enclosure, and thus the cordon was enabled rapidly to take up its position to close every outlet.

In a very few minutes the king was carried forth in his state cradle with a small following, and, escorted by the troops, he proceeded hurriedly to the *palaver*-ground. The queen-mother, similarly escorted, followed shortly after, as well as all the chiefs. They were then marshalled in a line, with a limited number of attendants each, in front of the governor, Mr. Maxwell, C.M.G., who was seated on a dais, together with Colonel Sir Francis Scott, K.C.B., and Colonel Kempster, D.S.O.

A square of British troops was formed all round, backed by Houssas and the native levy.

Then the doom of the nation was pronounced in a set-scene, and amid dramatic incidents such as could not fail to impress both natives and Europeans alike.

Through the medium of interpreters—Mr. Vroom, Secretary for Native Affairs, acting for the governor; Albert Ansah for the king—the conditions of the treaty to be imposed upon the Ashantis were demanded of them.

The first of these was that Prempeh should render submission to the governor, in accordance with the native form and custom signifying abject surrender. This is a ceremony which has only once before been carried out between the Ashantis and a British governor, namely. Governor Rowe. On that occasion the king deputed officers of his court to perform the actual ceremony; but in this case it was insisted that the king must himself personally carry it out.

Accordingly, with bad enough grace, he walked from his chair, accompanied by the queen-mother, and, bowing before Mr. Maxwell, he embraced his knees. It was a little thing, but it was a blow to the Ashanti pride and prestige such as they had never suffered before.

Then came the demand for payment of the indemnity for the war. Due notice had been previously given, and the Ashantis had promised to pay it; but unless the amount, or a fair proportion of it, could now be produced, the king and his chiefs must be taken as guarantee for its payment.

The king could produce about a twentieth part of what had been promised. Accordingly, he was informed that he, together with his mother and chiefs, would now be held as prisoners, and deported to the Gold Coast.

The sentence moved the Ashantis very visibly. Usually it is etiquette with them to receive all news, of whatever description, in the gravest and most unmoved indifference; but here was Prempeh bowing himself to the earth for mercy, as doubtless many and many a victim to his lust for blood had bowed in vain to him, and around him were his ministers on their feet, clamouring for delay and reconsideration of the case. The only " man" among them was the queen.

In vain. Each chief found two stalwart British non-commissioned officers at his elbow, Prempeh being under charge of Inspector Donovan. Their arrest was complete.

But there was still an incident coming to complete the scene. The two Ansahs, although they held a large hand in causing the trouble

Submission of King Prempeh, January 20th 1896

between the British and Ashantis, appear in their own country to have little or no influence with the people, and, indeed, were looked on with jealousy and suspicion. These were surveying the scene—their handiwork—with a somewhat curious look, half amused, half nonplussed, when the governor added to his remarks the suggestion that the present might be a suitable occasion for the arrest of these two gentlemen on a charge of forgery; and before they had fully realised between them that the charge was actually being preferred against them, they found that Mr. Donovan had adroitly handcuffed them wrist to wrist, and the scene was complete.

During the performance of this act another had been quietly preparing behind the scenes. Parties of the native levy had been withdrawn from the parade-ground, and were added to the cordon already drawn round the palace. All was silent there, and all the many doors were locked. But a path from the jungle leading to the back door, also locked, brought one within sound of the buzz of many men talking within, and of the soughing of bellows of smelting fires. At the close of the palaver on the parade-ground, two companies of the West Yorkshire Regiment, under Captain Walker, were detailed to take possession of the palace, clear it of all people inside, and to collect and make an inventory of all property found inside.

One company was accordingly sent to stiffen the cordon of native levies, and with the other company I proceeded to effect an entrance by a back way, which I had previously reconnoitred.

There had been reports of the palace being undermined, and it was natural to expect that if this was so, the main entrance would be the spot selected for the mine, and that at any rate the place where the inmates were collected would be safe. Accordingly, making its way through the deserted garden, this company proceeded to the back entrance, and burst open the door. This opened into a large courtyard. Not a soul to be seen! Everything silent. Two painted doors in a side wall were kicked in by soldiers, and immediately after Tommy Atkins' persuasive voice was sounding, "Come out of that, you blatherskiting idiot; d'ye think I want to eat you?" and so on, as a frightened flock of natives were dragged out into the daylight. They were placed in the courtyard under sentries, while the remainder of the company proceeded to search every corner of every court and alley of the palace—and these were many—for further occupants. A hundred or two of these were taken, and then the work of collecting valuables and property was proceeded with.

There could be no more interesting, no more tempting work than this. To poke about in a barbarian king's palace, whose wealth has been reported very great, was enough to make it so. Perhaps one of the most striking features about it was that the work of collecting the treasures was entrusted to a company of British soldiers, and that it was done most honestly and well, without a single case of looting. Here was a man with an armful of gold-hilted swords, there one with a box full of gold trinkets and rings, another with a spirit case full of bottles of brandy, yet in no instance was there any attempt at looting.

It need not be supposed that all the property found in the palace was of great value. There were piles of the tawdriest and commonest stuff mixed indiscriminately with quaint, old, and valuable articles, a few good brass dishes, large metal ewers, Ashanti stools, old arms, &c. But a large amount of valuables known to belong to the king had disappeared, probably weeks previously—such as his celebrated dinner service of Dutch silver, his golden hat, his golden chair of state, and, above all, the royal stool, the emblem *par excellence* of the King of Ashanti.

These were all probably hidden, together with his wives, in various hamlets in the remote bush. The "loot" which we collected was sold by public auction, excepting golden valuables, which were all sent home to the Secretary of State.

The term "palace" has merely been used to denote the residence of the king. In reality there is very little that is palatial about it. It consists of a collection of the usual wattle-and-daub huts, with high walls and enormous high-pitched thatched roofs; endless courts, big and little, succeed each other, with narrow entries between, and with little or no attempt at architectural design or ornamentation.

The foundations of the old palace, built on more substantial principles, and destroyed in the last campaign, are still to be seen in the centre of the present place in a disused court.

Finding so little of real value in the palace, it was hoped that some treasure might be discovered in the sacred fetish-houses at Bantama, the burial-place of the kings of Ashanti, about a mile out of Bantama. This place had also been piqueted, but all its priests had disappeared previously, and when we broke in, only one harmless old man was found residing there. No valuables—in fact, little of any kind was found in the common huts that form the sacred place. In the big fetish building, with its enormous thatched roof, when burst open, we only found a few brass coffers—all empty The door, which was newly sealed with mortar, showed no signs of having been quite freshly closed up, and it may therefore be inferred that the treasure had been removed some weeks previously.

Then, in accordance with orders, we set the whole of the fetish village in flames, and a splendid blaze it made. The great fetish-tree, in whose shade hundreds of victims have been sacrificed, was blown up with gun-cotton, as also were the great fetish-trees on the Kumassi parade-ground. Among the roots of these there lie the skulls and bones of hundreds, and possibly of thousands, of victims to the *régime* which today, (as at time of first publication), has so dramatically been brought to a close.

Chapter 14

After Events

Kumassi, 22nd January,

It has given us some amusement here to read the statements of Mr. Hogan and others who, according to the last received budget of papers, have been enlightening the British public on the subject of Ashanti. They have, however, condemned themselves out of their own mouth, their prophecies have been altogether stultified by the outcome of events, and their general statements are equally wide of facts. Prempeh and his chiefs did not escape into the interior, partly because steps were taken to prevent them doing so, and chiefly because up to the last they had not been sure of the line that they would adopt. That the Ashantis would not fight could not have been foreseen, but could only have been guessed at, as subsequent events have shown.

It is now known that had it not been for the presence of the two white battalions in the expeditionary force, the Ashantis would have attacked, and might very possibly have stopped any column sent up. Eight thousand men had been collected in Kumassi only ten days before our arrival there, and are today not altogether disbanded. They were, as our scouts reported, waiting about in neighbouring villages ready for the call of their chiefs who were in Kumassi. But the *coup* of Mr. Maxwell in arresting in full palaver the king, queen-mother, and all the leading chiefs, has utterly demoralized them, and the nation is now like a flock of sheep without a leader. Had the people even guessed beforehand what the result of the *coup* was to have been, there is not the smallest doubt that they would have fought to prevent it.

When we arrived here on the 17th inst., Kumassi was full of its ordinary inhabitants. On the 19th there was suspicion in the air. Numbers were trying to make their way out of the town; all the fetish priests at Bantama fled; there is little doubt, had the roads and the palace not been carefully guarded all that night, that Prempeh and other important personages would have been missing in the morning. By the evening of the 20th, the day of the arrest, there was not a soul left in Kumassi. With his characteristic promptness the governor intimated that the force could now move down again, taking with it its string of prisoners, and on the 21st orders were issued for the move next day.

A prison had been improvised by isolating a suitable collection of huts near the headquarters camp. All surrounding houses were levelled to the ground, and a guard was mounted to make it secure on all sides. Precautions had also to be taken, not only against escape or rescue, but against the suicide or assassination of the king; the disgrace, and more especially fetish and superstition, made it desirable to the king and to his people that he should not be removed alive from Kumassi.

Yesterday evening (the 21st) more reports came in of armed men being in neighbouring villages, and there were whisperings of possible reconnaissances during the night. Bantama, about a mile and a half from Kumassi, was the headquarters of the levy, and it was there, at two in the morning of today, I paraded a reconnoitring force—four companies of the scouts under Major Gordon, two companies of Houssas under Captain Mitchell, a Maxim gun in charge of Armourer-Sergeant Williams. Then we started; a long, silent string of men gliding past the outposts of the troops in camp, down through the deserted lanes of Kumassi, and out into the bush beyond. Suddenly our path becomes muddy, and then watery—we try to keep dry-shod, but in vain; ere long we are ankle-deep, then knee-deep, and deeper, and so we wade on and on through the cold and evil-smelling water swamps that lie below Kumassi.

Once past it, our way lies through the densest bush by a narrow, winding foot-track, whose line we guess at by feeling with a stick. Streams, fallen trees, and high-growing roots obstruct our way at every step, and our progress naturally is extremely slow, and, cold and miserable about the legs, we creep along, hour after hour, mile after mile, in deepest silence; frequent halts while scouts examine points ahead, or to allow some closing up in rear. At last the dawn begins to show itself in the thick and dripping mist around us. The men all have their orders what to do on arrival at the village. The scouts will gain both flanks through the bush, followed by a section to either hand of Houssas; the Maxim takes the centre with the remainder of the Houssas, while the rest of the levy face about and guard the rear. The ammunition is ready, and we really hope that now at least a brush will be our reward.

Presently the scouts bring in a capture, a wild-looking native talking in a strange upcountry tongue. He is a slave, who has just made his escape from a village near our path, and which at this moment is full of armed Ashantis; but it is not the place we came to take. Here we know that 400 men are mustered, and so we press on faster in the gradually lightening gloom. Now we are near, the scouts check to reconnoitre, and the column closes up on tiptoe. Forward! A cry from the scouts. Too late! They've gone; got wind of our coming, and the place is empty. Nothing for it but to munch our biscuit and chocolate, and after a few minutes' rest to march our weary way back—back through the bush, back through the long, wet, foetid swamp, and so to the camp.

Here we find the tail of the column just moving out upon its downward march, and we prepare to form the rearguard. But other orders wait us. Another village has just been reported to be full of men and treasure, so, after an hour's rest and breakfast, once more the scouts turn out, and, backed by a fresh company of Houssas, proceed to visit the newly-designated point. Once more we ford the filthy swamp, which, with its repeated stirrings by many feet, has now "a fine old crusted" reek. Luckily we have not far to go—two miles will bring us there. A running scout was sent before to spy the place, and presently he meets us with the news we half expected—the enemy have gone, leaving five men there and heaps of boxes. So we press on silently. Our scouts capture one of theirs without a sound. Then we rush the village, and catch three men who have hidden away their arms.

Among the huts lie strewn a host of boxes broken and empty. Within the little courtyards are piles of articles in jumbled-up confusion. The place itself was Prempeh's country house, and his furniture was chiefly feather-beds, plates, dishes, and despatch-boxes. Delft of the commonest make strews the place, and is evidently looked upon as valuable by our men, who, after asking leave, proceed to pile themselves up with the largest dishes they can find. The place looks like a jumble auction sale. Old chairs and curtains, common decanters, a bust of Her Majesty, common cotton cloths, gin bottles in profusion. At first it looked as though a hurried attempt at packing up had been made by the inmates, but one of our prisoners told another tale. Valuables and jewellery had been securely packed in all the boxes here and placed in charge of a Sefwi slave, the king's head drummer. The day before our arrival this man had come, with others of his tribe, and had systematically looted the whole of the valuables, and was by this time miles away, hidden in the bush.

Once more we turned back to the camp, a disappointed crew; and on arrival there we found the Union Jack was flying half-mast high. Good Prince Henry! a martyr, if ever there was martyr, to his sense of duty. And then we started on our coastward march, not as we had pictured it, light-hearted and rejoicing, but tired and disappointed, and very sick at heart at this last crowning blow.

CHAPTER 15

The Coastward March

Prahsu, 26th January,
The retreat is generally more fatal than the advance. In its retirement from Kumassi the expeditionary force has still had the same two foes to contend against that it had in the advance up to that place. On the one hand, it had to be prepared against the Ashantis; on the other hand, against fever.

The danger from Ashantis on the return journey lay in any attempt that might be made to effect the rescue of their king, or of one or more of their chiefs from the custody of the English, or, failing a rescue, in the endeavour which it was more than probable they would make to assassinate Prempeh. It would be a great blow to the prestige of the Ashanti nation, and destructive of the one national superstition, if the king were to be taken even across the Sberri River, which surrounds Kumassi, and then on, altogether out of the country. So that as long as he was still in Kumassi, or in Ashanti territory, there was every chance that an attempt would be made, if rescue were impossible, even by single individuals to take the king's life. Nor would there be an end to this danger when he had passed out of Ashanti territory, for then he would travel through first the Bekwai and later the Adansi countries, where people were quite as ready to shoot him, although from another cause, namely from a desire to pay off old scores and wipe out the blood of relations who had been the victims of sacrifice at some of the king's "customs."

The narrow path that constitutes the "Great North Road," and the dense bush hedging either side of it, affords a perfect cover for such ambuscade, whether of an individual or of even a large body; consequently special precautions had to be taken to make all secure for the safe passage of the prisoner. He was escorted by white troops on the path, while all the by-paths for miles round were occupied by piquets of the levy, and the bush itself was thoroughly searched by them previous to and during the passage of the convoy of prisoners. The levy also visited outlying villages, where gatherings of armed men were reported, and drove them off in all directions. There was plenty of evidence that the precautions taken were no more than were necessary, and the additional toil was compensated by the entire success of this our last task of the campaign.

The other enemy—the fever—was not defeated with such success. Since turning its back on Kumassi for the coastward march, the force has come to feel the clutch of sickness. The weather is no worse than it was for the march upcountry. It is, in fact, even more healthy just now, and the men themselves, after their long march, should now be in far better, harder condition than when fresh landed, soft from shipboard life. It is, therefore, not so much from physical causes that the men are becoming a prey to sickness; it is rather due to mental depression. It is the result of the feeling of absolute disappointment which now pervades the force. They have worked hard, marching through the poisonous tangle of rank forest and swamp, bearing up under the enervating heat, and fighting against sickness, simply with the pluck and determination that are characteristic of the Briton bent on achieving the task he has set before himself.

To see the Special Service Corps, at the end of a long day's march, suddenly prick up their ears, as it were, and press on at the double because they thought they heard firing in front, was a sight that may well be recorded. Their one idea has been to get at the enemy to give him a real good drubbing; and whatever may be said of the morality of such an aspiration, none the less it spurs Tommy Atkins to great deeds, that so he may win the medal. Now all their hopes and all their aspirations are dashed to the ground. Wearied and dispirited, they are now dragging their way back along the hateful, depressing road, and between them and the coast there lie many miles of malarial bush, through which but few can pass untouched by the poison in the air. But they plod along pluckily through the foetid forest.

As I passed one loaded hammock among the many on the line of march today, a haggard, bearded face within looked out with burning eyes, and the sick man asked, "Do you think, sir, they will give us a medal for this?" At my "No doubt they will," he sank back in some relief to dream it over. The men have suffered and endured even more than if they had had fighting, for the consequent excitement would have carried them through much that affects them now.

Cape Coast Castle, 8th February, 1896.

The march up to Kumassi was a weary, toilsome business, even in spite of the excitement and hope which buoyed the men up. What, then, can one say of the march down, when the same long depressing road had to be re-traversed by men whose spirits were now lowered by the deep disappointment they had suffered, and whose systems were gradually giving in to the attacks of the ever-resent fever fiend? In truth, that march down was in its way as fine an exhibition of British stamina and pluck as any that has been seen of late years. For the casual reader in England this is difficult to realise, but to one who has himself wearily tramped that interminable path, heartsick and footsore, the sight of those dogged British "Tommies," heavily accoutred as they were, still defying fever in the sweltering heat, and ever pressing on, was one which opened one's eyes and one's heart as well.

There was no malingering *there*; each man went on until he dropped. It showed more than any fight could have done, more than any investment in a fort or surprise in camp, what stern and sterling stuff our men are made of, notwithstanding all that cavillers will say against our modern army system and its soldiers.

To one fine young fellow—who, though evidently gripped by fever, still was doggedly marching on—I suggested that his kit was very heavy, whereat he replied, with the tight-drawn smile and quavering voice one knows too well out here, "It ain't the kit, sir! it's only these extra rounds that I feel the weight of;" these extra rounds "being those intended for the fight which never came. The never-ending sameness of the forest was in itself sufficient to depress the most light and cheerful mind, and thus it was a great relief at length to get to Mansu, where the bush begins to open out, and where there is more of the light and air of heaven. But the change is not altogether for the better. The forest, it is true, is gone, but the road is open to the sun, while the undergrowth on either hand is denser now than ever, and forms a high impenetrable hedge that seems to shut out every breath of breeze. Acting on the experiences of the upward march, this portion of the road was now traversed by the troops by night, and consequently heat apoplexy and sunstroke were not encountered. But the string of loaded hammocks grew longer every day!

On the downward journey the discomforts of the march were added to by the clouds of flies, which up till now had never bothered us; but their presence was only natural, considering the refuse of so large an expedition, which attracted them in spite of every care that was taken to ensure the camp-grounds being kept in clean condition. At every rest-camp an officer and a guard of West Indians had been posted for this work during the expedition, and here one saw something of the thankless jobs that fall to troops on service, and which were, nevertheless, performed with all the zeal and thoroughness that characterized the work in front.

Mansu, Dunkwa, our marching was really coming near its end at last. How eagerly we listened for the first sound of the distant thundering surf, and longed for the first whiff of the sea breeze! And in due course they came. At length, between two hill-tops we saw the grey hazy horizon of the sea, and anon the great white ships all lying ready to take us home. In one short hour our life seemed changed; out of the dank bush and the shadow of disappointment we had come into the sunshine with hopes of home before us.

Cape Coast Castle lay as usual sweltering in the sun, but redeemed by the sea breeze which blows with steady regularity during the middle hours of the day, but maddening to the sick with its native clamour, heat, and smells. Never since the last expedition had the town been so full of life and business. First to arrive from the front were the gangs of supply carriers to be paid off. Under the charge of Captain Donovan and his lieutenant of the same name, the army of nigh ten thousand of them marched in in military order, and in two days had all been settled up with, paid, and dismissed to their homes.

Soon after them arrived the levy. We had accomplished the march from Kumassi to Cape Coast in seven days. Immediately on arrival the men handed in their arms and ammunition, and on the following morning were paid up and were marched out of the town by companies on their homeward roads. As has been before described, the levy was formed of contingents from half a dozen different tribes. The Bekwai, Abodom, and Adansi contingents had been discharged *en route* as the regiment passed through their respective countries. The latter, who had chiefly performed the scouting duties, received as "dash" or reward the guns with which they had been provided by government.

This was at Prahsu. They then went on as a guard of honour to the remainder of the levy, firing salutes as they went, until the village was reached in which their king resides. The king—a decrepit but loyal old man—came out to receive his men from me, and in his conversation showed his gratitude to the British for getting back for his people their own country about the Adansi hills, and stated it as his intention to return there and re-establish the Adansi capital in its former site at Fommenah. Although the men were glad to get back to their homes, the parting between them and their three white officers was full of regret on both sides, for in the short time they had been enrolled they had already picked up such discipline and drill as had made them a useful and reliable body of men, and it seemed a pity that now, just when they had attained a good standard of efficiency, their services should have to be dispensed with.

There was now a pause in the arrivals at the base for several days, but business was very brisk in the castle—the business of closing up the accounts of the expedition, checking returned stores, condemning and selling those for which there was no longer any further use. Indeed, hard work had been the order of the day there ever since we had left it to go up-country, and fever had been as obstructive at the base as it had been in the bush, but by transfer to the hospital ship *Coromandel* those who were affected were the more easily enabled to shake it off, and were, as a rule, soon back at their work again.

Here one was able to see something of the English newspapers and thus to learn something—in addition to the general news of Europe and the world at large—of what we ourselves had been doing in Ashanti. It is a notable fact that, with camps spread about as ours were over a large tract of country, one does not gather all the news that is going, and accompanied as the expedition has been by correspondents of every class and variety, it was natural to find the news was often served up in astonishing and entirely novel form. The departure of one officer from the coast to the next depot at Mansu was headed "A Plucky Dash into the Interior;" hut-building, we are told, was much interfered with by the presence of "serpents;" an illustrated paper gave views of the troops landing at the back of the castle, where no landing is possible; another showed us Prempeh surrounded by camels and horses, animals unknown at Kumassi, and so on *ad infinitum*; and doubtless we have yet to hear more of the personal feelings of some of those gentlemen who have reason to believe that they have not been treated with the respect due to their merit as word-painters. To "those who know" it should be amusing reading.

Soon after daybreak on February 5th, the West Yorkshire Regiment marched into the town from Dunkwa, having in their midst King Prempeh and the captive queen and chiefs. These were marched directly to the beach, where eight large surf-boats were lying ready for

The Embarkation of King Prempeh

their embarkation, A few marines and Houssas were posted in each boat to act as escort and to ensure the safety of the prisoners, for it was considered possible that the *kroo* boatmen might, in the excess of their hate, contrive to upset Prempeh in the surf, and hold him down till dead! However, all went well. The boats were quickly paddled through the surf, looking, with their paddles—six a side— like beetles crawling over crumpled satin, and ere long the prisoners had been transferred aboard H.M.S. *Racoon*.

This was to them the climax of their troubles. Awed and nervous at their first sight of the ocean and their first experience of boats and ships, at the utter breaking up of all their royal prestige, and their ignorance of what it might portend, they huddled all together, chiefs and attendants, in one close, frightened group; and presently, as the ship steamed out, their trials were increased by sea-sickness. An hour's run along the coast brought them abreast of Elmina Fort, and here, much to their relief, the surf-boats took them off and landed them at their final destination.

A harsh, unpromising place it looked to European eyes—a grim white fort on the surf-lashed strand, whose inner court, which forms the prison, is not inaptly termed the "Bear-pit." Here will Prempeh and his chiefs remain; but attended as they are by a fair allowance of wives and slaves, and with all their wants supplied, their confinement will in no way be a hardship to them. Before Prempeh had, reached his prison-house, his late escort, the West Yorkshire Regiment, were already installed on board the transport *Manila*—such of them as were well, but a long string of sick was sent aboard the *Coromandel*. So many that, the following day, when the Special Service Corps arrived, they had to divide the regiment between the two ships for conveyance home, and local steamers called up from neighbouring ports by telegraph were utilised to carry drafts of officers and men according to their various capacities.

The bearer company embarked on the *Manila* ere she sailed on the 6th. The immediate headquarter staff are on the *Coromandel*. Today the last of the sick from the base hospital at Conor's Hill have been swung on board, a sick-roll of close on twenty officers and 200 men. Of these nearly all are fever cases, the balance being dysentery; and it is curious to note that the percentage of sick among the officers is greater than that among the men. It is a sight to sadden any eyes to see these pale, limp forms who, but a few weeks back, were men selected for their vigour and robustness to join the expedition.

But the medical arrangements all along the line have been faultless, and have worked without a hitch. Medical attendance and stores have been abundant, sick transport has been carried out with comfort and rapidity, and once on board the hospital ship, with its comfortable, airy wards and its excellent service of hospital orderlies and nursing sisters, the invalids have every chance of speedy recovery. And perhaps the best medicine to the majority of them will be the sound of the screw and the rushing of the seething waters as we steam away out of the "smokes" that envelop this pestilential coast with their noxious haze.

CHAPTER 16

Homeward Bound

Las Palmas, 16th February,
So long as the water supply runs well, the plumber is not thought of.

The expedition to Ashanti, having succeeded without hitch or hindrance, one is apt to lose sight of the difficulties that were quietly overcome in its prosecution, and of the important results of its consummation; whereas, had the preparations been a little less complete in their character, these difficulties would have been more apparent, and disasters possible, and, perhaps, even greater credit would have redounded in the end to those charged with the conduct of the whole. As a matter of fact, this expedition now stands among the many small expeditions of late years as a pattern one for punctuality and rapidity of progress. To these points its success was entirely due, and they were the result only of careful preparation and thorough organisation; and though every branch distinguished itself by playing its part in a manner as nearly as possible approaching to perfection, the following services have without doubt scored for themselves a record performance—namely, the Transport, Supply, Medical, Telegraph, and Special Service Corps.

The Transport organised in a very few days, one might almost say hours, a larger force of human transport than has before been attempted, and its working has from the first been as eminently satisfactory as it has been vitally necessary to the progress of the expedition. The Supply, ordnance as well as commissariat, has similarly been an unqualified success. Abundance of stores of the right kind have been available from first to last at every stage of the operations. Nothing seems to have been forgotten, and nothing superfluous or useless seems to have been brought, which is no small triumph where some

14,000 men of most varied nationalities and requirements had to be catered for in a land whose products consisted of a very meagre supply of plantains.

The medical arrangements were as complete and efficient as could be devised: medical officers and sick hammocks distributed among the corps, bearer company for transport of sick and wounded, field hospital close up, hammock train laid in, relieving posts for rapid transport of sick to the coast, excellent base hospital at Cape Coast Castle, with sea transport to the capacious and well-equipped hospital ship, the *Coromandel*. The Field Telegraph was an unqualified success. It was laid with surprising rapidity, and thus permitted the advanced force to be within rapid communication with headquarters during the whole of the advance to Kumassi. The Special Service Corps—the object of much criticism in England—gained a reputation for itself that must have caused the liveliest satisfaction to the hearts of its supporters. Its small tactical units were eminently suited to the work on hand; the care which had been exercised in the selection of its men as possessing stamina and other qualifications to meet the peculiar conditions of service on the Gold Coast enabled the corps to maintain its strength and efficiency to a marked extent when contrasted with the ordinary line battalion employed on the same duty; and the emulation of each unit working with all the energy begotten of *esprit de corps* was productive of the best results in practice.

Perhaps one might also add to this record of "records" the fact that the local government worked throughout most effectively and loyally in assisting the expedition. Its *employés* had already effected much before the head of the expedition proper had even set foot in the colony. The telegraph had been laid—and in a very substantial manner—as far as Mansu; the whole of the material for the bridge over the Prah had been collected at Prahsu, and merely required to be roped for use; the road had been cut and made, and rest-camps set up from the coast to Prahsu, and the work of collecting natives to act as carriers or native levies had been effected with good results. These were points which an ordinary eye would look at as the natural aim of the local officials, but how seldom do we see them giving their aid in this way, even though the success of an expedition means everything to them.

And it must be a source of gratification to many a taxpayer (and I, alas! am one of them) to see that our departments can "run a show" of this kind in a way that transcends anything that has been done in Madagascar, Abyssinia, or Cuba. It is true that it is but a small one, but if your workman "can make a watch, you bet he can make a clock."

With all these organisations thus perfected, the expedition did not, as it could not, fail to succeed; and yet a few faults in previous preparation or a very little mismanagement might have produced a very different result. One need only look to the history of the strip of territory next to Ashanti, namely, Dahomey, or to the late conquest by France in a similar climate against a similar enemy, namely, Madagascar, to see what terrible expense in life and money has been avoided by the use of a well-planned organisation endowed with thorough efficiency in all its working parts.

The secret of the perfection in the preliminary arrangements lies in the fact that most of the heads of the staff at the War Office were themselves employed in the previous campaign in Ashanti, and have been therefore able to order things in accordance with their own personal experience of the country and climate; and the viciousness of this climate is shown by the fact that, in spite of all the forethought and precautions that were taken, no less than fifty *per cent*, of the men and something like eighty *per cent* of the officers were attacked by fever. The practical result of the efficient organisation of the expedition was the "rushing" of the Ashantis. At best the Ashantis are slow to mobilize, and on this occasion they were also doubtful how to act pending the return from England of the envoys they had sent there, and consequently had till then only partially mobilized their army.

Within two hours after the returning envoys had crossed the Prah on their journey to Kumassi our advanced force had also crossed and followed close upon their heels. The information given by these envoys to the expectant people in Kumassi was to the effect that the British force had been overrated, and was still a long way off. Armed men were then called up, and a raid was organised against the Bekwais, who showed signs of defection; but before the orders had been fully carried out, the Ansahs arrived with fresh information of the British force of white troops being well on the road, and Bekwai itself was suddenly occupied and prepared for defence by our force on the very day on which the Ashantis were to have attacked it. Additional columns were, at the same time, reported as advancing against the capital from the north and from the south-west.

There was consequently panic among the leaders; orders and counter-orders were issued—one day it was to be war, the next day peace. Envoys were sent to meet the troops with orders to make every effort to delay their advance till something could be done; but in vain.

The stream of invasion flowed steadily and rapidly forward. There was nothing for it but to distribute all the treasure and valuables for concealment in different parts of the country till the troublous times were over; and then king and chiefs must satisfy the British with whatever promises they might find necessary, so long as they could induce them to go away again. The whole *régime* was disorganised by the rapid inroad of the expedition; and the panic of the country reached its climax at the arrest and deportation of Prempeh and his chiefs.

From the foregoing it will have been deduced that the success and bloodless victory of the expedition was due to the rapidity and the completeness of the movements of the force, and that this rapidity was in its turn the result of a thoroughly planned and well-equipped organisation. But then arises the question. *Cui bono?* What is the good of this victory when you have won it? What return is there for the half million that will have been spent upon it?

Inter alia, one may at once point out that it has, at any rate, put an end to the practice of human sacrifice, which up till within three months ago had gone on with all the unchecked force that it had ever enjoyed. Fetish superstition has an immense hold on the untutored children of the bush, and tradition and custom decreed that human sacrifice was the best form of propitiation of the fetish demons. Moreover, the men of the country have no kind of diversion or employment beyond very poor hunting and an occasional raid on a neighbouring tribe. Bloodlust, like many another vicious habit, rapidly takes root and grows on a man who is without other occupation. A bloody spectacle was naturally to the Ashantis a most attractive form of amusement, especially as at the same time it satisfied their superstition.

The popularity of human sacrifice was none the less great because it gave a direct impetus to the slave trade. As a rule, the victims of fetish sacrifice were slaves, and the supply had to be kept up to the demand. How great that demand was we may, perhaps, never know, but that it was little short of enormous may be guessed partly from the deposit of skulls and bones about the fetish groves, and partly from the fact that two streets in Kumassi consisted of the houses occupied by the official executioners. The suppression of this abuse has been one result of the expedition, and the disintegration of the Ashanti kingdom into its minor kingdoms will insure its non-revival. This alliance of lawless chiefs into a common band, under the direction of the Kumassi king, has hitherto acted like a dam to a reservoir.

Within five days' march of Kumassi, to the northward, the poisonous bush country comes to an end, and on beyond there lies the open country, rich and populous, which stretches thence to Timbuctoo. The natural outlet for this country's trade is by the Kumassi road to Cape Coast Castle and the sea. This is the reservoir which the Ashanti dam has kept closed up so long. In breaking down the Ashanti gang we have broken up the dam, and the stream which will now begin to flow should, in the near future, well repay the expenses of the machine with which it has been cut. An encouraging example lies to hand in the colony at Lagos, where, as a direct result of the Jebu campaign, the trade has in a single year leaped up to double what it was before.

The British prestige has, moreover, now extended its effect into the back country among tribes who were hitherto wavering with their future allegiance in the balance, and it may be inferred that they will not delay to come under our protectorate. This in its turn will mean the extension of our boundaries till they touch the Niger, and will thereby save the Gold Coast Colony from being shut out from up-country trade, as had been threatened, by the junction of the two French forces in Dahomey and in Timbuctoo. Indeed, the colonial party of our friends across the Channel are just beginning to suspect that, using Prempeh as a nail to hang our cloak upon, we have quietly beaten them in the race for the Gold Coast Hinterland—that instead of Dahomey joining hands with the French Soudan, the Gold Coast will ere long have marched its boundary on to that of the Royal Niger Protectorate. In gaining this enlarged territory, we may very probably also gain the assistance of a ready-made force with which to hold it, namely, the army, horse and foot, of Samory.

Thus, in the course of a few weeks, an enormous change has been wrought in the history of this part of Africa, and the *vista* of a great future has been suddenly opened to the Gold Coast Colony. And yet this great result has been gained by the use of a mere handful of men, and it is only when one realises the magnitude of the result that one sees with something akin to awe how much might have been lost by a little mismanagement or by a single false move.

CHAPTER 17

The Formation of a Native Levy

There may be those among my readers who would be glad to receive some information regarding the organisation and work of the levy, and who, on the other hand, have not the leisure or inclination to wade through the foregoing pages in search thereof. To save them this trouble, I have thought it right to append the following brief account, extracted by the kind permission of the editor, from the *Journal of the Royal United Service Institute* for March, 1896:—

> Our frequent little wars in all parts of the globe necessitate continually the raising of native levies, and yet one looks in vain for any book that may give one details of organisation, or even the experiences of previous efforts, and that may serve as a guide to similar work when occasion demands it.
> It is, of course, impossible for any hard and fast organisation to be laid down to suit all cases. For example, to attempt to impose some new form of discipline and tactics on a levy of Zulus or Swazis would be to hamper a people already well-grounded in their own form of warfare; whereas with a levy of less warlike folk, such as the West African Coast tribes, some system has to be arranged by which they may be kept in hand by the few white officers available for commanding them.
> It may, therefore, be of interest to many to learn what were the lines upon which the native levy in the recent campaign in Ashanti was organised, and what was the scope of its work.
> On the arrival of the expedition at Cape Coast Castle, on December 13th last, I was ordered to raise and organise a native levy.
> Fortunately, I was given the invaluable assistance of an officer

who had already some experience of the country and its people, namely, Captain Graham, D.S.O., 5th Lancers.

Also, through the kind offices of Captain Donald Stewart, I obtained the services of Chief Andoh of Elmina, who proved himself a most loyal and trustworthy adviser on all points of native custom and character.

The material at hand for forming the levy consisted of some 300 of the Krobo tribe, under their king, Matikoli, and about 100 of the Mumford tribe, under Chief Brew. The Krobos had in former times distinguished themselves as a comparatively warlike race, and they furnished a satisfactory contingent to the native levies in the last campaign against Ashanti. The Mumfords were merely coast fishermen, splendid in physique, but absolutely useless, as they rather proudly admitted, for anything but sea-fishing. They were fitted with—

Iron sinews, but hearts of mice.

Upcountry, on the Prah, there were already collected 100 warriors of the Adansi tribe. These warriors had already been armed by the civil government with 'Dane' guns, that is, long flint-lock trade guns, and supplied with a few kegs of powder and bars of lead for ammunition. A store of these arms was lying ready at Prahsu for arming the remainder of the levy as soon as it should arrive there. Two or three days were required to collect the men at Cape Coast Castle, and it was only by adopting somewhat vigorous methods with the chiefs that this time was not prolonged to a week or more.

The native was apparently incapable of grasping any idea of punctuality; lying was the natural form of every statement or promise he made; lying was the natural attitude assumed by his body, especially when any work was to be done.

Moreover, in the present instance, the trade gin of the metropolis had come sweet to the lips of the countryman just called up from his village, and his natural stupidity was thereby rendered doubly dense. One good point about these warriors was their cowardice; the least hint of an intention of backing up an order with force ensured its prompt obedience, but this was a trump card which had to be held up with discretion until the frontier was crossed and desertion had become impossible.

In the meantime, extreme patience, coupled with firmness, was required; exasperation and a rising gorge had to be smoked or whistled down. (There is nothing like whistling an air when you feel exasperated beyond reclaim.)

It is a West Coast proverb which says, '*Softly, softly, catchee monkey.*' This was suggested jokingly as a suitable motto for the stealthily creeping corps of native scouts, but its spirit soon came to be adopted as a guiding principle in practice in all our dealings and actions. Its meaning might be construed into 'Don't flurry! Work up to your point quietly and steadily.' In a word, 'Patience!'

The Krobos and Mumfords had at length been coaxed into assembling by the evening of the 16th, and on the following day they were roughly organised in companies under headmen of their respective villages. They were then supplied with red *fezzes*, paraded for the inspection of His Excellency the Governor, and marched off for the interior.

The ultimate organisation that was found to be best adapted for all purposes, whether for pioneer work, drill, reconnaissance, or outposts, was the division of each tribe into small companies of from twenty to thirty men each.

Each tribe was under the orders of its chief, and he, or his orderly, understood English, and acted as the adjutant of his detachment, taking all his instructions from the white officer. Each company was under a 'captain,' assisted by an under-captain.

No specific duties beyond those of acting as scouts had been assigned to the levy; but as we made our way upcountry, it became evident that much pioneering work would be necessary, in order to make the road passable for troops through the dense bush and to prepare clearings and huts for rest camps. Therefore, whenever we saw a chance of obtaining tools of any description, we did not fail to avail ourselves of it; but in the end, the quantity and quality of our equipment did not amount to anything very considerable, and it was greatly due to the further system applied to our organisation that the levy was able successfully to carry out the pioneering work which it eventually accomplished. Our tools consisted mainly of machetes (long, heavy knives), naval cutlasses, spades, picks, and a few hatchets and felling-axes.

The companies were permanently detailed to certain kinds of work: thus, one was charged with the work of building bridges, another with making huts, another with digging the road

NATIVE LEVY BUILDING A FORT.

and draining it where necessary, another with felling timber and log-cutting, and so on; so that every man knew his proper work, and with a few days' practice, became proficient in it. But at first much instruction had to be given in the method of using felling-axes, spades, levers, and in knotting ropes—or, rather, the substitute for rope, the kind of creeper known as 'monkey-rope.'

Each 'captain' was made responsible for tools used by his company (and these had to be checked daily, both before and after work), and also for the presence of all his men during working hours, which, with the exception of two hours' rest for the midday meal, generally lasted from daylight till dusk. It was some time before this idea of responsibility for the working of their men could be instilled into the captains, but once it had been grasped by them, and the system had got into working order, all went smoothly and efficiently, so long as a white officer was at hand to keep the rate of progress up to the mark.

The practical outcome of the pioneer work of the levy was the cutting of over fifty miles of road beyond the Prah through the bush to Kumassi, the bridging of numberless streams, the corduroying of swamps, and the ramping of numerous giant tree-trunks that lay across the path; and also in the clearance of camping-grounds, erection of huts, and the building of three forts; and, lastly, in a piece of work that was comparatively light and yet of paramount importance, namely, in the clearing of the bush round the palace at Kumassi, which enabled that place to be surrounded, and so prevented Prempeh's intended escape when he was 'wanted.'

Of course, strong measures had at first to be taken to bring the amount of work up to the standard required, and the punishment for non-obedience of orders was supposed to be fining; but the native, unaccustomed to much regular payment of any kind, and totally ignorant of payment in arrear, could not understand the meaning of deductions and stoppages, and their infliction was not carried out; more tangible punishment had to be substituted.

Rations were not issued to the levy, but in order that they might live without raiding when in strange territory, the men were paid three pence a day, and this sufficed to buy them sufficient yams and plantains to satisfy their wants. In addition to this subsistence, the Krobos, Elminas, and Mumfords also drew, in arrears, daily pay at sixpence a man and eighteen pence for a captain. This was less than the pay of carriers, but more than would be given to levies in any other part of our dominions; for, surely, it would seem the duty of warrior-subjects to turn out when called upon for the defence of their country, as a return for our protectorate over them.

This latter rule was carried out with part of the levy, namely, the Adansis, Bekwais, and Abodoms, and they worked none the less satisfactorily for it—perhaps all the better, as they hoped, by good work, to obtain a good 'dash' or reward at the end of the campaign.

While the main body of the levy had been undergoing organisation and equipment about the Prah, as above described, the Adansi contingent of four companies had been acting as scouts and outposts to the front of the Adansi Hills, three-quarters of the way to Kumassi from the coast.

They were a wild, uncivilized crew, living entirely in the bush, and therefore well adapted for this particular duty.

It was only necessary to show them a system to work upon, and they readily grasped it. Briefly, the plan for outpost duties was this: Each company formed a piquet, and during the day it had sentries out for all paths leading to it. These sentries were concealed in the bush close by the path, and within reach of recall by the horn sounding at the piquet. Patrols of two or three men went out for the whole day on every path. No individual work could be got out of natives at night—the bush was too full of fairies and fetish devils for that. Therefore, after dark, instead of the day sentries and patrols, small detached posts of half a dozen men each were bivouacked on every path, at a distance of about a mile from the piquet.

In addition to their watchfulness, the Adansis, and also the Bekwais and Abodoms (who were afterwards added to them for detached duties), distinguished themselves by their quickness in detecting the presence of an enemy, and by the rapidity with which they conveyed the news not only to their commander, but also to neighbouring piquets and parties.

Their faculty, too, for finding their way in the forest, whether by day or by night, was surprising. They could not explain it themselves, but, like the forest tribes of South-Eastern Africa, they were in no way guided by sun or stars—some natural instinct brought them through.

In the meantime, the Krobo portion of the levy had been armed with Snider rifles, and, in the intervals of work and on the march, the companies were instructed by Captain Graham in the use of their arms and in the elements of drill. This instruction bush. A few simple whistle-signals were employed to signify 'Halt,' 'Advance,' 'Rally,' 'Cease firing,' &c., and these were readily learnt by the men.

The supply of ammunition was kept up by means of an ammunition carrier to each company. Every man was allowed five rounds only, loose in his pouch, with another five rounds tied up. This would, it was hoped, do something to check indiscriminate blazing away. Unfortunately, the work told upon Captain Graham, and in the midst of it he was struck down, and for a time incapacitated by fever; and the same fate befell two more officers who were thereupon successively attached to the levy for duty, namely, Captain Williams, South Staffordshire Regiment, and Captain Green, Gold Coast Houssas. Major Gordon, 15th Hussars, then joined us, and would have been an ideal leader for the men had it been our fortune to come to blows with the enemy.

The levy eventually was composed as follows;—

    8 companies of Krobos,
    2 ,, ,, Mumfords,
    1 company of Elminas,
    4 companies of Adansis,
    2 ,, ,, Bekwais,
    1 company of Abodoms,

having a total strength of 860. Of these eighteen companies, eleven were more or less disciplined, armed with Sniders, and equipped with tools for pioneering. The remaining seven companies were irregulars, armed with flint-lock guns, and specially useful as scouts and for outpost and reconnaissance work.

The first actual test of the marching and scouting power of the levy and of its discipline was the march to the assistance of Bekwai. This was carried out by night as well as by day, and in the presence of an outpost and scouts of the enemy. The levy was backed up by two companies of Houssas, and this no doubt helped to give it the confidence it displayed, and which contributed to its rapid and successful completion of the duty.

After this experience there was no doubt of its ability to work, if not in a bold and dashing manner, at least warily and usefully; and this was borne out in the final advance on Kumassi, when the levy forming the advance guard was divided into three parties and approached the place by three different routes. The central party on the main road cut the path for the troops. Its covering party being sent to within a short distance of Kumassi, the remainder was distributed in cutting parties at intervals along the track; by this disposition the last six miles of road were cleared in two hours. On arrival at Kumassi the levy formed outposts to cover the arrival of the main body, and continued to find the outposts all round the camp during the stay of the troops there.

These outposts were partly employed for the purpose of protecting villagers bringing in supplies to the market, and partly to prevent native followers from going out to raid on their own account, and they were also useful, especially at night, in preventing the escape of Prempeh and his chiefs from Kumassi. It was certainly due to their vigilance that Prempeh did not escape on the night before his arrest.

The palace had been reconnoitred soon after the arrival of the troops, and we had then found that its garden adjoined the bush at the back, and that a small postern existed in the fence, and led by a footpath through this bush, across the swamp and into the forest beyond.

The levy therefore went to work with machetes, and in a few hours had cut away a broad open space all round the palace enclosure; and thus, when the time came, it was found possible to draw a cordon of men rapidly round the place, to prevent not only the escape of its inmates, but also looting parties from gaining an entrance.

On the night before the arrest the piquets on all the roads were reinforced, and an extra patrol was stationed to watch what went on at the palace. Messengers from the palace and others were caught trying all the roads, and during the night one of the Ansahs was captured by the piquet on the so-called 'secret' path.

There had been some difficulty in obtaining information as to where the queen-mother resided, but at three o'clock in the morning the patrol saw her come out of the palace and go to her home in the town, and there they marked her down with a piquet until she might be wanted.

There is good reason to suppose that the palace party had intended to escape that night, but were obliged to abandon their plan on finding every road stopped.

The last pioneering task carried out by the levy was the very satisfactory one of levelling the smouldering walls of the burnt fetish houses at Bantama.

Then part of the levy made a night march and reconnaissance to a place five miles beyond Kumassi, where 400 of Mampon's men were reported to be encamped, but these got wind of our coming, and slipped away; and a reconnaissance the same day to Maheer, the king's summer residence, only arrived there to find that the place had already been looted by the slaves left in charge of it.

Next came the march down to the coast with all the royal and other prisoners. The part taken by the levies in the early portion of this march was not an unimportant one, since to them fell the duty of searching the bush and of holding all by-roads, to guard against attempts which we had reason to expect would be made to assassinate Prempeh. They found numbers of individual men in the bush, but these always came in asking for news, and were evidently runaway slaves rather than would-be assassins.

On the 22nd January the levy marched out of Kumassi; on the 29th it arrived at Cape Coast Castle, thus completing a march of 150 miles in seven days, which in that climate is not a bad performance.

This brief *résumé* of the work done by the levy will tend to show to what extent it was capable of being useful in the short period of its enrolment, after being organised on the principles above stated.

It is not claimed that such organisations could also go so far as to put pluck into the men, but it is only reasonable to infer that if they had been brought into actual conflict with the Ashantis, they would at least have shown themselves no worse than their enemy; they would, at any rate, have been perfectly under control of their officers; and they would probably have been emboldened to a very useful extent by the possession of better arms and by their superiority in tactical power.

A reliable authority on the subject has stated that, in his opinion, West African tribes are worse than useless as levies, for two reasons: one is that their natural cowardice will lead them when the fight is going against them to run away at the critical moment, and in their panic in the narrow bush path to overrun and bear back with them the steadier troops in support; the other is that in a winning fight their want of discipline will, on the other hand, lead them to commit excesses such as would be unbecoming in allies of the British.

But in dealing with a native levy in any part of the world, one or other of these difficulties, often both, will have to be encountered by the white commander; and the sooner he realises that other means must of necessity be used for enforcing discipline than ordinary commands or requests, the sooner he will find himself properly obeyed. These have to be resorted to occasionally as the lesser of evils, up to the point of shooting one's own men; but when resorted to they should be the result only of deliberate and fair consideration of the case. Strict justice goes a very long way towards bringing natives under discipline. A very few lessons suffice, as a rule, to show them that an order is not to be trifled with; and once this idea has been engrafted into their minds, they become very amenable to discipline.

In the late Ashanti expedition, although we had no fighting to do, the pioneering, scouting, and outpost work performed by the native levy were sufficiently valuable in their results to justify very fully its enrolment, in spite of the fact that it was composed of the much-abused West Coast tribes.

Policy and Wealth in Ashanti, 1895
By Sir George Baden-Powell.

In 1895-96 we wage the fourth serious Ashanti war within half a century. The cost in blood and treasure, in valuable lives, felt so heavily by the august head of the nation, as well as by the nation at large, and in valued money, should be a very special concern to the representatives of the people. The ultimate unit, the taxpayer—whether home or colonial—looks for two groups of results as his reward. On the one hand, he hopes to see Christianity and civilization *pro tanto* extended; and, on the other, to see some compensating development of industry and trade. Unless he or "his servants the government" secure either or both these results, the question must be plainly asked, has he the right, and is he right, to wage such wars? In relation to Ashanti, the solution of this problem in politics has a very present and direct importance, as well as an indirect and more general significance.

First of all, the place in history of Ashanti as it stands today is remarkable. The "Gold Coast" was the one part of the African coast which attracted the earliest navigators of Western Europe, because of its gold.

The very first English traders—Windham, Lok, Hawkins, and others—visited Guinea for gold. This legitimate commercial adventure was, however, promptly superseded by another and even more profitable trade, namely, that in slaves. The one crying need of the gold mines and plantations, which European enterprise was just then opening up in tropical America—in the West Indies, in Mexico, in Peru, in Brazil—was black labour. From the days of the Greeks and Romans right down to modern times, Africa was the one great slave preserve; and to Africa came the Europeans to filch that human labour they so much needed in the New World.

The trade speedily assumed enormous proportions, and overwhelmed all other forms of enterprise and commerce. The very lowest traits of the native races were thereby cultivated, and the most ruinous of all industries was developed. The south-east and the northeast trade-winds competed, as it were, to waft from Africa to America these human cargoes; and the heavy blight of the slave trade hung over Africa and over all attempts at European settlement or civilization from the sixteenth to the middle of the nineteenth century. All along that portion of the coast of Guinea which runs eastward from Cape Palmas to the Delta of the Niger, 1000 miles in length, where the natives brought down gold and ivory as well as slaves, European forts and factories were established from the earliest times.

But, confining ourselves to the present century, we come to the period referred to by Mr. C. P. Lucas in his most admirable *Historical Geography of the British Colonies* (vol. iii):—

The English went for generations to Africa to follow up the slave trade. Then they went again to put it down.

The putting an end suddenly to this great and vigorous trade burdened the nation with the responsibilities of the slave-trading merchants. Their forts and factories and settlements at once fell to the ultimate charge of the Home Government, and for the succeeding fifty years we see the British Government, with the steady vacillation of a pendulum, alternately taking over administration from and handing it back to the traders.

Early in this century the government found Cape Coast Castle itself to be rented from the Fantis. But the Ashantis were attacking the coast tribes, and setting up a very effective *suzerainty*, and claiming all rents and tributes; nor did they hesitate boldly to attack the whites.

In 1816 the Ashantis actually blockaded Cape Coast Castle, and in the following year the traders sent an embassy to Kumassi, where they made a convention recognising the suzerainty of the Ashantis, but stipulating for a British Resident at Kumassi. The following year the Home Government sent an embassy to Kumassi, and there was great friction between the government and the merchants on the coast. The Ashantis, hoping to profit by these dissensions, made a formidable invasion of the small British territories in 1821.

In 1824 came the *first* Ashanti war. Sir Charles McCarthy led a British force, chiefly composed of native troops, across the Prah; but the force was completely demolished, and he himself slain. The consequence was a fresh Ashanti invasion, and they were only beaten off in their attack on Accra by means of the newly-introduced war-rockets, which are said to have had a widely-spread effect among the natives, who took them to be lightning and thunder in the hands of the white men. In 1831 followed a treaty freeing all the forts from Ashanti suzerainty. At this period Governor Maclean, under the rule of the merchants, established a quasi-British authority along a great stretch of coast, and set up sovereign claims. He maintained unbroken peace with the Ashantis.

In 1840 the Home Government once again took complete charge of the Gold Coast, and after this commenced the policy of buying out the smaller Dutch and Danish possessions.

In 1863 another attempt at armed interference with Ashanti took place. The *second* invasion was made; but the result was a terrible military disaster, chiefly due to the undertaking of operations at the wrong season, and the consequent abandonment of the expedition owing to the terrible ravages of sickness among the troops.

The trend of opinion in England at this moment was against the widening responsibilities of empire, and in 1865 the House of Commons adopted the notorious resolution of withdrawal from the West Coast of Africa, in which it was declared:—

> All further extension of territory or assumption of government or new treaties offering any protection to native tribes would be inexpedient . . . with a view to ultimate withdrawal from all (West African possessions) except, probably, Sierra Leone.

But this "Little Englander" resolution proved mere waste paper in the face of the actual work in process on the West Coast. As a matter of fact, the purchasing of the smaller foreign settlements marked a great consolidation and strengthening of the British power at the very moment when the self-sufficient representatives of the people were passing their most impracticable and impossible academic resolution.

But this first consolidation of British power twenty-five years ago on the Gold Coast found the powerful Ashanti nation—one versed in all the worst forms and practices of fetish and barbaric tyranny—closely hemming in all our settlements and small protectorates. Some great conflict between the two powers became inevitable.

In 1873 occurred the *third* Ashanti war. When Sir Garnet Wolseley arrived at Cape Coast Castle, he found the Ashanti forces at its very gates. Commodore Commerell had been seriously wounded by an Ashanti ambush at the very mouth of the Prah; and Sir Garnet fought his first pitched battle with the enemy at Abrakampa, not eight miles from Cape Coast Castle.

Thus twenty-five years ago on the Gold Coast the Queen's authority barely extended outside the forts and factories established 250 years before.

But the results of the Wolseley Ashanti war were very significant. By a series of brilliant actions and marches, Sir Garnet very speedily captured the Ashanti capital, and dictated terms to the king. The military work done was all that could be desired: the political action which followed was the very reverse. We had seized and occupied the fountainhead of Ashanti barbarism; we had it in our power completely and finally to purify the whole stream of Ashanti influence. Instead of this, we retired, imagining, in our folly, that a nation steeped to the lips in barbarism and savagery would abide by and carry out the terms of a paper convention.

The consequences of our folly developed rapidly and surely, and in twenty years came to disastrous fruition. Every vice, every evil, every terror known to savagery came to be rampant over all Ashanti. The main clauses of the convention—the war indemnity, the abolition of human sacrifices, the keeping open of the roads, and the freeing of trade and traffic—remained a dead letter.

Thus, in defence of the interests of our own colony and of numerous natives, we were compelled once again to use force, and enter upon the *fourth* Ashanti war.

The one permanent gain due to the 1873 campaign was that the British frontier was carried up to and across the Prah River.

But the whole of the area behind our own possessions, with a boundary running by the Hinterland of the New German acquisitions in Togoland, past the eastern ends of French Guinea and the French Soudan, round by the borders of the Niger Company's territories, down to the frontiers of the new French possessions in Dahomey—all that area, where not overrun by the mysterious Moslem forces headed by "Samory," was in 1895 under the domination of the Ashanti king, Prempeh.

His rule involved all the insecurity inevitable to active slave-raiding; all the cruel misery and drain of population incidental to the system of wholesale human sacrifices; all the destitution and retrogression due to ruthless repression of industry by the ruling powers; no profits of industry or trade were safe; no man could be sure of reaping what he sowed, or of retaining the price he obtained for the wild but valuable products of the forest. All gold found or obtained by any form of work had to be delivered up to the chief or king. All was stagnation, poverty and cruelty. The mere putting an end to such a state of affairs would be even a noble reason for conquest by force of arms. And when, for the other reasons of broken treaty-pledges and the material damage done to our own interests and to those of the natives for whom we had become responsible, armed interference on our part became necessary, then those among us who had watched such affairs recognised a grand opportunity for doing a great and good act on the part of the British power.

In 1823 we sacrificed the lives of our own men and the lives of the enemy without securing any good in return for so much evil.

In 1863, again, we sacrificed 1000 lives on our own side and untold numbers of the foe, but no permanent good results follow.

In 1873 once again we embark on a campaign against the same Ashantis, at a human sacrifice to ourselves of 300 killed and wounded and an untold loss to the enemy.

Each time we press our frontier a little forward. But, to the disgrace of our statesmen, each time, even this last time in 1873, we retire from and surrender to the despotism of savagery all the area of Ashanti proper; and in so far make our own country responsible for all the fetish practices, the human sacrifices, the slave-raiding, and other such curses, which have brooded over that land and its unfortunate inhabitants for the past quarter of a century.

Here again, as in many another instance, the philanthropy of the British nation has seen and judged aright of the evils of such barbaric despotism, and has set itself, regardless of cost, to crush such despotism. But here again, as in so many other instances, the statesmen in office, as a rule, through craven fear of electioneering results, have ignored the further moral obligation of setting up some better power in the stead of that which we have destroyed.

As in Zululand in 1881, so in Ashanti in 1873, we crushed a great native organisation and retired, setting up nothing in its place. The invariable consequences follow, namely, a recrudescence and intensification of previous cruelties and barbarities, further dishonour to the national credit, and ultimately fresh expense, fresh expeditions, and fresh human sacrifices in war.

Such must not be permitted to be the result of the 1895-96 expedition. We are bound in honour to the natives to provide them with some better form of government than that from which we have saved them by force of arms. We have crushed the barbaric despotism, but we have yet to make our conquest over the demoralizing agencies of slavery, savagery, and drunkenness. We have yet definitely to set up the queen's peace over all this new area; yet definitely to establish law, order, and security. And to accomplish these ends, all we have to do is to *administer*. The means to this end are elastic, and must be suited to the special circumstances of each district and date.

The whole area must at once be divided into provisional districts, and a white chief placed over each. Armed support each must have, and white assistants, as many as he needs, be always available. Gradually must be instilled the leading ideas of our civilization—the sanctity of private property; individual liberty; security for person and property, and so forth. There are instruments to this end to be found in native courts, armed police, legitimate revenue-raising, and so forth.

Another side to the political aspect must be at once taken in hand. We must cultivate the most friendly relations with the independent powers bordering on this our province—with the German and French colonies on either side, and with the daring and independent chief "Samory" at the back—and with them not only make mutual and final demarcations of frontier, but also institute such combined arrangements as shall prohibit and prevent the deleterious trades in spirits, arms and ammunition, and all other infringements of the salutary ordinances of civilized authority.

Such is the policy of honour we must pursue; and it is the policy of common sense as well.

Over this Ashanti area, which now comes definitely under our flag, there exists, according to indisputable evidence, abundance of wealth, mineral, vegetable, and animal. The following records of exports indicate what has occurred before and after our Gold Coast Colony spread its administrative *ægis* as far as the Prah, and this will give some indication of results in progress and prosperity which the spread of British jurisdiction can bring over all the Hinterland of that colony:—

	Exports from the Gold Coast Colony,	
	1882.	1892.
	£	£
Palm Oil	179,000	179,000
Palm kernels	50,000	104,000
Rubber	—	167,000

Monkey skins	4,000	35,000
Gold	62,000	99,000
	£295,000	£584,000

The value of the colony as a new market for British produce is seen by remarking that ten years ago the imports were less than 300,000*l.*, and now they are close upon 600,000*l.*

But the figures of actual trade hardly indicate what is the main feature in the wealth of an expanding colony, and that is the corresponding power of the expansion of trade. The following table gives at a glance the records of expansion at twenty-year periods of the Gold Coast Colony:—

	1853.	1873.	1893.
Area (square miles)	6,000	29,000	39,000
Population	150,000	410,000	1,474,000
Tonnage	36,000	180,000	831,000
Imports	£60,000	£360,000	£718,000
Exports	£125,000	£321,000	£722,000
Index numbers	43	130	408

In rough result this colony, which nearly trebled its commercial value in the twenty years preceding 1873, has nearly quadrupled its commercial value in the last twenty years, and three-fourths of the total trade is with the United Kingdom.

But this new province has as yet had no more exploiting than a "mere scratching of the earth." In all the staples there has been no systematised production as yet. We have indications of many minor products of value, such as grain, ivory, quicksilver, and petroleum; but in regard to the staples, much remains to be done before this area can be said to be producing anything like its legitimate output.

Take *gold*, for instance. As I have said, hitherto the chief or king took all the gold that was found—a far heavier levy even than that of the English Crown on the gold miners in Wales. And yet there are indications in numerous old works, and, above all, in the undoubted fact that natural nuggets, indicating alluvial gold deposits, abound among the native hoards, that we have not yet got hold, in any appreciable degree, of the natural stores of the precious metal which gives its name to all the coast.

One word more as to gold. It has often been a fact of history that the value of the output of gold in a given country has not exceeded the cost, that in some cases the gold obtained at a total cost of 5*l*. the ounce has, of course, fetched in the market only 3*l*. 17*s*. 6*d*.; and yet the district or country prospered exceedingly. The fact is, that the raising of gold means considerable success to a great many incomers. It also means considerable loss by means of considerable expenditure to a great many others. But it means in the aggregate the coming into the district of the successful and the unsuccessful, and the expenditure there of much wealth by both classes. The consequence is, a great many other industries spring up, and many hitherto unnoticed local resources become developed.

It is the same with other industries, as, for instance, that of timber-getting; and it is certain that portions of the Ashanti forests consist of valuable African mahogany.

A word must be said on the modern method of discovering and developing the unknown resources of such a country. This is nowadays done by means of concessions from the government. In regard to these, the very first point is to discover that any particular concession is obtained fairly and squarely; and the second point is to see that the financial arrangements are equitable.

The most modern proposal is, that the government should only grant concessions for which large sums are paid, which the government undertakes shall be expended in the public works necessary for the carrying-out of the concession, such as roads, bridges, railways, telegraphs, and water supply. But in making such stipulations it would be foolish and wrong on the part of the government to insist on too high a price for concessions. In untried and unknown countries the development of any industry is carried on at considerable and unknown risk, and the commercial value of an untried concession must be calculated with due consideration of these unknown risks, and a balance struck by prospectively large profits. In short, as large a margin of possible profit must be left to the investor, or he will not face the possible losses. Nor should he alone be saddled with expenses, such as those of providing improved means of communication, which necessarily benefit so large an area of country and so many other persons.

With an official policy of development, based on sound financial principles, and controlled by adequate knowledge of such countries, there should be no difficulty in securing the rapid industrial opening up of all Ashanti.

In two matters, however, the government must take action forthwith. A light railway must at once be constructed to the Prah, with a view to ultimate extension right into the Hinterland; and a sufficient breakwater must be built, probably at Accra, to render easier the landing and shipping of goods.

In this work of the political and industrial regeneration of Ashanti, the missionaries, to say nothing here of their immediate and great religious work, do give invaluable aid. They are, as they have been before, ready to establish stations at all available centres over the interior, and thus to set up the standard of Christian and civilized lives for all men to look at. And they become, as they are already in the more settled districts, invaluable in all matters connected with the education of the natives.

As is proved by the recorded results in all other cases, thus to set up the British idea and British administration over all this great new area is bound very speedily to yield handsome returns in commerce and finance, to the great advantage, not only of the traders and ship-owners already engaged, but also to the exporters and manufacturers of the mother country. It is no mean advantage to them to discover, even in Ashanti, a new market which, if properly organised, should take in a few years probably from two to three million pounds' worth of British produce each year.

Moreover, in thus setting up strongly and definitely the queen's peace over this great native area, in the place of the degrading, demoralising, and pauperising *régime* hitherto dominant, we shall be bringing to perhaps four or five millions of natives all the advantages of peaceful industry and commerce, and teach them, in the most practical manner, the benefits of attaching themselves to a civilization which, as they will then very speedily come to see, has its roots in those high principles of law, order, justice, and goodwill for all men, which are, after all, the guiding lessons taught by our firm national religion.

The nation, therefore, has good cause, whether from the religious, the philanthropic, the financial, or the commercial point of view, for very great gratitude to those who, at great risk of life and health, have so signally and speedily crushed the opposing barbaric forces which stood in the way of a wholesome and profitable regeneration of all Ashanti.

In Ashanti the British nation can now do a piece of work of inestimable material benefit to themselves and to the natives, and which can become an invaluable object lesson both for ourselves and for foreign nations, in the extension to tropical areas of the benefits of Christianity and civilization. George Baden-Powell.

www.ingramcontent.com/pod-product-compliance
Lightning Source LLC
Chambersburg PA
CBHW021958160426
43197CB00007B/176